OPENING

OPENINGS

*Narrative Beginnings
from the Epic
to the Novel*

A. D. NUTTALL

CLARENDON PRESS · OXFORD
1992

Oxford University Press, Walton Street, Oxford OX2 6DP
Oxford New York Toronto
Delhi Bombay Calcutta Madras Karachi
Petaling Jaya Singapore Hong Kong Tokyo
Nairobi Dar es Salaam Cape Town
Melbourne Auckland
and associated companies in
Berlin Ibadan

Oxford is a trade mark of Oxford University Press

Published in the United States
by Oxford University Press, New York

British Library Cataloguing in Publication Data
Data available

Library of Congress Cataloging in Publication Data
Nuttall , A. D. (Anthony David)
Openings: narrative beginnings from the epic to the novel / A. D. Nuttall.
Includes index
1. Openings (Rhetoric) 2. Narration (Rhetoric)
3. Epic poetry—History and criticism 4. Fiction—History and criticism.
I. Title
PN2 12.N88   1991
808–dc20   91–20192
ISBN 0–19–811741–8

Typeset by Taj Services Ltd., U.P. India
Printed and bound in
Great Britain by Biddles Ltd.,
Guildford and King's Lynn

In memory of
E. R. Dodds

Preface

'If on a winter's night a traveller . . .'. These words plant
certain hooks in the reader's mind. 'If' implies an indefinite
multitude of possible apodoses—'then' clauses, which could
follow; winter is more mysterious and therefore, paradoxically,
more pregnant than summer; a traveller is necessarily a liminal
figure, moving from this place to that as he passes from past to
future. The words therefore compose an excellent opening.
Italo Calvino made them the title of a book which systematically frustrates the reader's wish for natural sequence and, at the
same time, lavishly rewards the appetite for formal brilliance.
The reader is given first a title like an opening, and then opening
after opening; but Calvino never explains what happened to the
traveller. There was a time, perhaps, when a minstrel might
have been killed for that (even if the fool, meanwhile, might
have known how to get away with it). Calvino himself, indeed,
ends on a note of humorous desperation.

Certainly, there is an immense distance between Calvino,
with his word processor (?) and, say, Taillefer, who sang at the
Battle of Hastings. Taillefer—'Cut-Iron'—is said to have ridden
out before the Norman army on that October day, hurling his
sword into the air and catching it; as he rode he sang 'of
Charlemagne, of Roland, of Oliver and their followers, who
died at Roncesvalles.'[1] On the one hand we have, in Calvino,
structures dissolving before our eyes; on the other, in the heroic
figure of the singer on his great horse, we have structures
forming, hardening.

This book is a study of the ground which lies between these
extremes (although chronologically, it begins with a poem
written long before Taillefer was born). It is in part an
investigation of the various tensions which exist between the
formal freedom to begin a work of fiction wherever one likes
and an opposite sense that all good openings are somehow

---

[1] Wace, *Le Roman de Rou*, 8013–18, Société des anciens textes français, 3 vols.
(Paris: A. and J. Picard, 1970), ii. 183.

naturally rooted, are echoes, more or less remote, of an original
creative act: *in medias res*, as against 'In the beginning'. I have
chosen to follow a path very different from that adopted by
Edward Said in his *Beginnings* (1975). Where he sustains a
simultaneous onslaught on a great number of interrelated texts,
I have concentrated on a canonical—almost a dynastic—
sequence. The resulting spectacle of alternating (male) authority
and (male) rebellion will certainly be unpleasing to some people.
Harold Bloom is hardly mentioned in my text, but his influence
will be evident. The same is true of Gabriel Josipovici's *The
World and the Book* (1973). My third major influence, Frank
Kermode's *The Sense of an Ending* (1967), is more fully avowed,
in my last chapter. Behind these lies a yet deeper debt, to E. R.
Dodds. I am conscious as I write this that the age of Dodds (and
Bruno Snell and A. W. H. Adkins) has to some extent been
superseded by the generation of Hugh Lloyd Jones and Jasper
Griffin; a period of keen interest in the otherness of older
literatures has been succeeded by a phase in which common
preoccupations have been re-emphasized. I write nevertheless as
one only half converted, remembering still not only the charm
and brilliance but also the sheer intellectual cogency of Dodds as
he lectured to us in the 1950s on Aeschylus and Homer.

In this book as in others I have written in conscious
opposition to full metaphysical formalism, that is to the notion
that nothing exists but discourse (or text), with the consequence
that verisimilitude becomes wholly a matter of convention. If it
is said, 'You are attacking what no one believes,' there is a sense
in which I must at once agree. In the preface to my *A New
Mimesis* (1984) I conceded that pure formalism is a doctrine
which no one can operate in daily life. Nevertheless formalist
principles are frequently if intermittently avowed and are
sometimes given unjust—almost theological—authority.
Although increasing numbers of theoretically minded critics
now welcome the idea of negotiations with reality (here Peter
Brooks' *Reading for the Plot* (1984) may serve as a distinguished
example) the thesis; 'There *is* no uninterpreted reality' continues
to be accorded uncritical assent in conferences, tutorials, and
seminars, often enough in juxtaposition with critical practices
which presuppose the existence of separate objects of mimesis.

In his *Fictional Truth* (1990) Michael Riffaterre writes, 'Far be it from me to suggest that verisimilitude in fiction is always independent of readers' assumptions about reality, of their pragmatic knowledge, of their experience of people . . .'. Yet elsewhere in this same book, on page xiii, he defines verisimilitude as 'a system of representations that seems to reflect a reality external to the text, but only because it conforms to a grammar', and on page 84, 'fictional truth spurns referentiality . . . [it] relies entirely on the text itself'. The juxtaposition of a radical with a moderated formalism is to be found, in particular, in Frank Kermode's *The Sense of an Ending* (1967). This work, which I take to be one of the great critical books of the century, has a force and influence which seems to extend indefinitely. This whole of my book may without strain be construed as a response to Kermode's. The matter indeed is made explicit in my final chapter.

I have been helped by John Batchelor, Bernard Brugière, John Burrow, John Carey, Rachel Falconer, Robin Lane Fox, Stephen Gill, Estelle Haan, Charles Martindale, Stephen Medcalf, and Lino Pertile. I am deeply grateful to them all. The surviving errors and absurdities are, of course, all mine.

I am grateful also to Cambridge University Press for permission to reprint some pages from a contribution I made to *The Enduring Legacy*, edited by G. S. Rousseau and Pat Rogers (1988), to Macmillan for permission to reprint material from *Addressing Frank Kermode*, edited by Margaret Tudeau-Clayton and Martin Warner (1991), and to Edinburgh University Press for permission to reprint in my last chapter part of an essay on Shakespearian openings written as a tribute to Professor G. K. Hunter for the volume, *Arts of Performance in Elizabethan and Early Stuart Drama*, edited by Murray Biggs and others. That a study of openings should terminate in Shakespeare is perhaps not surprising. I have suggested that Calvino with his uncompleted narrative is somehow quintessentially modern. Yet Shakespeare, who notoriously could do anything, did this too. *The Winter's Tale* takes its name not from its own major content, but from a story, never finished, of sprites and goblins.

MAMILLIUS   There was a man,—
HERMIONE   Nay, come, sit down; then on.

MAMILLIUS   Dwelt by a churchyard. I will tell it softly.
             Yond crickets shall not hear it.
HERMIONE   Come on then,
             And give't me in my ear.
             Shakespeare, *The Winter's Tale*, II. i. 29–32.

                                        A. D. N.

Contents

I

The Beginning of the *Aeneid*

THE VOICE OF THE MUSE AND THE VOICE OF THE POET

'Arma virumque cano . . .'

'Arms and the man I sing'; the voice of Virgil breaks suddenly from the silence, to begin the song of Aeneas. Before these words there is nothing; after them, the story of a journey from dubiety to imperial glory, from burning Troy, through spectral cities, turbulent seas, ruined pastoral, human love trodden underfoot, through the slaughter of the young to the marble clarity of Rome, to certainty and power. We think today of Virgil as the silver-tongued poet, smooth in his cadences, yet these opening words are strangely abrupt. There are signs, as we shall see, that contemporaries found them uncomfortably bald, were disconcerted by their sudden loudness. Yet they work. As we listen or read, we are instantly subdued by a larger-than-human voice. The lyric poet Propertius felt this in Virgil's own century. There is, I think, no irony in the famous line of homage: *Nescio quid maius nascitur Iliade*, 'Something here is being born which is greater than the *Iliad*' (II. xxxiv. 66).

Propertius speaks of birth, and in doing so opens a perspective on the poem's prehistory. When he daringly suggests that Virgil is more than a match for Homer, we know that the poet has, before his mind's eye, not a simple rivalry of peers but rather a more painful image: a son defeating his father. In this way the silent darkness from which the voice arose begins to be peopled with (male) parental shapes. Already, there is a kind of irony: all the world knows that Virgil revered *pietas*, which is almost a way of saying that Virgil revered reverence. *Pietas* has none of the adverse connotations of the English word 'piety'; it

---

All references to Virgil are to Sir Roger Mynors's Oxford Classical Text (Oxford: Clarendon Press, 1972 corr. repr. of 1969 ed.). For the *Appendix Vergiliana* I have used the Oxford Classical Text, ed. F. W. Clausen, F. R. D. Goodyear, E. J. Kenney, and J. A. Richmond (Oxford: Clarendon Press, 1966).

comprehends a loving and dutiful submission to gods, ancestors, parents, and the home. Notoriously in the *Aeneid* the linear relationships of father and son (Anchises with Aeneas, Aeneas with Iulus, Aeneas with Rome itself, of which he is progenitor) override the lateral relation of sexual love (Creusa, Lavinia, and, most of all, Dido). There can be no doubt that Virgil's attitude to Homer was one of profound literary *pietas*. Yet (such are the anxieties of influence) in this instance the child, almost against its own will, proves to be in certain respects stronger than the parent. Virgil, we begin to see, does not after all speak from an absolute silence. He starts with a pious echoing of the 'first' epic and, even as he does so, he transforms what he touches: the imitation is a revolution.

Homer is the point at which European literature becomes visible to posterity. Before the *Iliad* and the *Odyssey* there must have been—we cannot say poems, exactly, since in an oral culture there is no stable continuity of text—but innumerable singings of tales. Some think Homer himself (themselves, if the name really connotes a plurality of bards) could not read or write and that the *Iliad* and the *Odyssey* were somehow committed to writing by teams of scribes. Others believe that Homer could write but, so to speak, only just: that his method of composition is still grounded in the very different psychology of oral poetry.[1] The writing down of the *Iliad and the Odyssey* was an event of momentous literary importance. As the stylus raced the poem froze, became canonical for posterity.

Virgil conjures the spirit of his own literary father, the Father of Epic, in two Latin words: *arma virumque*, 'arms and the man'. The *Iliad* is about war (think here of the pathologically literary C. S. Lewis who said to himself as he stumbled through the smoke of the trenches of Arras, 'This is War. This is what Homer wrote about.')[2] The *Odyssey*, meanwhile, is very much about one hero, Odysseus, and begins with the Greek word *andra*,

---

[1] Jasper Griffin, following Ruth Finnegan's *Oral Poetry* (Cambridge: Cambridge University Press, 1977), esp. pp. 66–7, has cast doubt on the existence of a clear dividing line between oral and written poetry; see his *Homer on Life and Death* (Oxford: Clarendon Press, 1980), p. xiv. See also J. B. Hainsworth, 'The Criticism of an Oral Homer', *Journal of Hellenic Studies*, 90 (1970), 90–8. Griffin adds, however, that in Germany, where Homeric criticism is especially strong, the oral theory appears to be catching on.

[2] *Surprised by Joy* (London: Collins, 1959), 158.

'the man'. But while Homer had left two epics, Virgil knew that he could make only one, and must therefore combine the *Iliad* and the *Odyssey* in a single structure. It has long been noticed that the first six books of the *Aeneid*, telling of the wanderings of Aeneas, are 'Odyssean' and the last six books, recounting the Latin wars, are 'Iliadic'. Notice that in the poem itself the order is 'man' → 'arms' but that, curiously, the first line defers instead to the past, Homeric order rather than to the order of the ensuing Latin. The commentator Servius, writing his commentary on the *Aeneid* at the end of the fourth century AD, speaks of the multitude of voices, disputing the question of why Virgil began with 'arms'.[3] The *Odyssey* was deemed from the first to be subsequent to the *Iliad*, not so much because readers were aware, in a sophisticated fashion, of the signs of later composition as because it deals with a later stage of the Great Story, after the sack of Troy.

Virgil's opening words are, then, an act of deference or even of homage, but already there is a rebellion at the level of grammar, this rebellion consisting literally in an assertion of *ego*. For, where Homer begins with a second person singular prayer-imperative, 'Sing, goddess, of the wrath' or 'Tell, Muse, of the man' (the bard so to speak emptying his personality to make way for a voice greater than his own) Virgil uses the declaratory first person singular, 'I sing'. In due course he will call upon the Muse for aid, but not until the eighth line. The grand sequence of the poem, arms and the man, the long sufferings of the journey from Troy to Latium, the Latin wars, the building of Rome's high walls, and the founding of the race—all these are governed grammatically by 'I sing'. The Muse is called upon when the poet begins to search for the obscure causes of divine resentment against Aeneas—not as a primal source of power but as an ancillary *aide-mémoire* or expert witness. In noticing this shift away from Homer we are not imposing anxieties exclusively available to the hypercritical twentieth century. The ancient commentator Servius felt impelled by the oddity of what was before him to say that the

[3] *Servianorum in Vergilii Carmina Commentariorum*, Editionis Harvardianae, ed. E. K. Rand *et al.* (Lancaster, Penn.: Lancaster Press), ii (1946), 5. Vol. iii. containing the commentary on *Aeneid* iii–v, appeared under the Oxford University Press imprint in 1965. Vol. i seems not to have been published.

Aeneid had two *principia*, or 'openings'; the second is the ordinary epic opening, which Servius calls, 'invocative' (*invocativum*) because in it the Muse is invoked; the first, Servius decides is 'professive' (*professivum*).[4]

Here, perhaps, is the first visible mark of a developed literacy. The oral or almost-oral poet, who is in some ways like the performer or executant of a pre-existent though fluid body of song, will as a matter of empirical fact experience his own performance as flowing from sources above or beneath ego-control. It comes naturally to us to ascribe such unsupervised feats of creativity to the unconscious mind. It came naturally to the early Greeks to ascribe it to a Muse. The 'cash' difference between the two conceptions may be less than it appears. One rises from below, the other descends from above. A spatial metaphor—a flourish of *Aberglaube*[5]—is all that separates them. But these are large issues, to which we shall return. Meanwhile the 'writerly' poet of a later, fully literate generation can read back, tinker with, and reflect upon the process of composition. In this way the poet becomes privy to the genesis of his own art and, as a consequence, the conscious mind appropriates the poem. Servius's word is a good one: Virgil has become the pro-fessor of his poem.

It is probably too simple, however, to ascribe this radical transformation to the growth of literacy alone. Between the times of Homer and Virgil we can watch the gradual replacement of a language which accounts for human emotion and behaviour in terms of gods by a psychological language. This prepares the way for the use in our time of such potentially contradictory conceptions as 'unconscious mind' ('unconscious conscious'). We cannot say, indeed, that Homer has no psychological language. Words like *tharsos* and *thumos* ('aggression', 'spirit') are, quite certainly, the names of inner states, not deities, though gods will again and again be found to have 'breathed' such impulsive energies (lying outside ego-control) into human subjects. Ever since E. R. Dodds wrote his famous

---

[4] Ibid. 6.

[5] 'Extra-belief' is Matthew Arnold's term (drawn from Goethe) for the mythopoeic, concretizing impulse in literature. See his *Literature and Dogma*, ch. 2, in *The Complete Prose Works of Matthew Arnold*, ed. R. H. Super, 11 vols. (Ann Arbor: University of Michigan Press, 1960–77), vi. *Dissent and Dogma*, 202–13.

essay on 'Agamemnon's apology'[6] it has been clear, first, that for Homer the ego is, so to speak, a smaller area, lying *within* the self, and that the self, in its turn, is not as straightforwardly exclusive of 'external' agencies as we (perhaps uncritically) deem it to be. The Greek word for ego is, smoothly enough, *ego* and the Greek word used to express 'self' ('myself', 'herself', etc.) is *autos* (as in *autobiography*). Later in the *Iliad* Agamemnon is brought to the point at which he must explain how it was that he compensated himself for the loss of a mistress by robbing Achilles of *his*. Agamemnon's words, translated as literally as possible, are,

Not I (*ego*) was the cause of this act, but Zeus and my lot and the Fury who walks in the dark; they it was who in the assembly put wild *atē* ('infatuation', 'madness') in my wits, on that day when I myself (*autos*) took Achilles' prize away from him. (xix. 86–9)

The modern reader is likely to experience the speech as confused or evasive. But, as Dodds observed, Agamemnon is not trying to avoid responsibility. This is made clear by his offer, immediately after these words, to pay compensation. It could even be that Dodds's own word, 'apology', is misleading: that Agamemnon is really not so much defending or excusing himself as explaining what happened. The crucial thing is that, when the explanation is given, no contradiction is felt between 'Zeus [not I] did this, in me' and '[I] myself did this'. It is not that the supernatural beings referred to are felt to be *metaphors* for mental events.

Some three hundred years later when Euripides wrote the *Hippolytus* there may well have been a faint, nascent sense that Artemis and Aphrodite and the story of an anti-erotic personality are not simultaneous truths but, conceivably, alternative languages, so that one may by metaphor be substituted for the other. Artemis and Aphrodite stand as emblematic statues on the stage. At the same time, they figure as agents in the drama; yet, because the person destroyed in the play is a young man of extreme chastity, the audience senses the growing possibility of a complete psychological translation of this very agency: from

---

[6] In his *The Greeks and the Irrational* (Berkeley and Los Angeles: University of California Press, 1963), 1–27. The book is based on lectures given in the autumn of 1949.

'Aphrodite reacted because Hippolytus offended against her' to 'The libido of Hippolytus reasserted itself after excessive repression.' In Homer an act of blind folly or aggression will indeed be seen, simultaneously, as an event within the self and as real divine agency. The self is therefore an arena within which deities may contend. Note that here, even as the agency of the ego is curtailed, some room is after all made for the 'modern' preposition *within* (as opposed, say, to 'down from above'). The third word of the *Odyssey*, *ennepe*, which I translated 'tell', is strictly speaking a compound not a simple verb: *en(n)-epe*, 'in-tell'. It is hard to know whether this prefix carries any hint of interiority. The same word is certainly used by Homer with reference to the ordinary exchange of information by human beings. In these instances, although full 'interiority' is out of the question, there seems frequently to be an implication of relative privacy, a sense that the information given is, in some degree, a confidence, or designed for the individual recipient. It is the word used by Telemachus, the hard-pressed son of Odysseus, when he quietly asks if there is any news of his father (*Odyssey*, iv. 317). In the twenty-third book of the *Odyssey*, the hero has come home again and declares his true identity to the beloved, faithful Penelope. The old nurse, Eurycleia, helps to prepare the marriage bed for them and then withdraws to her own room. After they have made love, Odysseus and Penelope tell their own stories (*enepontes*, the same verb, 301). In all these cases the simple translation 'tell' (with no special colouring of privacy) may in fact be wholly adequate and accurate. But it is also possible that, in the opening address to the Muse, there is a suggestion that the Muse *privately* communicates that which the poet publishes. The common modern assumption of hermetic insulation of the self according to which an event is unequivocally either internal or external, is not to be had in these early texts. Again the curious unfolding, in the twentieth century, of psychoanalysis may make it a little easier for us to entertain the old model. If my Oedipus Complex is identical with Peter's and with David's, when I act from that complex does the action have an internal or external source? For Freud, the traffic of the self, which certainly extends far beyond the artificially illuminated conscious area, is in a manner prepersonal, for much of the time.

Near the end of the *Odyssey* Phemius, the minstrel, says, 'I am self-taught (*autodidaktos*); a god planted all sorts of songs in my mind' (xxii. 347). Dodds comments,

The two parts of his statement are not felt as contradictory: he means, I think, that he has not memorized the lays of other minstrels, but is a creative poet who relies on the hexameter phrases welling up spontaneously as he needs them out of some unknown and uncontrollable depth; he sings 'out of the gods', as the best minstrels always do.[7]

Dodds is perhaps too absolute in his assumption that memorial performance is a godless affair, for in an age without books remembering is a partly mysterious, highly dynamic thing, in which the Muse may play a vital part. But on the essential point he is surely right. Predictably, however, when Dodds must convey 'the reality' to twentieth century readers, what for Phemius surely descended from above must now well up from below.

Homer is quite capable of drawing a contrast between individually based or extra-personal motivation. Medon says of Telemachus, 'I do not know whether some god set him on or whether his own spirit stirred him to go to Pylos' (*Odyssey*, iv. 712–13). It is instructive to compare with this two lines of Virgil, which are too often cited in commentaries as a simple derivate from the Homeric formula. In Book ix of the *Aeneid* two young Trojan warrior-lovers, Nisus and Euryalus, fretting at inaction, are each seized by an impulse which seems rather to be given to the subject than formed by him—and yet at the same time is vividly internal in its operation. Nisus says,

> Dine hunc ardorem mentibus addunt,
> Euryale, an sua cuique deus fit dira cupido?
>
> (ix. 184–5)

For Medon there are two mutually exclusive alternatives; either a god made him go or his own spirit sent him; one or the other must actually have happened. Nisus's words are much less down to earth. Indeed, they are touched by a distinctively philosophical anxiety. He is, as it were, suspended between the matching of rival, factual possibilities and the very different

---

[7] Ibid. 10. For the phrase, 'out of the gods' see *Odyssey*, xvii. 518.

matching of rival languages. By the first of these models he is saying, as Homer might have said, 'Do the gods put this ardour in us or does our own spirit produce it?' By the second he is saying, 'When such ardour arises in human beings, is it really because of the gods or do *we* turn something which is properly our own into "divine agency"?' The crucially un-Homeric word, spanning the novel transition, is *fit*, 'becomes', 'is made'. The sense 'is made', moreover, is now beginning to carry, unmistakably, a nuance of human creativity: *verum factum*[8]: *verum fictum*; 'truth made, truth feigned'.

It is impossible to plot in detail the transformation of Mediterranean thought which lies between the Homeric and Virgilian passages. The suspicion that 'god language' might be susceptible of translation into psychological language certainly found occasional expression. Long before the *Hippolytus* of Euripides the pre-Socratic philosopher, Heraclitus (about 500 BC) says, in a surviving fragment, 'Character is a man's destiny god', or rather 'Character is what a man's destiny god really is' (*ēthos anthrōpō daimōn*).[9] That the second—reductive—translation is not forced is attested by the fact that Plutarch (*Moralia*, 999e) cites the Heraclitean tag in express contrast with the authentic divine spirit which, he believes, animated Socrates. As a good Stoic he is repelled by the irreligious character of the Heraclitean aphorism. In the same passage Plutarch offers a similarly tantalizing fragment of the comic dramatist Menander (later 4th century BC), *Ho nous gar hēmōn estin en hekastō theos*,[10] 'Our mind is in each of us a god'. This may look like a shining example of the converse, Stoic impulse to re-annex for theology territory by this date claimed by the psyche, that is, like a serious deification of the rational element, but Plutarch saw it as tainted with the earlier Heraclitean psychologizing

---

[8] See Giambattista Vico, *Dell'antichissima sapienza italica*, in *Opere*, ed. Fausto Nicolini (Milan: R. Ricciardi, 1953), 248.

[9] Fragment 94 in M. Marcovich, *Heraclitus: Greek Text with a Short Commentary* (Merida, Venezuela: Los Andes University Press, 1967), 500 (no. 119 in the Diels-Kranz numbering). For the date, see W. K. C. Guthrie, *A History of Greek Philosophy*, 5 vols. (Cambridge: Cambridge University Press, 1962–78), i. 408.

[10] Gnom. mon. 434, fragment 762K in *Menander*, with an English translation by Francis G. Allinson, Loeb Classical Library (London: Heinemann, 1921), 530; in T. Kock (ed.), *Comicorum Atticorum Fragmenta*, 3 vols. (Leipzig: Teubner, 1880–8), iii. 214.

reduction. Every schoolchild used to know that Latin has two ways of expressing 'either . . . or': '*aut . . . aut*' and '*vel . . . vel*'. The first is used to express exclusive, practical alternatives ('Either she saved her mother or she did not'). The second is used for alternative, competing expressions, having reference to the same thing ('She is the mother or guide of us all.') The transition from Medon's to Nisus' words could be described as a move from an '*aut*-mentality' to a '*vel*-mentality'.

Meanwhile the contrast between the Homeric 'Sing, goddess' and the Virgilian 'I sing' looks curiously absolute, though we have seen enough of Homeric phraseology to sense that, while the Muse may be fundamentally other than the poet's ego, she may well have operated within the poet's 'self'—within his *autos*. Nevertheless, if we read literally as E. R. Dodds would have us do, certain bizarre consequences swiftly present themselves. For example, Homer's personal ego-contribution to the *Iliad* and the *Odyssey* is remarkably brief—eight lines at the beginning of the *Iliad* and ten at the beginning of the *Odyssey*. The poet *in person* must call up the Muse, who presumably cannot invoke herself, but once she has been conjured, *her* voice takes over. This would mean that *Iliad*, i. 1–8, is 'by Homer' and i. 9–xxiv. 805 (less a few secondary invocations) is 'by the Muse'. We live in a historical period which has been variously deluded by spuriously clear conceptions of authorship and attribution, so that the transition I have just caricatured is much more rebarbative for us than it would have been for an ancient Greek. The style and the metre of 'the bit by Homer' is identical with the style and metre of 'the bit by the Muse'. Many centuries later George Herbert was to create a similar problem of liminal poetry, that is of lines placed at the threshold of the work: the dedication of *The Temple*:

> Lord, my first fruits present themselves to thee,
> Yet not mine neither, for from thee they came,
> And must return . . .

Herbert the poet comes with a creaturely gift for his Maker and then finds, true Protestant that he is, that the poems he thought his to give were wrought in him by God. Here, similarly, the situation may be caricatured (if we take Herbert at his word) by saying that Herbert wrote the dedication of *The Temple*, and

God the rest. Moreover, in the case of Herbert, we cannot say that the distinction is blurred. It is characteristic of Protestantism to sharpen these questions until they draw blood; accordingly, *The Temple*, unlike the *Odyssey*, continually and painfully negotiates and renegotiates moral and poetic initiatives. It is indeed in the seventeenth century that the thought becomes a source of general anxiety. One cannot believe that the original listeners to Homer were in any way troubled by it. Homer after all is there throughout. singing to them, *autodidaktos*, self-taught and inspired.

Virgil was not the first poet in the epic tradition to switch to the first person singular. The *Ilias Parva* or 'Little Iliad' begins with a wholly unapologetic 'I': 'I sing of Ilium and of Dardania with its fine horses.' The *Ilias Parva*, a poem belonging to what is called 'the Epic Cycle', is early enough in date—about seventh or sixth century BC—to make one wonder whether Homer himself performing on some other occasion might not, after all, have begun with the words 'I sing'. But, if he had, the hearers would still have supposed the song to be *ek theōn*, 'out of the gods' (*Odyssey*, xvii. 518). With Virgil's *cano* there is no such religious security or underpinning.

In Alexandria, a city famous for its library, for literacy and literary disputes, in the later third century BC, Apollonius Rhodius composed his sophisticated epic, the *Argonautica*. This begins indeed with a first person singular, but the verb is modified and guarded by a curious flourish of ambiguity.

> Archomenos seo, Phoibe, palaigeneōn klea phōtōn
> Mnēsomai

Beginning from thee, Phoebus Apollo, I will recount the glorious deeds of those born long ago

Apollonius, belonging as he does to a critical age, brings to bear an explicitly literary consciousness and therefore refers as if from outside to the origin of the poem. At the same time, however, it may be that we are confronted by a problem of interpretation. The Loeb translator, R. C. Seaton, renders the phrase 'beginning with thee, O phoebus',[11] presumably meaning 'beginning by mentioning you' or 'beginning with my

---

[11] Apollonius Rhodius, *The Argonautica* (London: Heinemann, 1919), 3.

invocation of you'. But the ghost of another, much more ancient meaning cannot quite be exorcised: 'beginning from you as source of my song', 'inspired by you'. To pursue this question is to become involved in minute and seemingly very dry questions of linguistic usage; but anyone who wishes to understand the conception the old poets had of the way epic poems begin—who wishes, in short, to know *what a Muse was*—will want answers to these questions.

It must be granted at once that *archesthai ek Dios*, 'to begin out of Zeus' (*ek* is a preposition) and *archesthai theon*, literally 'to begin of-the-gods' (no preposition; *theon*, 'of the gods', is a simple genitive) are by Apollonius's time conventionally established idiom, employed by poets as well as by people talking about poetry. Pindar in his fifth Nemean ode (line 25) telling of a song sung long ago *by the Muses themselves* described them as *Dios archomenai*, 'beginning of-Zeus'. Those who believe that Homer's concept of passionate motivation was wholly theological (intervening divine powers) and not in any degree psychological encounter a curious difficulty when they meet the passionate, quarrelsome gods of Olympus; for when *Aphrodite*, say, experiences an erotic impulse, *she* cannot have been 'breathed in' by a (higher) Aphrodite; were it so, an infinite regress of motivating deities would instantly be generated. One might as a consequence of this absurdity recoil to the almost equally odd alternative conclusion that Homer was able to deploy in connection with gods something which he was as yet unable to conceive in the human sphere, a truly interior system of motivation—a scheme which, most strangely of all, could scarcely have been drawn from any other source than human beings themselves! Yet something of this sort is implied in Feuerbach's famous, pre-Marxian version of *Entäusserung*, or *Entfremdung*, 'alienation', according to which religion is pro-duced by a sort of willed self-deprivation, a collective ascription of characteristics properly human to a divine order.[12] So it is with Pindar's Muses. If the Muses are no longer inspiring but

[12] 'Man first of all sees his nature as if *out of* himself, before he finds it in himself . . . The divine being is nothing else than the human being . . . made objective . . .'. Ludwig Feuerbach, *The Essence of Christianity* (*Der Wesen des Christentums*, 1841), trans. George Eliot (New York: Harper and Row, 1957), 13–14.

are themselves inspired we might smell just such an absurd
infinite regress of motivating deities; Pindar has already referred
us on, to Zeus. But it may well be that Pindar really does mean
'beginning *by speaking of* Zeus'. Even so, however, the problem
is postponed rather than resolved. For a preliminary mention of
Zeus or 'prelude to Zeus' as the Loeb translator puts it[13] would
surely have been an invocation of Zeus, and gods are invoked in
order that they may *inspire* the subsequent song. The phrase
'beginning of/from the god' recurs in other Hellenistic poets
contemporary with Apollonius, for example, Aratus,
Phaenomena, 1, and Theocritus, *Idylls*, 17. 1. A. S. F. Gow in
his commentary on this passage gives numerous further
parallels.[14]

Apollonius was nothing if not learned and would undoubted-
ly have written not only from a consciousness of the Homeric
roots of the notion but also from a knowledge of the accreted
scholastic commentary which had gradually encrusted the text
of Homer. It is likely, as we have seen, that Homer's phrase
theon ex, 'out of the gods', refers directly to inspiration. Closer
still to the phrasing of Apollonius is Homer's account of the
Phaeacian minstrel, Demodocus, in Book viii of the *Odyssey*.
Odysseus calls upon Demodocus to sing, in effect, another *Iliad*,
but this time concentrating on the story of the Wooden Horse
(which Virgil himself will sing in the second book of his
Aeneid). Homer describes the response of the minstrel in these
words: *hormētheis theou ercheto* (viii. 499), literally, 'having been
stirred/made to rise of-the-god he began'. The sentence
continues, 'taking up the tale from the point at which the Greeks
set fire to their huts'. There is an initial difficulty (which may be
found in the long run to make little difference) as to whether
theou, 'of-the-god', is to be taken with *hormētheis*, 'having been
stirred', or with *ercheto*, 'he began'. E. Schwyzer[15] and P.
Chantraine[16] both take *theou* with *hormētheis*, but J. B.
Hainsworth[17] says that such a usage is post-Homeric and

[13] *Pindar*, with an English translation by Sir J. E. Sandys (London: Heinemann,
1919), 361.
[14] *Theocritus*, 2 vols. (Cambridge: Cambridge University Press, 1952), ii. 327.
[15] *Griechische Grammatik*, 4 vols. (Munich: C. H. Beck'she, 1953–71), ii. 119.
[16] Pierre Chantraine, *Grammaire homérique*, 2 vols. (Paris: C. Klincksieck,
1942–53), ii. 61, 65.
[17] In Alfred Heubeck, Stephanie West, and J. B. Hainsworth, *A Commentary on*

accordingly he does what Apollonius appears to have done, that is, he takes *theou* with *ercheto*. The Scholiasts (the ancient commentators on Homer) exhibit confusion on precisely this point in their glosses. The 'Hamburg Scholiast' (known as 'T') explains *hormētheis* as meaning *ex theou empneustheis*, 'breathed in/inspired from the god', adding that the minstrel gets his powers and his start from the god. The 'Palatine Scholiast', on the other hand ('P') takes *theou ercheto* together in what we have guessed is the Apollonian manner. His comment is mildly indecisive: ' "Inspired by the Muse" or else "Beginning from the god" '.[18] Thus, even when *theou*, 'of the god', is taken with the verb, the scholiast does not go unequivocally for the sense, 'began by speaking about the god' but reverts (uncertainly) to the idea of divine inspiration. We appear to have been set down in a linguistic labyrinth in which, however carefully we choose from the precisely defined paths before us, we are always led back to the same ambiguity.

It is entirely possible, therefore, that the radical notion of inspiration (whether as the object of a literary nostalgia or as in some way reflecting the experience of composition) is still operative in Apollonius, despite his 'proto-Virgilian' choice of a first person singular. The argument for the existence of this possibility has been based so far on Apollonius' learned 'inwardness' with Homer and Homeric commentary. There are, however, other corroborative signs of a less tangible kind that Apollo was a vivid reality to Apollonius, or at least that the god was something more to him than a literary convention. The epiphany in Book ii (669–713) when the golden-haired god causes the earth to quake at his tread and sea-waves to mount is quite extraordinary. Apollonius seems almost to have surprised himself, for at 708–9 he interjects a strange and sudden address of his own. The whole passage has a power not easily matched, unless by the rape-epiphany in Euripides' *Ion*, 887–901.[19]

There is one curious footnote to be added. Apollonius in due course attracted his own *scholia* whose task it was to explain (as

---

Homer's Odyssey (Oxford: Clarendon Press, 1958), 379. This is the first volume of what is to be a 3-volume commentary on the *Odyssey*.

[18] For both scholia see W. Dindorf (ed.), *Scholia Graeca in Homeri Odysseam*, 2 vols. (Oxford: Clarendon Press, 1855–60), i. 396.

[19] I owe this comparison to Mr Robin Lane Fox.

I, in 1989, am seeking to explain) Apollonius' *archomenos seo*, 'beginning from/of/with thee'. The Apollonian Scholiast suggests two meanings: first, 'I, making a start from you' (what does *that* mean?) and second, 'being elected by you' (*archairesiazomenos*, a political word). The retreat from a full assertion of inspiration to a more distant notion of prior election is interesting. He adds that *archomenos* may be a *periectic* ('comprehensive') use of the verb incorporating both active and passive senses.[20] We are being asked to think not only of Apollonius starting his poem but of Apollonius *being started*, in which case, note, the notion of prior, divine agency lives on.

POLYSEMOUS EPIC

'Arma virumque cano . . .'

Even as Virgil asserts his own power over the huge work which is to follow, there is an undertow of submission, an acknowledgement of the Homeric passiveness, a receptivity towards both a Maker and a Poem larger than the merely human subject. For all that, we are now in a different world. The individual voice is now urgently, almost scandalously present and the relation with the Muse is curtailed, relegated to a secondary status. Where, then, is the element of submission? We sense, in fact, the presence of an implicit invocation of another kind—an invocation of previous literature; one can almost say, *Virgil's real Muse is no goddess, but is Homer*. The goddess is there, we surmise, only because the true authority, Homer, prescribes her presence. But indeed the relation of Virgil to Homer is different from that of Demodocus to the god. Virgil's relation to the dead, Greek father of epic is, as we have seen, partly antagonistic. He knows that in 'writing the *Iliad* and the *Odyssey* again' he must transform his material. The wanderings and homecoming of the hero, the war for the city must be changed so that they become instinct with a larger, historical significance, the making of Rome. He was telling his Italian auditors their own story. C. S. Lewis was right when he said that Virgil

---

[20] See C. Wendel (ed.), *Scholia in Apollonium Rhodium Vetera* (Berlin: Weidmann, 1935), 7.

virtually invented the Great Subject.[21] The *Iliad* is about Achilles, or, if it is about war, it is about war at any time. Behind this hesitation there lurks no doubleness or ambiguity in the Homeric material. The *Aeneid* is about Aeneas who as he travels, bewildered, from Troy to Italy, is in fact building, block by block, the future of his race, the present of the poem's audience; here there is, always, a kind of doubleness. Aeneas is preceded by the shadow of a future immensity, which stalks before him like a Brockenspectre. Within the poem, Rome is pre-echoed by a series of ghost cities: the rising splendours of Dido's Carthage (destined to become the great antagonist of Rome), the doomed, plague-stricken attempt to build Pergamum on Crete (iii. 132), Helenus's sad, miniature Ilium at Buthrotum (iii. 349–51)—and, of course, burning Troy itself. Sometimes the Virgilian doubleness crystallizes as a kind of typology, as when Dido prefigures Cleopatra or Aeneas, Augustus. The 'Pathetic Fallacy' whereby nature mirrors the failings of human subjects, as in the storm in which Dido and Aeneas come together in the cave, is deeply congenial to Virgil and foreign to Homer. Ruskin, who gave us the term 'Pathetic Fallacy' actually loved and admired the unsympathizing manner in which the earth which covers the dead brothers of Helen is still described as 'life-giving' by Homer (*Iliad*, iii. 243).[22] By the Pathetic Fallacy, for all its apparent capriciousness, a sense of an echoic conspiracy *in rebus*, in the shaping of actual events, may be subliminally enforced. It has been said that Ruskin's use of the word 'fallacy' is odd, since no one was ever deceived by the tamarisks which wept when Gallus died (*Eclogues*, x. 12) but with the larger, less distinct doublings of the *Aeneid* (written after the pastoral *Eclogues*) one can begin to feel that an obscure but far-reaching deception is indeed afoot—terminating in nothing less than historicism itself. I here mean by 'historicism' something which is profoundly the opposite of Homer's grim,

[21] *Preface to Paradise Lost* (London: Oxford University Press, 1960), 27–33. Lewis had in mind the idea of a great *historical* subject, a significant event projected in epic form. As far as one can judge from the surviving fragments, the historical *Annals* of Ennius were not about Significant History in the Virgilian manner.

[22] *Modern Painters*, part 4, ch. 12, in *The Works of John Ruskin*, ed. E. T. Cook and Alexander (A.T.O.) Wedderburn, 39 vols. (London: George Allen, 1902–12), v. 213.

unmeaning turbulence, something which on the contrary ascribes to history a determined—perhaps an ordained—shape, to be expounded by theologians or political prophets. Without Homer (though Virgil without Homer is almost unimaginable) Virgil might have written Annals, like his Roman predecessor, Ennius. As it was, the mere fact of cross-reference to a mode of epic now historically remote would of itself have tended to precipitate him into typology and ulterior significance—the whole business, in short, of literary latency.

If, however, the *Aeneid* is considered as a system of human figures standing in a hall of mirrors, it rapidly becomes apparent that, again and again, the glass is disturbingly flawed. An unappeasable distress for a green world destroyed continually thwarts the triumphal closure of images and survives the end of the poem, in the reverberation left by the unconsenting (*indignata*) death of Turnus. The recurrent image of a stricken deer refuses the grand historical typological assimilation: the first thing Aeneas does when he lands in North Africa is to kill a deer (i.189); Dido, whose heart he breaks, is compared with a wounded deer at iv. 69. The Latin War breaks out when Iulus, Aeneas's son and a kind of repetition of his father, hurts the stag which belongs to Silvia ('the woodland girl') at vii. 496–502. Aeneas brings law and order, incongruously, to an Arcadian kingdom whose subjects are spontaneously righteous (vii. 203). When Aeneas arrives in Latium, without consulting the inhabitants he marks out the land with boundary lines (vii. 157). In the *Georgics* Virgil sees the first marking of the earth as a species of violation (i. 126). Yet, in spite of all this, the adumbrated Imperium dominates the poem.

So Virgil wrote not annals but a poem which simultaneously mirrored and smashed Homeric epic. Never was there so loving, so pious an iconoclast. The opening section of Virgil's poem (the Muse still uninvoked) ends with the powerful un-Homeric assertion of the story beyond the immediate story:

> genus unde Latinum
> Albanique patres atque altae moenia Romae. (6–7)

whence the Latin race, the Alban fathers and the walls of high Rome.

Thus far we have a personal voice, inchoating a theme which thereafter opens upon successively greater but always historically specific vistas. Meanwhile, however, there is an 'opening behind the opening'. Donatus, the author of a fourth-century life of Virgil, and Servius, the Latin commentator of the same century, both cite four supposedly cancelled opening lines, which lead, by an unbroken grammatical sequence, into the standard *arma virumque* opening, forming a single complex sentence. The lines are as follows (I mark the canonical opening with a capitalized word):

> Ille ego qui quondam gracili modulatus avena
> carmen, et egressus silvis vicina coegi
> utquamvis avido parerent arva colono,
> gratum opus agricolis, at nunc horrentia Martis
> ARMA virumque cano, Troiae qui primus ab oris
> Italiam fato profugus Laviniaque venit
> Litora, multum ille et terris iactatus et alto
> vi superum, saevae memorem Iunonis ob iram,
> multa quoque et bello passus, dum conderet urbem
> inferretque deos Latio; genus unde Latinum
> Albanique patres atque altae moenia Romae.

That man am I who, having once played his tune upon a slender reed, emerging from the woods compelled the neighbouring fields to submit even to the greediest farmer, a work welcome to husbandmen, but now Mars's bristling ARMS and the man I sing, who first from the shores of Troy by fate a fugitive came to Italy and the Lavinian shore—much suffering, too, in war, till he should found the city and bring his gods to Latium; whence the Latin race, the Alban fathers and the walls of high Rome.

The account Donatus gives of the extra lines is a complex one: the grammarian Nisus, he explains, had heard from his 'elders' that Varius, the friend and literary executor of Virgil had excised the first four lines leaving the opening we all know. Scholars are to this day divided, some thinking the lines Virgilian (F. A. Hirtzel's Oxford Text of 1900 actually had the printed text begin with them), some regarding them as spurious. Various intermediate positions are possible. For example it is conceivable that the lines are indeed by Virgil but that he disliked them; *he* may have intimated to Varius that the poem had better begin at *Arma*. A responsible editor, believing this, ought presumably to print *Arma* as the first word, out of respect for the author's wishes. The matter is certainly not settled by fact that early quotations reflect, and Pompeian graffiti humorously paraphrase, the *arma virumque* opening.[23] If Varius, with or without the authority of Virgil, had excised these lines the Latin world at large would have been given a poem which began with 'arms and the man'. What is harder to stomach is that Virgil, at whatever stage of provisional drafting, could ever have countenanced such a rambling, broken-backed period. In the entire ensuing poem there is no sentence as ill-formed as this.

Yet, in another way, what we are given is quintessentially Virgilian. If for a moment we can bear with the inelegancies of syntax and tempo there is something haunting in the very duplication. Our sense of the personality of the poet, already urgent, is now enhanced, the story of the epic emergence of Aeneas and Rome is pre-echoed in a coded literary story. The lines which tell of the reed and the woods are an allusion to Virgil's *Eclogues*, his first important work (in particular to the 'thin reed' and the 'woodland Muse' of *Eclogues*, i. 2) and the words which follow are a reference to his next work, the *Georgics*, which dealt with practical husbandry. Moreover, behind the literary pre-echo lies a more poignantly human and personal analogical narrative. The verbal reminiscence of Eclogue i may remind us of Tityrus, the shepherd cast out from his farm who according to tradition represents Virgil himself. The story is that after the Battle of Philippi, when agricultural land was requisitioned for the discharged veterans, Virgil was dispossessed. Thus, Tityrus is Virgil. It will be said that the tradition is open to doubt, but the habit of analogy it assumes and enforces is itself Virgilian. In the *Aeneid* it may be that the same essential story is subjected to a sudden dreamlike analogical expansion, since the theme of dispossession, of pastoral invaded and destroyed, is projected upon a Homeric screen, after which, as we have seen, the Homeric theme is itself made to shadow forth a national history. Aeneas, Evander, and Turnus may each in his turn step forward, as a magnified image of the grieving poet, deracinated from a loved landscape.

The radical alternative is that the lines cited by Donatus are

---

[23] See R. G. Austin, 'Ille ego qui quondam . . .', *Classical Quarterly*, NS 41 (1968), 107–15, and the same author's note in his commentary, *Aeneidos Liber Primus* (Oxford: Clarendon Press, 1971), 26.

not by Virgil but by some other hand, writing after his death. This is perhaps the most plausible hypothesis, but it makes less difference than one might have expected. For whoever wrote these lines was, so to speak, full of Virgil's poetry. It is as if the habit of indistinct typology, set in motion (perhaps) by the first Eclogue and the audacious historical allusiveness of the *Aeneid*, together with the strong initial assertion of the author as individual, generates a kind of 'after-poetry', like the after-images we see when we stare at a light and then close our eyes. The live poem continues to grow, after the poet had laid down his stylus, but not through a process of communal revision and extension as ballads grow, but rather through the assistance of readers who, paradoxically enough, are excited precisely by the actual personal and historical provenance of the poem, and have caught its technique of mirroring.[24]

In the *Appendix Vergiliana* there is a poem which few now would believe to be by Virgil himself, in which the poet laments his expulsion from his own land, the *Dirae* ('Curses' or 'Furies'). Five lines in it especially stand out:

> Hinc ego de tumulo mea rura novissima visam,
> hinc ibo in silvas: obstabunt iam mihi colles,
> obstabunt montes, campos audire licebit:
> 'dulcia rura valete et Lydia dulcior illis
> et casti fontes et, felix nomen, agelli'.　(86–90)

From this mound I shall look for the last time at my lands and then go into the woods, now hills will block, now mountains, but the levels will still be able to hear, 'Goodbye, sweet country places and Lydia sweeter still, goodbye, chaste springs and you little fields of happy name'.

These lines stand out from the relatively coarse, sub-Virgilian versification of the *Dirae*. Eduard Fraenkel went so far as to say that whoever wrote these lines could not be the poet of the *Dirae*, and he stressed a connection, indirect but nevertheless intimate, with the authentically Virgilian fifth Eclogue.[25] The passage is remarkable for its subtle hypallage from subject to

---

[24] Annabel Patterson has argued that Virgil deliberately defaced himself in order to necessitate reinterpretation by other poets. See her *Pastoral and Ideology, Virgil to Valéry* (Oxford: Clarendon Press, 1988), 4.

[25] 'The Dirae', *Journal of Roman Studies*, 56 (1966), 142–55, 152.

object, not all of which can be conveyed straightforwardly in an English version. For example, the Latin does not actually say, 'I shall look for the last time at my lands'; it says, 'I shall look at my newest (latest) lands'; the character of the looking (looking for the last time) is ascribed to the thing looked at. This is not a mere trick or metrical convenience. It is *used* poetically.

Partly, the effect is of an extreme subjectivism: where the *pathos* of the viewer is as strong as this, it can, so to speak, appropriate the object in an act of wilful perceptual tyranny, but at the same time this is a poem about expropriation and we are aware that this small, defiant movement of the imagination is futile. The notion of a last embrace, hackneyed in English, but poetically powerful in the *Aeneid*, may lie behind the thought here. Thus, together with the rhetorical appropriation we sense the opposite of appropriation: that the subject is drained, that a richness of identity properly his has passed into the landscape. There is even a faint paradox within the single word *novissima*, where, because this is a time poem, we hear for an instant the basic sense, 'newest', before it is contested and defeated by the dominant sense 'last'. But then we have a firmly personal assertion: *ibo in silvas*, 'I shall go into the woods', followed at once by *obstabunt iam mihi colles*. I translated these words, with all the inelegance of a studied neutrality, as 'now hills will block'. In ordinary Latin *obstabunt* following *ibo* must mean 'will bar my path'. But the context of intense subjective perception, of looking and listening (or being heard) ensures that we do not take it so. It is as if the poet is walking with head turned, so that *obstabunt* can mean (as the Loeb translator takes it) 'will block *my view*'. The agency is mysteriously transferred, once more, from the subject moving through the landscape, to the landscape itself. We cannot quite say that the poet makes the hills move (these hills are not like the striding mountain in the first book of Wordsworth's *The Prelude* (1850, i. 412)). Yet the repetition of the verb and the changing scale of its subject (first hills then mountains) suggest as it were a covert action on the part of the landscape, as if the ground moves to interpose its masses when the poet is not looking. In these lines we have, then, a certain linguistic and logical oddity, deployed to a subtle literary effect. These hints are then allowed to flower in the full-blown poetical figure of the levels still hearing the poet's melancholy valediction, a version of the quintessentially Virgilian trope of the Pathetic Fallacy, since we infer sympathy in the listening fields.

If these lines are not by Virgil they are by someone who, as they used to say in the sixteenth century, was deeply inward with his work—though the *Dirae* never lost its place in the Virgilian *corpus*, it seems to have been little taught in the Roman schools and to have escaped the kind of learned commentary which accreted round his *Eclogues*, *Georgics*, and *Aeneid*. These lines especially are thoroughly Virgilian in their subtle manipulation of subject and object and in their heart-tearing sense of place. Virgil is rightly famous as the poet of *idem in alio*, who reworked the war and the wanderings of Homeric epic until they became instinct with futurity, with the divine history of a single city, Rome. At the same time, as I have suggested, Virgil was aware of a correlative personal history, of his own eviction, wandering, and homecoming. This is picked up and accented in the *Dirae*, together (it must be confessed) with a quantity of substandard writing of quite another order.

Here too we can see the operation of a 'ripple effect', started by the distinctive assertion of Virgil's genius in the *Eclogues*, *Georgics*, and *Aeneid*. The idea that the figurative technique should be extended at times to comprehend the poet's own life (a curious fusion of biographer's interpretative metaphor—'Mr Micawber is Dickens' father'—and poet's metaphor) is authorized, I suggest, by the Virgil –Tityrus identification in Eclogue i, to which we may now add the Virgil–Menalcas identification in Eclogue ix. But the tradition, I conceded, may be doubtful. In particular, the story so dear to the early biographers and commentators on Eclogue i that Octavian, the future Emperor, restored Virgil's lands to him may not be true. Moreover it has often been observed that in Eclogue ix the disinherited free citizen, Meliboeus, is a closer analogue to Virgil than Menalcas, the freed slave, could ever be. Some suppose that the gloomy reflections at *Georgics*, i. 197–9, work against the supposition of restitution: 'I have seen seeds, carefully selected, go wrong . . . fate causes all things to degenerate, to slip back; it is as if an oarsman, rowing upstream, were to relax and be swept back . . .'. It is in fact impossible to infer with confidence from such passages of generalized melancholy that Virgil's lands were never restored to him. In truth we do not know. Meanwhile, note, the original dispossession motif remains firmly in place. Moreover Tityrus is a poet. This instantly enforces a relation between the artful city poet and the somehow miraculously natural singer within the green world which has enriched pastoral poetry ever since. Even E. Brandt's ingenious suggestion that the extra lines were written to accompany a frontispiece showing Virgil himself is not outside the bounds of possibility.[26] The interesting thing is that here, yet again, it is Virgil's technique of over spilling significance which permits the curious syntactic joinery, whereby the legend under the picture is grammatically merged with the poem.

In the *Appendix Vergiliana*, especially, as we have seen, in the *Dirae* and also in *Catalepton*, viii, a new species of literary piety found it natural to extend—and, it must be admitted, to coarsen—the queer, fruitful mingling of personal and impersonal which we find in Virgil's poetry. The way was being prepared for one whose faithlessness and subsequent return (to Beatrice and to God) would be projected on an even larger screen in medieval Italy.

How, then, shall we sum up the effect of this *Ille ego qui quondam* . . . 'That man am I, who having once . . .'? This 'coded literary autobiography' is indeed in typological relation with the poem which follows; this syntactically gauche anticipatory doubling of clauses, is, in all but its clumsiness, an essentially Virgilian thing, even if Virgil did not write it. Virgil's achievement, which is nothing less than the invention of subjective epic[27] has charged his first readers with a strange power—and power mishandled may still be power. The collision of pronouns—*ille ego*, 'that man I'—in the first foot of the first line is itself fascinating. I have pressed so far in my argument for the importance of the first person singular in Virgil's proem. Yet the *very* first word of this prelude is a distancing word, apotropaic, propelling the poet's identity far from him into history and public discourse. The gesture does not hold, however, for the grammar of the sentence which follows, which could easily have been third person. 'I am that

---

[26] 'Zum Aeneis-Proemium', *Philologus*, 83 (1928), 331–5.
[27] See Brooks Otis, *Virgil: A Study in Civilised Poetry* (Oxford: Clarendon Press, 1964), 41–97.

man who *has* . . .', is immediately reinvaded by the first person.
'I am that man, I, who *have* . . .'. Virgil or his surrogate writes
not *coegit* but *coegi*.

THE BEGINNING OF THE STORY

I have spent many words on Virgil's proem, with the general
presumption that in doing so I have been discussing the
beginning of the *Aeneid*. It is time to remind ourselves that
many of the ancients, especially, perhaps, those closest in spirit
to Homer, construed all this quite differently. For them the
Aeneid, that is the story of Aeneas, has not yet begun. We have
been engaged exclusively on the maieutic preliminaries, on that
which the poet must do to induce birth. The poem itself starts,
even here, when the Muse begins to sing, to recount the causes
of divine anger. To us having before our eyes a block of print of
which the irregular right hand margin proclaims verse form, it
is merely obvious that the poem begins with the first line
printed. As long, however, as epic had living links with oral
performance (and it is worth reflecting that even as literary an
epic as the *Aeneid* was, almost certainly, always read *aloud*) this
becomes less obvious. I do not claim that the sense of
disjunction is as strong as that which for modern readers
separates, say, '© Oxford University Press' from 'Chapter 1.
Dawn crept slowly over the golf course . . .'. Nor, to approach
the real conditions of ancient primary epic more nearly, is the
proem as clearly separate from what follows as is say, the tuning
up of a guitar from a song, though where this includes
preliminary half-experimental chords the analogy shows after
all some signs of life. Nevertheless the sense that the proem is not
the beginning but precedes it, is one which we should foster in
ourselves, if only to understand the manner in which Virgil, by
his act of self-incorporation, began the gradual transformation
of European poetry, leading us in due season to poems which
are, in a way, *all* 'personal beginning', such as Milton's *Lycidas*.
  The story of Aeneas begins with these lines:

> Urbs antiqua fuit (Tyrii tenuere coloni)
> Karthago, Italiam contra Tiberinaque longe
> ostia, dives opum studiisque asperrima belli,
> quam Iuno fertur terris magis omnibus unam

posthabita coluisse Samo. hic illius arma,
hic currus fuit; hoc regnum dea gentibus esse,
si qua fata sinant, iam tum tenditque fovetque.
progeniem sed enim Troiano a sanguine duci
audierat Tyrias olim quae verteret arces;
hinc populum late regem belloque superbum
venturum excidio Libyae; sic volvere Parcas.
id metuens veterisque memor Saturnia belli,
prima quod ad Troiam pro caris gesserat Argis—
necdum etiam causae irarum saevique dolores
exciderant animo; manet alta mente repostum
iudicium Paridis spretaeque iniuria formae
et genus invisum et rapti Ganymedis honores:
his accensa super iactatos aequore toto
Troas, reliquias Danaum atque immitis Achilli,
arcebat longe Latio; multosque per annos
errabant acti fatis maria omnia circum.
tantae molis erat Romanam condere gentem.
 Vix e conspectu Siculae telluris in altum
vela dabant laeti et spumas salis aere ruebant,

(i. 12–35)

There was an ancient city (Tyrian farmer-settlers held it) facing Italy
and the Tiber estuary across the sea, rich in wealth and hard in the
pursuits of war. This city Juno is said to have favoured most with her
presence, more, even, than Samos. Here were her arms, her chariot
and that this (the fates somehow permitting) should be the city which
would rule over the nations was even at that time her cherished aim.
But she had heard that a progeny drawn from Trojan blood would one
day throw down the towers of Carthage; that from Troy a people,
broad-ruling, proud in war, would come, to the ruin of Libya. So span
the Fates. So Saturn's daughter, fearing this, remembering the old war
she had fought at Troy for her beloved Greeks—nor yet, either, had
the things which caused her anger and fierce pains yet fallen from her
mind, for there yet remains, shelved deep in her recollection, the
judgement of Paris and the hurt of her beauty despised, the hated race
and the high favour shown to the ravished Ganymede—set burning all
the more by these things, she began to keep the Trojans back, far from
Latium—those Trojans who were tossed to and fro over the whole
sea, the remnant left behind by the Greeks and the pitiless Achilles;
through many years they wandered, driven by the fates, round all the
seas. So massy and so heavy a thing was it to found the Roman race.
 Hardly out of sight of Sicilian soil they were joyfully setting sail for
the deep sea, cutting the salt foam with brazen prow

It is as if we are not really under way until the very last sentence: the poem moves with the brazen prow of the ship. *Urbs antiqua fuit*, 'There was an ancient city' is not the first movement of narration but 'scene-setting', and the scene—Carthage—in its turn generates the need for prior explanation, in terms of the mind of its presiding goddess, the history of the Trojan war and injuries older still.

This, it may be said, is thoroughly Homeric, for the *Iliad*, after its proem, tells how Apollo stirred up the quarrel because Agamemnon had insulted his (Apollo's) priest, Chryses: 'For one day Chryses came . . .' and the major narrative begins. Thus there is a transition, involving divine motivation, between the proem and the narrative proper. In the *Odyssey* there is, again, a transition, this time more elaborate. First we have a swift summary of the sufferings and journeyings of Odysseus leading to the death of his companions, because they ate the oxen of the Sun God; then we are brought down to Odysseus himself, now companionless, wanting his wife and his home, held captive by the amorous Calypso. But neither of these Homeric transitions has the scale and sense of graduated, recessive 'deep' causality that we find in the *Aeneid*. The shadowed, alien perspective, the temporal vistas opened by the Virgilian subjunctive verbs are un-Homeric. The *Iliad* indeed betrays almost at once the need for a full account of two events which led to the famous quarrel, but solves the problem by making over the preceding insult to Apollo's priest, at once, into foregrounded human narrative, so that the explanation and the beginning of the action are Homerically one. Erich Auerbach's contention[28] that there is in Homer no background, no latency, is open to attack at many points, but it holds here.

Virgil, conversely, loves the sense of recession, of psychological and historical spheres within spheres. The backward vista of prior causes is made by the poet to open upon a future which the poem itself will never fully narrate, for the end of Book xii leaves the formation of the Roman race still in process, not yet accomplished. This in its turn permits, in place of the urgent

[28] *Mimesis: The Representation of Reality in Western Literature* (New York: Doubleday, 1957), 1–20.

objective sequence of Homer, a Virgilian poignancy of contrast, when the ship at last sets sail. For this dispossessed remnant of a ruined city is first seen, with curious abruptness, in a state of joy. Here there is an implicit pathos, a chiaroscuro in the contrast with the shadowed preceding lines, evoking other traditional narratives.

None the less the major act of deference, from the Roman poet to the Greek is there, in the *in medias res* opening, the opening 'into the midst of things'. It is strange that Homer whom we regard as primitive should leave as a legacy this obligation to thwart the ordinary serial logic of 'telling' with so audacious a stroke of art. The phrase itself, *in medias res*, was produced by Horace in about 20 or 19 BC, at the very time when Virgil was working on the *Aeneid*. Horace, at the point in his *Art of Poetry* at which the phrase appears, is anxious to differentiate good poets from bad, and, with this end in view, takes Homer as his guide and beacon. He begins by putting the first lines of the *Odyssey* into Latin:

> 'Dic mihi, Musa, virum, captae post tempora Troiae
> qui mores hominum multorum vidit et urbis.'
> Non fumum ex fulgore, sed ex fumo dare lucem
> cogitat, ut speciosa dehinc miracula promat
>
> .   .   .   .
>
> Nec gemino bellum Troianum orditur ab ovo,
> Semper ad eventum festinat, et *in medias res*
> Non secus ac notas, auditorem rapit[29]
>
> (*Ars Poetica*, 141–9)

In Ben Jonson's translation:

Speak to me, muse, the man, who, after Troy was sacked,
Saw many towns, and men, and could their manners tract.
He [the good poet] thinks not, how to give you smoke from light,
But light from smoke; that he may draw his bright
Wonders forth after

.   .   .   .

               nor Troy's sad war begins
From the two eggs, that did disclose the twins.
He ever hastens to the end, and so

[29] The Oxford Classical Text, ed. E. C. Wickham and H. W. Garrod (Oxford: Clarendon Press, 1901).

(As if he knew it) raps his hearer to
The *middle of his matter*[30]

Both Horace and Virgil, virtually simultaneously, are learning from the Greeks not just superficial tropes and motifs but a profoundly un-Roman (and also un-Hebraic) principle of autonomous artistic order. Where other cultures follow the seemingly unexceptionable advice of the King of Hearts, 'Begin at the beginning, and go on till you come to the end; then stop',[31] Greek culture, led, it would seem, by Homer, said, 'No. Begin half-way through.' Aristotle praises Homer for his interventionist openings and scorns the low writer who imagines that unity is to be obtained by recounting 'all the things that happened to Theseus' (*Poetics*, 1451a 16–22).

We seem to be confronted by a primary assertion of the priority in literature of form to matter. The laws of poetry are not the laws of nature and their radical autonomy must be declared, in a gesture of proud discrepancy. The beginning of the poem must never fuse with a known beginning in nature. Although all these terms are potentially problematic they are in a way appropriate to what is here set down as a first impression. A kind of hostility to the natural can be discerned in the progression of Horace's language, from the (despised) biological beginning of the egg, by way of the excitingly insubstantial images of smoke and light, to the blankest of all Latin words, *res*, 'things'—the matter, in which the poet intervenes, now reduced to a grey, abstract uniformity. We begin to sense in the history of European literature an enormous tension between (say) 'In the beginning God created the heaven and the earth' and 'Hardly out of sight of Sicilian soil they were joyfully setting sail', that is, between a natural and a formal beginning.

In another place Horace wrote, *Naturam expelles furca, tamen usque recurret*, 'You may drive out nature with a pitch-fork, but she will come running back' (*Epistles*, i. x. 24). Even as he opts for the Greek interventionist opening Virgil betrays a certain nostalgia for the 'deep' natural beginning. We have seen how in the *Aeneid*, beyond the chosen narrative shape of the poem,

---

[30] 'Horace, of the Art of Poetry', in *Ben Jonson, The Complete Poems*, ed. G. Parfitt (Harmondsworth: Penguin Books, 1975), 359.
[31] *Alice's Adventures in Wonderland*, in *The Complete Works of Lewis Carroll* (London: Nonesuch, 1939), 114.

beyond the story of Aeneas, a larger, more cosmic history is continually hinted. This is un-Homeric. With due concessions (for example, the *Theogony* of Hesiod starts with the beginning of time) we may allow ourselves to say that the drive toward origins, and to a 'shaped' history is Hebraic. At the time of the expulsion from Troy the ghost of Creusa appeared to her widower Aeneas and said,

> Longa tibi exsilia et vastum maris aequor arandum,
> et terram Hesperiam venies, ubi Lydius arva
> inter opima virum leni fluit agmine Thybris

(ii. 780–2)

A long exile is thine, and a vast tract of sea to be ploughed; and thou shalt come to the Western Land where between rich fields of men the Tiber flows with gentle motion . . .

The ideas of Exodus and the people's Promised Land apply themselves directly to the *Aeneid* and equally refuse to be fitted to either the *Iliad* or the *Odyssey*.

I have used the word 'nostalgia', 'home-pain', which may remind us that the *Odyssey* is a poem about going home. *Nostos*, 'home-coming', is precisely what is withheld from Odysseus, and it is the need for home which drives him through the seas. But 'home' in the Odyssey is utterly concrete and specific. It is Ithaca. Notoriously, when Dante treated Odysseus ('Ulisse') in the *Commedia*, he turned the emotion inside out, creating a figure of unappeasable restlessness, who cannot stay at home but must sail out once more on a last voyage into unknown seas. Homer's Odysseus is a wanderer by necessity, Dante's by temperament. Virgil's Aeneas, however, framed in the first six books on the model of Odysseus, renders the very notion of nostalgia problematic. He is torn from Troy, the home he knows, and sent wandering in search of a home for which he can feel no natural nostalgia (for he has never seen it) but which is yet more anciently his than Troy was. Apollo tells Aeneas when he puts in to Delos, *Antiquam exquirite matrem*, 'Seek out your ancient mother' (iii. 96). Thus the *telos* or end of Aeneas's wanderings is itself a primal origin, or beginning. This means that the un-Homeric drive in the poem to 'the walls of high Rome' is really, in the 'deep structure' of the poem, a reference to origin, to the *real* beginning.

This proleptically adumbrated conclusion-which-is-itself-a-beginning is thoroughly historical in character, though the history is entangled in myth. It is quite distinct from the opening of the Biblical Genesis (or Hesiod's *Theogony*, or the *Metamorphoses* of Ovid). Nevertheless it shares with such creation myths a sense of extra-poetic shaping, of a religious determination. It is interesting to compare this version of extrinsic, prior mythopoeia on the part of the gods (who, so to speak, write their Poem with real people, not words) with the interior, inspiring mythopoeia of the Homeric Muse. That there is meanwhile a 'pull' in Virgil towards the primal Genesis story is shown by the line in the *Georgics* in which he links a description of spring to the childhood of the world: 'the great world was keeping Spring, and the East-winds spared their wintry blasts, when the first cattle drank in the light and man's iron race reared its head from the hard fields, and wild beasts were let loose into the forests and stars into heaven' (ii. 339–42).[32] The same feeling is present in the line in Georgics, i, about the day when Deucalion (the classical analogue of Noah) 'threw stones into an empty world' (62) and in the curious passage in *Georgics*, ii, in which Virgil pays tribute to the Epicurean poet Lucretius, the enemy of religion, happy because he knew 'the causes of things', and immediately joins that philosophic felicity to the happiness of the man who knows the rural gods (490–3). It is there, most importantly of all, in the *Aeneid*, in the song of the poet within the poem: Iopas, the Carthaginian minstrel, unlike Homer's Demodocus, sings of the origin of men and beasts, a creation song (i. 740 f.).[33]

In Virgil there is a tense poetic negotiation between the Greek interventionist opening and a divinely ordained natural beginning. This is associated with a displacement of divine causation, leaving the poet strangely free to sing with his own, learned voice (this it is that links the first person proem with the 'enlarged' subsequent narrative). The thematic pre-existence of a shaped history, a *natural* story, is answered at the formal level by the pre-existence of the Homeric poems, themselves so

---

[32] The translation is that of H. Rushton Fairclough, *Virgil,* Loeb Classical Library, 2 vols. (London: Heinemann, 1965), i. 139.

[33] In Apollonius Rhodius Orpheus sings a song of creation to the Argonauts (*Argonautica*, i. 496 f.). Greeks, too, can be 'Hebraic'.

differently conceived. The poetry of *idem in alio*, likeness in difference, is born. The very words *in medias res* begin themselves to take on a new meaning. The idea, so important to Dante and later to Eliot, that we are ourselves *in mediis rebus* is planted. Note that in the Horatian formula *res*, 'things', refers not to the chaos of reality in general but to the ordered sequence of the story of Troy; but in Virgil general reality itself—history—ceases to be a chaos and can therefore become *res* in what is in fact an expanded application of Horace's word. We are living in The Great Story, overarching and containing both the sufferings of Aeneas and the imperium of Augustus, our benevolent leader.

After Virgil, at the ordinary technical level, it became increasingly difficult for a literary work to 'sound professional' if it did not begin *in medias res*. This remains true to the present day. There will indeed always be some dogged spirits who resist such assertions of *les lois du texte* over nature. Thus Grote found the 'Hebraic' opening of the *Theogony* satisfyingly ordered, in agreeable contrast with what he saw as the scattered allusiveness of Homer; Hesiod, he affirmed, made a genuine attempt 'to cast the divine foretime into a systematic sequence'.[34] When Dickens, as we shall see, resists the Horatian imperative by beginning a novel with the words 'I am born', with genesis, this is immediately felt as witty, as a wilful counterploy.

To say this, however, may be to ascribe too absolutely to Virgil a revolutionary efficacy which is not his alone. Other poets before Virgil availed themselves of the Pathetic Fallacy. In certain ways the 'deepened' Epic, with its ulterior significance, may result from the fact that Virgil read his Homer in books carrying marginal comment which was sometimes allegorical.[35] This may suggest that Virgil did not *create* doubleness in the *Aeneid* but rather transposed and integrated in his poem a pre-existing doubleness. The scholiasts had invested Homer with 'significance' before the *Aeneid* was begun. This presentiment will bear some weight but not much, as can be verified by

[34] George Grote, *A History of Greece*, 10 vols. (London: George Murray, 1888), i. 11.

[35] See Robin R. Schlunk, *The Homeric Scholia and the Aeneid: A Study of the Influence of Ancient Homeric Literary Criticism on Virgil* (Ann Arbor: University of Michigan Press, 1974), esp. 41 f., 45–7.

anyone who tries to read the leaden disquisitions of the commentators and turns from them to the richly sombre polyphony of the *Aeneid*. It is because Virgil is so canonical a text, so often read, so often imitated, so often expounded in the Roman schools, that it still makes sense to locate in him, if not the exclusive invention, at least the central point of growth of a new literary 'phylogenetic tree'.

We may reject the historicism of Virgil. The world, after all, has seen too many dreams of power translated into spuriously authorized fact. Thus W. H. Auden wrote,

> No, Virgil, no:
> Not even the first of the Romans can learn
> His Roman history in the future tense,
> Not even to serve your political turn;
> Hindsight as foresight makes no sense[36]

Nevertheless the literary and cultural power of the Virgilian combination of hindsight and foresight is hard to deny.

The Greeks, meanwhile, remain Greek. For the sophisticated Apollonius and for the super-sophisticated Heliodorus two hundred years after the time of Virgil, history is still a sad, sunlit, meaningless flux. The beginning of Heliodorus's *Aethiopica* is a brilliant excursion from the *Odyssey*. Its first sentence is like a first sentence from one of the *middle* books of the *Odyssey* ('So soon as rosy-fingered Dawn' and so on): 'The smile of day was breaking and the sun just catching the mountain tops, when some men, armed to the teeth like pirates . . .'. The unnamed men are 'discovered' (the theatrical term has a certain appropriateness) peering over a ridge. At first they see nothing but then notice a ship fairly close at hand. On the ship are many corpses and some who are still alive together with the remains of an interrupted feast. All is still. The ship, strangely, has not been robbed of her cargo. This they can tell because she is riding low in the water.[37] Heliodorus has given us an extreme version of the *in medias res* opening. The bewilderment of the reader is repeated in the pirates, who have to 'read'

---

[36] 'Secondary Epic', *Collected Shorter Poems, 1927–57* (London: Faber and Faber, 1966), 296.

[37] See Heliodorus, *Aethiopica*, ed. Aristides Colonna (Rome: Typis Regiae Officinae Polygraphicae, 1938), 3–5.

what is before their eyes. It is almost as if Heliodorus, ahead of
history, first works out one of the standard nineteenth-century
novel openings, 'Two persons might have been observed', and
then at once hits on the idea of making the persons observed by
the reader themselves observers. Then what confronts them is a
seeming interruption, an event arrested half-way through and
strangely frozen. The modern reader 'can scarce forbear to
think' (as Dr Johnson would say) of the mystery of the *Marie
Céleste*.

The men then rush upon the ship and find a young woman,
who is ecphrastically described (an *ecphrasis* is a description
within a literary work of another work of art, a sculpture, say,
or a picture): 'the elbow of her other arm rested upon her right
thigh, while on its palm she rested her cheek'.[38] She is gazing,
like Patience on a monument, at a prostrate young man. His
eyes, we are told (the tense is a frequentative, almost timeless
imperfect), were weighed down by suffering but (ever and
anon) were raised to return her look. The pirates decide that she
cannot be a goddess on the interesting ground that no goddess
would kiss a corpse (for so they take the young man to be) so
passionately. The wondrous pair are Theagenes and Chariclea,
who are to figure largely in the ensuing story. Thus the
narrative is fully under way.

As we read on we discover that the *Aethiopica* is a nest of
stories and it is only at the end that we learn that Chariclea is
really the long-lost child of the King and Queen of Aethiopia.
Here, at x. xii–xiii, we are at last given a true account of
preceding events, an account which replaces an earlier false
narrative. Yet in all this bravura display of narrative latency and
readerly involvement there is no hint of the Virgilian Major
Theme or Great Story. No one reading the *Aethiopica* could ever
have been gripped by the thought, 'This is the story of us all.'
The intricacies of Heliodorus, like the *entrelacement* of Spenserian epic narrative, are uniform, golden, and somehow continuously *present*. Perhaps the Greeks by this date were
collectively just too old to learn from a Roman. It is as if Virgil
had never sung of arms and the man.

---

[38] Ibid. 5.

2

The *Commedia*

INTERVENTION: POETIC AND DIVINE

> Nel mezzo del cammin di nostra vita
> mi ritrovai per una selva oscura,
> che la diritta via era smarrita.

In the middle of the journey of our life I came to myself in a dark wood, for the straight way was lost.

This, the greatest of all *in medias res* openings, precipitates the reader or listener into the action without any kind of preliminary courtesy. The first verb of the first sentence of the *Commedia* is in the narrative past tense and proves indeed to be the start of the major story. Together with the suddenness and the bewilderment there is, we soon learn, a definiteness, located squarely in historical time. The date is Easter, 1300. The poet-pilgrim is half-way through his life at the point at which the *visio* begins. The allotted span is three-score years and ten and Dante was born in 1265 (somewhat unusually for a medieval man, he seems to have known this, clearly and distinctly).

The impression is of a confused intermediacy invaded by clarity and necessity. Already we may begin to think of Horace's *ex fumo dare lucem*, 'to give light out of smoke' (*Ars Poetica*, 143). We are aware, if we are reasonably good readers, of being at the beginning of a huge poem which is in some ways like an ancient epic, is in some ways a comedy (happy-ending vernacular poem) of the spirit, and in yet other ways a *visio*, a 'vision-poem', likely to prove in some degree allegorical. The sense of actuality, the feeling that the bewilderment is experienced in real darkness, is certainly strong. Twentieth-century readers who have never strayed beyond the range of a street

All references to Dante's *Divina Commedia* are to *The Divine Comedy,* translated, with a commentary, by Charles S. Singleton, 6 vols. in 3 (Princeton: Princeton University Press, 1970–5).

lamp will do well to imagine what it is really like to be in a wood at night, when one has inadvertently left the path. But this specificity is countered by the generalizing *nostra*, not 'my' life but 'our' life, which forewarns us that this is a figurative journey, in which case the wood may be a figurative wood. We thus begin to apprehend the Dantean inversion: *the poet is here the matter of the poem*. He, not Aeneas, appears in mid-journey, and the journey in which he is surprised is that of life itself, whose poet or maker is not Dante but God. Life, we begin to guess, may be broken in upon by something which is other than—more than—'our life'. In relation to that Other, present actualities may suddenly seen insubstantial. This is the first hint of the immense subversion of reality-ascription of which Auerbach wrote in his essay, 'Figura': 'It is we who are the shadows . . .?'[1]

But the growth of this apprehension is gradual. Dante is not directly and immediately surprised by God, or Beatrice, or even Virgil, who will in due course take him lovingly by the hand to guide him through the gates of death. For the moment it is sufficiently arresting that the *visio* begins, not with a falling asleep (as in Cicero's *Somnium Scipionis*) but with a kind of awakening. When Langland later in the fourteenth century wrote the major English *visio, Piers Plowman*, he began with a falling away into slumber, under a warm sun:

> In a somer seson whan softe was the sonne,
> I shoop me into a shrou[d] as I a shepe weere;
> In habite as an heremite, unholy of werkes,
> Wente wide in his world wondres to here.
> As on a May morwenyinge on Malverne hilles
> Me bifel a ferly of fairye me thogte;
> I was wery forwandred and wente me to reste
> Under a brood banke bi a bourn[e] syde,
> And as I lay and lenede and loked withe watres,
> I slombred into a slepyng, it sweyed so murye.
> Thanne gan I to meten a merveilouse swevene[2]

---

[1] 'Figura', p. 2, in Erich Auerbach, *Scenes from the Drama of European Literature* (New York: Meridian Books, 1959), 11–78. For a different view of Dante's use of *figural*, see A. C. Charity, *Events and their Afterlife: The Dialectics of Christian Typology in the Bible and Dante* (Cambridge: Cambridge University Press, 1966), esp. pp. 161, 179–207.

[2] Prologus, 1–10, in William Langland, *Piers Plowman: The B Version: Will's*

Indeed Dante, from an initial hostile darkness, moves to what is unequivocally an intensified, enlarged state of consciousness. In the words *mi ritrovai* the prefix *ri*-directs us to the interior character of what is described, not just 'I found myself' but 'I came to myself'.

The intuition of an asseverated reality which is not weakened but rather intensified by generalization is strong. Here we must remember Auerbach's cardinal distinction between the medieval tradition of *figura*, by which certain real, historical persons bear, *objectively*, a certain significance which reaches beyond human time, and *allegoria*, according to which figures are *feigned*, in order to illustrate general truths. Dante, unlike de Lorris, say, with his erotic garden in the *Roman de la Rose*, works with historically existent Florentines who, in life, pointed to a reality profounder than that of history. This presents us with a degree of objectivism which is almost inconceivable in our age of endlessly elaborated subjectivisms. In the *Commedia*, the supposed source, the 'author' ('authority') is in fact the manipulated object of God's artistry. The book called *Comedy* will, then, mirror the book of the universe. Thus, at the end of the poem, we are told how the *visio* reached its summation when the Pilgrim gazed upon infinite goodness (*valore infinito, Paradiso*, xxxiii. 81):

> Nel suo profondo vidi che s'interna,
> legato con amore in un volume,
> ciò che per l'universo si squaderna

(Paradiso, xxxiii. 85–7)

In its depth I saw that it contained, bound with love in one volume, that which through the universe is scattered.

We are, it would seem, as far as it is possible to be from the radically labile, self-generating, modernist text. Yet something in this picture is false. That a great feat of the objectivist imagination is essayed in *Commedia* I do not doubt. But it cannot be the whole story.

We know from the start, in a low pragmatic fashion, that Dante, not God, is the author of the Italian words we read and

---

Vision of Piers Plowman, Do-Well, Do-Better and Do-Best, ed. G. Kane and E. Talbot Donaldson (London: The Athlone Press, 1988), 277.

that Dante has, in some degree at least, *feigned* the metaphor of the journey. Moreover, while the exhilarating grand conception may seem to have been cleanly achieved, details begin to nag. Beatrice is 'figural' in so far as there really was[3] a little girl in a red dress in the house of Portinari on that crucial day in 1274 when the child Dante fell in love with her—but the living Beatrice never uttered the marvellous words of anagnorisis: *Ben son, ben son Beatrice*, 'I really am, I really am Beatrice (*Purgatorio*, xxx. 73). These words are not part of the fabric of God's creation, but are feigned by Dante. Even in the final vision of a consummated unity, where it might be felt that the *Commedia* of Dante triumphantly fuses with the Book of God, Dante reminds us, in the wonderful phrase *si squaderna*, 'scatters itself', 'is scattered', of the fact that for our fallen awareness the leaves of the book are dispersed—'substances, accidents and their relations' (*Paradiso*, xxxiii. 88). There is in *si squaderna* what might be described as an inner vertigo. In that dispersal a space is made for the poetic art of Dante, the individual Florentine. Dante's bodying forth of himself as pilgrim within the poem is therefore a dynamic, fictive project rather than a divinely accomplished fact.

The result is that the precipitate concreteness of the immediate narrative is, after all, held within a distinctively human literary consciousness, within something very close to *wit* (God has complete intelligence but only the fallen have wit).

We soon learn that the date from which I began requires, if we think biographically, a pragmatic adjustment. The date within the poem (fiction) is indeed 1300. But Michele Barbi tells us that in fact the poem was probably begun in 1307.[4] There is a temporal interval between Dante the writer and Dante the written. Hence, indeed, the past tense. In God's grammar, we may surmise, there are no past tenses, no futures.

Take next the word *mezzo*, 'middle'. The commentaries rightly explain this as a reference to Psalm 89 [90]: 10, 'The days of our years are three score years and ten'. In his *Convivio* (IV. xxiii. 9) Dante imagines life as an arch, the highest point of

---

[3] The real historical existence of Beatrice is not accepted by all Dante scholars.
[4] *Life of Dante*, translated by P. Ruggiers (Berkeley and Los Angeles: University of California Press, 1954), 69.

which, for those of perfect nature, will be in the thirty-fifth year. Singleton points—surely appropriately since we are about to enter the *Inferno*—to Isaiah 38: 10, 'I said in the cutting off of my days, I shall go to the gates of the grave'. In the vulgate 'the gates of the grave' is *ad portas inferi*. At the same time, however. there are signs as we shall see, that Dante was also thinking in an unregenerate, secular, thoroughly literary manner: that he conceived his opening in relation to the openings of classical epic (Virgil himself, after all, will soon appear, to join hands with the pilgrim-poet).

Once one has become aware of the pattern of classical reference, it is hardly possible to avoid hearing in *mezzo* an echo of Horace's *in medias res*, 'into the midst of things'. This is the way Virgil, Rome's Homer, Dante's guide, began *his* poem. But of course Virgil, though he did this, *did not say that he was doing so*. For that, we had to wait for the critical (in a way, extra-poetic) verses of Horace. That Dante knew the *Ars Poetica* there can be no doubt.[5] In the *Vita Nuova* (xxv) he quotes from the very sentence in which the words *in medias res* appear, though he does not quote the phrase itself. If Dante has indeed built into his poem an echo of this literary-critical phrase, the consequence is spectacular. We have, once more, a reduplicative effect, but this reduplication is not Virgilian. The reader is pitched into a sequence already in process, and it is the 'hero', as if he were a projection of the reader, who comes to himself 'in the midst of things'. Thus far we might say that the result is an intensified—or a redoubled—'intervention effect'. What immediately follows, however, is a darkening, a relegation to obscurity and unimportance of the train of events preceding this 'middle', so that our sense that the poem's start may be matched with a real beginning of numinous significance may after all grow.

The foregoing sector of Dante's life—as of all our lives (*nostra*) untouched by spiritual illumination—is not a causally efficacious groundwork for the action of the poem. Here the implicit theology is Johannine: not an interlocked system of sin, repentance, and forgiveness but a huge discontinuity: peering

[5] See Edward Moore, *Studies in Dante*, 1st Ser. (Oxford: Clarendon Press, 1896), 197–206.

into darkness succeeded abruptly by a looking up, towards light.[6] Later in the *Inferno* there will of course be plenty of retrospection to the earthly lives of various damned Florentines, but very little, ever, to the previous life of Dante himself. This is not, therefore, a taking up of the lyre at some random or privately chosen point in the great saga. Rather, as Dante's poem begins, God's action of salvation begins and all that went before simply falls away. That is why the pilgrim awakes, and sees light on the mountain tops. Virgil's enlargement of epic to reflect a major historical sequence is here subjected to a root-and-branch revision far more ambitious in scope. We must learn to take a longer stride, from the benighted individual to the vision of God's shining universe. *Smarrita*, 'lost', applied to the path through the wood, is dynamically countered by *mi ritrovai*, 'I found myself', 'came to myself'. Notice that it is not the path which is found again; the symmetry is artfully flawed: the path is lost but the pilgrim is found. The movement is begun in the *middle* of a darkness but, before it is completed, its new nature, as the beginning of enlightenment, is so strong as to erase our sense of its originally intermediate character. What for fallen imaginations is an *in medias res* opening becomes, *sub specie aeternitatis*, a 'deep' beginning.

If we consider the *Commedia* in terms of the structure of classical epic we shall see at once that Dante did not seek, as Virgil sought, somehow to transpose the entire epic sequence of motifs into his vernacular. Virgil swallowed the *Iliad* and the *Odyssey* whole and, through a remarkable feat of the appropriative imagination, digested them. Dante instead takes a single element from the epic, the *nekuia*, and expands it so that it becomes the entire poem. The *nekuia* ('the dead') is that part of an ancient epic—*Odyssey* xi, *Aeneid* vi—in which the living hero leaves the light of day to visit slain heroes in the House of Hades. In Homer the *nekuia* can feel like a truancy on the hero's part or as a self-indulgent digression on the poet's. In Virgil one senses that the *nekuia* is growing stronger. Aeneas's journey to find his dead father is no mere exotic excursion but is crucial to

---

[6] See John 9: 41; 8: 42–3, 45, 47; 3: 18–20. See also Pierre Benoit, 'Pauline and Johannine Theology: A Contrast', *Cross Currents*, 15 (1965), 339–53, and Roger L. Cox, *Between Earth and Heaven: Shakespeare, Dostoevsky and the Meaning of Christian Tragedy* (New York: Holt, Rinehart, and Winston, 1968), 2–50.

his moral reconstitution. Before Book vi Aeneas is notoriously prone to error and infirmity of purpose, looking for Rome in Crete, hoping to find haven in the love of a Carthaginian queen. After Book vi, he is, at some cost to his humanity, a virtually unshakable instrument for the foundation of the Roman race. Even the Dantean reversal whereby the movement towards the next world is marked by an increase rather than diminution of light is anticipated in Virgil. When Aeneas first descends into the Underworld all is dark. As he moves forward the space round him seems to grow and the light gets stronger, until at last he comes to a place which has 'a bigger sky' (*largior aether*, vi. 640) than ours, with two suns set in it. It will be said that the proper Dantean comparison here is not with the light at the beginning of the *Inferno* but with the light of the *Paradiso*, since Aeneas is approaching the Elysian Fields. All this is true, but misses the point. For the light seen in the distance at the beginning of the *Commedia* is, imaginatively, the light of Paradise. The paradox of a death which is somehow brighter than what we call life is common to both poets, and wholly absent from Homer's *nekuia*. Moreover, while in Greek tales heroes had gone down into the Underworld as enemies of death, often to drag back by violence some loved person, Aeneas enters in a very different spirit. Charon, the ferryman of Hell, is alarmed when he sees Aeneas approaching through the shadows and throws out an aggressive challenge. But the Sibyl reassures him:

Nullae hic insidiae tales (absiste moveri)
. . . .
Troius Aeneas, pietate insignis et armis,
ad genitorem imas Erebi descendit ad umbras

(vi. 399, 403–4)

No such trickery as you fear is here . . . Trojan Aeneas, famous for both piety and heroism, descends to the bottom-most shades, in search of the father who begot him.

Not Heracles, not Theseus, not Pirithous, but pious Aeneas.

There is in consequence of this inversion a potential theology in Book vi which threatens to overthrow the logic of the entire *Aeneid*. The Telos, or End, of the *Aeneid*, that greatest thing for the sake of which all is done, is Rome itself. There must always have been a danger in this project—a danger that Virgil's audience sitting in the middle of Rome, with all its vulgarity, cruelty, and wealth, may have sensed that Aeneas's city, always receding from him like a rainbow, might have lost its lustre had it been subjected, so to speak, to a closer inspection. Some of the auditors may well have felt that there was something in the religious hunger voiced by Aeneas in the wilderness which is inadequately answered, both by the quarrelling divinities of the inherited Homeric Pantheon and by the realized imperial city. As it stands, the major design of the poem makes it necessary that Book vi should reach its climax with the spectacle of Rome's concrete, historical future, watched, in something curiously like a cinematic display, by the dwellers in Elysium. The snag is that Virgil has by this time found his way to a Platonist conception of an immortality better than such mere sequences of history, larger than time. An other-worldly conception of immortality has begun to oust a Pythagorean conception of immortality-through-continual-rebirth-into-this-world.[7] That is why the question arises with such urgency: 'Why should those who live in Elysium have this fearful desire to return to bodily existence?' (*Quae lucis miseris tam dira cupido?* vi. 750). Why, by like reasoning, should they be so hungrily interested in Roman history, past or future? In the *Commedia*, where all this is in a manner resolved, it is only the *dannati* who turn a famished gaze on this world—always retrospectively. Those in *Paradise* have turned away, to something better. It is only bad Virgilians who, forgetting the original context, suppose that *clausae tenebris et carcere caeco*, 'shut up in darkness and a blind prison' (vi. 734), refers to the prisoners of Tartarus. In fact the words point us to the world above, to *nostra vita* which is here indeed darker even than Dante's dark wood.

Thus Auerbach's notion of a figural reversal whereby the world of the dead is more real than our own, so that we in relation to it are mere shadows, begins to crystallize in the pre-Christian *Aeneid*, but does so, so to speak, *awkwardly*, because it cannot be integrated in the major project.

---

[7] For the transcendental conception, Virgil may have drawn on Plato, *Republic*, 611e–612a; *Phaedo*, 114c, from Pindar's 2nd Olympian Ode and from Cicero, *De Republica*, vi. xiv.

I have no doubt that Dante found Book vi the most exciting in the *Aeneid* and I am almost as certain that his second favourite was Book iv, the story of Dido. In Virgil's poem there is a tragic division between these books, because Dido is the enemy of Rome. When Aeneas finds her in the world of the dead, after she has died for love of him, she turns away from his faltering embrace to her own renewed *pietas*, to her former husband Sychaeus. Aeneas is left saying as she had said earlier, 'Is it me that you are fleeing?' (vi. 466; iv. 314). The pain is all the greater because in Hades Aeneas's proffered gesture of love is, if possible, hollower than ever, since by now he is virtually subject to the Roman, lineal influence of his father. I have said that Dido and the father are in tragic opposition, but the true situation is perhaps more complex. It has often been noticed that Book iv is like a Euripidean tragedy, Dido corresponding to Medea. Yet the tragic death of Dido, with its full declamatory bravura, is followed in Book v by the reticent, epic death of Anchises, the father. Our first formula was too coarse. Instead of calling the conflict tragic we should see how, if we are to speak accurately, the tragic principle is opposed—with infinite human pain—by another principle, itself anti-tragic in its implications. For Dante, Beatrice, his great love, is not a seduction but on the contrary leads him towards God. When the words of the Virgilian love story are reapplied by Dante, he echoes words which allude not only to the distracting love for Aeneas but also—and perhaps more strongly—to the pious authorized marriage with Sychaeus, which will be renewed beyond the grave:

conosco i segni de l'antica fiamma   (*Purgatorio*, xxx. 48)

agnosco veteris vestigia flammae (*Aeneid*, iv. 23)

When Dante at last turns from Beatrice to something even better, she can rejoice to be forgotten (*Paradiso*, x. 61).

For Dante there is no problem of Pythagorean return, or of redirecting the reader's energies to the significant processes of this world. Because Dante's poem is that product of a fallen imagination, by one who moreover (may we not say?) had never really visited Hell, Purgatory, Heaven, a preoccupation with Florentine and Italian history reveals itself in the poem. But now the tables are turned, and it is the medieval poet, not the classical, who is confused, in a converse manner. For Dante certainly writes amid the wreck of his imperial hopes to urge a conception of that Empire whose demise he refuses to accept. He descants on what are for him the great acts of betrayal: the Emperor Constantine's 'donation' of imperial power to the Papacy (*Inferno*, xix. 116), and Celestine's *gran rifiuto*, 'great refusal', to carry on as Pope (*Inferno*, iii. 60), thus leaving the way open for the vile Boniface and his bull, *Unam sanctam* (*Inferno*, xxvii. 105). Dante saw in Virgil a great forerunner, who had clearly perceived that history as a whole is shaped by the divinely authorized Roman *imperium*. As a reading of the *Aeneid* this is by no means unintelligent. A developing theory of empire whereby the office of emperor is increasingly spiritualized, eternized, and separated from the accidental imperfections of the individual holder of office,[8] is in a way appropriate to the *Aeneid*, which seems indeed to be groping towards a religious conception of *Romanitas* which, for want of a developed theory, it cannot satisfactorily conclude. It may be said indeed that this tendency in Virgil's thought found its true culmination, not in any medieval emperor or pseudo-emperor, but, precisely, in the Papacy; but this is an interpretation which Dante would resist to the death. In his treatise on monarchy, or 'single rule' (*De Monarchia*, especially I. xvi. 1–2) and in the famous *due soli* ('two suns') passage in the *Commedia* (*Purgatorio*, xvi. 109) Dante argues strenuously that the power of the emperor is not a secondary, lunar luminescence, a reflection of light received from the Papal Sun, but is rather parallel to the Papal power, derived, as *it* is derived, directly from God. That is why Brutus, who betrayed Julius Caesar, is placed in the lowest circle of Hell, with Judas who betrayed Christ.

Long after Dante's death the 'Donation of Constantine' was shown by the Renaissance humanist Lorenzo Valla to be a forgery. Valla proved his case from an analysis of the Latinity of the document, that is, by a remarkably early application of linguistic scholarship. For Dante the Donation was authentic but invalid: Constantine had neither the right nor the power to

---

[8] See E. H. Kantorowicz, *The King's Two Bodies* (Princeton: Princeton University Press, 1957), and Frank Kermode, *The Classic* (London: Faber and Faber, 1975), 32.

give away an office laid on him by God. The hated Boniface VIII, meanwhile, in his notorious bull, *Unam sanctam*, asserted the supremacy of the Church in the temporal realm. Dante's feelings in the matter are indeed extreme as is shown by his treatment of Celestine V. Celestine, a man of profound humility and piety, who lived a life of severe austerity, was elected to the papacy in his eightieth year. He had no taste for ecclesiastical power and feared that the office held moral and spiritual dangers. Boniface (then known as Benedetto Caetani) played upon this natural reluctance until Celestine at last made the 'great refusal' already referred to, the refusal to serve as Pope, for what most would regard as unexceptionable reasons. To be sure, Boniface's part in the business is another matter. The 'Florentine Chronicle' tells a grotesque story about Boniface, saying that he secretly rigged up a speaking tube over Celestine's bed, and spoke through it in the hours of darkness, pretending to be an angel, urging Celestine to give up the Papacy.[9] Celestine died a few years afterwards and was canonized in 1313. For Dante, Celestine's crime, simultaneously political and spiritual, consisted solely and sufficiently in the fact that he made way for the evil Boniface, who in his turn completed the ruin of the Empire.

Those who believe that the Christian Middle Ages were a time of rigid obedience to ecclesiastical authority may be advised to reflect carefully on the fact that, as E. G. Gardner observed, in the most famous of all medieval religious poems the first soul in hell is the canonized Pope-hermit (Celestine) 'whom the world extolled as a perfect type of Christian renunciation, and who died in the odour of sanctity; the first soul of the repentant is the king who died excommunicate, whose name was tainted with suspicion of incest and parricide' (that is, Manfred, in *Purgatorio*, iii).[10] John D. Sinclair, commenting on Gardner's words, observes that they enforce the idea that 'the soul's destiny lies in the soul itself, not in any ecclesiastical pronouncement on it'.[11] The really curious thing is

---

[9] *Cronica fiorentina compilata nel secolo XIII*, in *Testi fiorentini del Dugento e dei primi del Trecento*, ed. Alfredo Schiaffini (Florence: G. C. Sansoni, 1926), 142.

[10] *Dante* (Edinburgh: Edinburgh University Press, 1900), 104.

[11] *The Divine Comedy of Dante Alighieri*, with translation and comment by John D. Sinclair, 3 vols. (London: Bodley Head, 1958), ii. 54.

that Celestine based his refusal very precisely on the priority of the soul's claims over the claims of public office. Dante in judging Celestine as he does subordinates all this prating of souls to the obligations of office—with the implicit proviso that the immediately sequent obligation was to hold back the Papal power, to ensure that it did not encroach upon the imperial rule. The judgement is so eccentric and so fierce that some have doubted whether Dante really intended it to apply to Celestine (who is never named in *Inferno*, iii). Commenting in the fourteenth century Benvenuto da Imola was clearly shocked and believed that if Dante really did mean Celestine, he could not have heard of the old man's sanctity.[12] But the unanimity of early readers is insuperable. The poet's own son, Pietro di Dante, who in about 1340 began a commentary on his father's poem, says unequivocally that Celestine could have been as holy and spiritual in office as he had been in his hermitage, but pusillanimously renounced the Papacy, which is the seal of Christ.[13] There is no ambiguity about the reference to Celestine at *Inferno* xxvii. 105, where the point, once more, is that he failed to respect the task he had assumed. Manfred, meanwhile, is paradoxically honoured for a like political reason. He was the illegitimate son of the brilliant Emperor Frederick II (*stupor mundi*, 'astonishment of the world'). Until he was defeated at the Battle of Benevento in 1266 he was seen as the hope of Empire and after his death remained a hero of the Ghibelline (imperial) party. The politically driven extremism of Dante's relative placing of Celestine and Manfred becomes still clearer if one remembers that at Benevento an army of Saracens and Germans (Manfred's) went down before an army of Roman Catholics, under Charles of Anjou, virtually invited into Italy by two Popes in succession. Manfred, who died fighting like a tiger, was buried in an infidel's grave at the foot of a bridge over the Calore. In the *Commedia*, when he calls to Dante to turn his face, he slips into the dim light of dawn, a beautiful, wounded figure:

---

[12] *Commentum super Dantis Alighierii Comoediam*, ed. Giacomo Filippo Lacaita, 5 vols. (Florence: G. Barbera, 1887), i. 120.

[13] *P. Allegherii super Dantis ipsius genitoris Comoediam Commentarium*, ed. Vincentio Nannucci (Florence: G. Piatti, 1845), 69.

Biondo era e bello e di gentile aspetto,
ma l'un de' cigli un colpo avea diviso. (iii. 107–8)

Blond he was, and fair of face, noble in aspect, but one of his eyebrows
had been cloven by a blow.

One is tempted to say that the Virgilian future historical
projection is not available to Dante for a simple, practical
reason. Virgil was the child of an immense political victory;
Dante is the child of an unacknowledged but inescapable
political despair. The imperial cause was lost. Virgil's main
difficulty lay in the reconciling of a half-discovered transcendent
felicity with a temporal future of world-government. Dante, in
the major movement of the *Commedia*, resolves the difficulty
through a clear, prior allegiance to the transcendent. Virgil had
begun to realize that his New Jerusalem (it is always easy to
Hebraize Virgil) was nowhere on earth and, because it was a
place of perfect happiness, required no such violation of the
pastoral as was required by the rise of Rome out of Arcadian
simplicity. Therefore the dwellers in Elysium inhabit a green
world, not an urban. Likewise in Dante's solution the terminus
is not Rome but a garden, a *Paradiso*. All this is in accord with
the fundamental scheme of the poem. But, as we have seen,
Dante also has, as a minor theme, the idea of a political
imperium, and this is as unassimilable to the major scheme as,
conversely, Virgil's pastoral—timeless—transcendent vision is
to his civic, political theme. We must however be careful not to
exaggerate the symmetry of this comparison. Dante may place
Brutus beside Judas in Hell and set Justinian, the Roman
lawgiver, in Paradise, but we sense something shrill, something
strained in the assertiveness of the passages. Even if the Empire
were as directly from God as is the Papacy, the betrayal of
Caesar is clearly not truly parallel to the betrayal of Christ (for
Christ we would need to substitute Peter). The triumphal music
of *Cesare fui e son Iustiniano*, 'Caesar I was, and am Justinian'
(*Paradiso*, vi. 10), is strangely thwarted by an invading need to
justify this pagan figure in terms which are truly Christian. The
justification is accomplished by something extra-imperial,
belonging to a different universe—by faith (*la fede sincera,* 18),
planted in his mind by the blessed—and, again, far from
imperial, Pope Agapetus. Was *this* Pope, then, after all, closer to
God than Caesar was?

The formal collapsing of epic into its *nekuia* and subsequent expansion of the *nekuia* to become the universal ontology, the ultimate 'hard' reality, can leave only a temporary and provisional place for a political *imperium*, however immediate the relation of that *imperium* to God. And where the imperialist cause has met ruin and defeat, the political theme will be further weakened by relegation to the past, to retrospective rancour, or even a peculiarly fruitless species of revenge: the old idea that Dante paid out his political enemies by sending them to an idiosyncratically organized, *poetic* hell is, as far as it goes, true. It is necessary to add that he sent some of his best friends (for example, Brunetto Latini) to the same place. Most of the detail of Dantean politics is to be found in the *Inferno*, where the speakers, lacking hope, naturally reminisce. In the *Paradiso* there is one protracted narrative speech, and it comes from Justinian. Anchises, the father of Aeneas, was never thus. There it was the son who looked back and the old man who saw the city of the future. When Justinian comes at last in his story to the present behaviour of the Ghibellines his rhetorical and poetic energies, so far from coming together in a climax, seem to break down, in something very like gossip. Virgil, the poet of Empire, is Dante's guide in the world of the dead, but when the pilgrim draws near the gates of Paradise Virgil vanishes from his side; Beatrice comes to dry his tears and lead him upward (*Purgatorio*, xxx. 49–81).

I have said that Dante locates the consummation of his scheme not in a city but in a garden. This is true, but, so to speak, only just true. The very fact that Dante sees Virgil solely as the poet of Empire shows that he was not naturally responsive to the pastoral vision. There is no sense in his poetry of any poignant nostalgia for an innocent landscape, for something movingly antithetical to the City; there is no pathos of distance. Perhaps the most tantalizing line in the *Aeneid* is that which tells us that Aeneas left the Underworld by passing through the ivory gate of false dreams (vi. 898). Many readers in modern times have felt that this cannot but imply a radical disbelief in his own paraded vision of future imperial success.[14]

---

[14] See Jasper Griffin, *Virgil* (Oxford: Oxford University Press, 1986), 90–1, and Adam Parry, 'The Two Voices of Virgil's *Aeneid*', *Arion*, 2(4) (1963), 66–80.

Even in the twelfth century Bernardus Silvestris could explain the passage as a coded (*occulte*) sign to the reader that the poem had lied.[15] But Dante, though he sensed Virgil's pessimism (*Purgatorio*, xxx. 107), never fully perceived the anti-Virgil in Virgil.

We have uncovered in the first lines of the *Commedia* not just a human, spiritual reference, but also a literary reference, to Virgilian example. The initial categories, Christian/Classical, religious/literary, led us in their turn to further antinomies: political/ecclesiastical, poetry of Empire and poetry of Faith. The commentaries allow that before Virgil himself enters the poem (at *Inferno*, i. 61) there is verbal reminiscence of the *Aeneid*. Singleton plausibly traces the *selva oscura*, 'dark wood', of the second line to the *nekuia* of the *Aeneid*:

> Itur in antiquam silvam, stabula alta ferarum
>
> . . . .
>
> atque haec ipse suo tristi cum corde volutat,
> aspectans silvam immensam, et sic forte precatur:
> 'Si nunc se nobis ille aureus arbore ramus
> ostendat nemore in tanto!'
>
> (vi. 179, 185–8)

They pass into an ancient wood, the deep resting places of wild creatures . . . Aeneas himself revolves these things in his sad heart, and thus by chance he prays, 'If only now that golden bouth would show itself to us on its tree, in so great a forest!'

If, however, Dante is thinking not only about the matter of the epic *nekuia* but also about the manner of the epic opening (and *mezzo*, as we have seen, with its echo of *in medias res*, strongly suggests that his mind was moving simultaneously along this other path) then *selva* may refer, also, to the wood of which we read in the cancelled, 'Donatian' opening of the *Aeneid*:

> Ille ego qui quondam gracili modulatus avena
> Carmen et *egressus silvis*

That man am I who, having tuned his song upon a slender reed, *came out from the woods.*

---

[15] Bernardus Silvestris, *The Commentary on the First Six Books of the 'Aeneid' of Virgil*, ed. J. W. and E. F. Jones (Lincoln, Nebraska, and London: University of Nebraska Press, 1977), 127. The attribution of this work to Bernardus Silvestris is disputed by some scholars.

Virgil's breath can, perhaps, already be felt upon the poet's ear. Dante not only knew but was deeply interested in Donatus's *Life of Virgil*. It is no very great stretch of the literary imagination to suppose that Dante was here conscious of an analogy: each poem begins in a wood.

Virgil's literary progression from pastoral to heroic is here reinterpreted, according to the Christian scheme of the *Commedia*: Dante's emergence is to something higher than just another kind of poetry. Nevertheless, Benvenuto da Imola, the best of the medieval commentators on Dante, also saw *mezzo* as a key word, a classical, organizing directive (as is the Donatian 'prelude') this time with reference to what *will* be accomplished. Here, he says, Dante *prohemizatur ad totum opus*, 'gives us the proemium to the whole work'.[16] He goes on to explain that *mezzo* implies a triptych structure, Vice, Penitence, Bliss, which is indeed reflected in the structure of the poem: *Inferno, Purgatorio, Paradiso*. The initial contrast with the Virgilian proem shrinks still further. We may think of the triple conclusion of the epitaph which Virgil is said to have dictated as he lay dying:

> Mantua me genuit, Calabri rapuere, tenet nunc
> Parthenope; cecini *pascua, rura, duces*

Mantua gave me birth, Calabrians carried me off, the maiden city of Naples holds me now; I sang *pastures, tilled soil, captains: (Eclogues, Georgics, Aeneid.)* (my italics)

Although Dante perceives a classical proemial reference in *mezzo*, his use of the word 'middle' is not like Horace's. For Horace 'middle' does not generate an organized formal trinity but rather an unfocused dynamic (smoke before fire).

If Dante is indeed building from the Donatian prelude, he may be said to contrast strongly with the next major poet to tread closely in Virgil's footsteps, *il sommo poeta Inglese*,[17] John Milton. In *Paradise Lost* Milton chose to restore that in Virgil which was retrospective to an older, Greek tradition. In *Paradise Lost* the Muse grows strong again. He reserved his own, distinctively Miltonic reworking of the Donatian *ille ego* opening for the lesser, later miniature epic, *Paradise Regained*.

---

[16] *Commentum*, i. 21.   [17] Inscription at Vallombrosa, in Italy.

Dante, in seizing on the strange, half-allegorical reduplication of the poet's own story in the epic story, was instead pushing poetry forward, discovering something in Virgil which would foster new growth.

We have travelled, so far, only two lines into Dante's poem. The beginning is barely begun. After the arresting surprise of that first, narrative sentence in which clarity supervenes on bewilderment, the poet falls back, in fear of his own enterprise: 'What a hard thing it is to tell what that wood was like . . .'. But then, at the thought of the good he found in the forest (8) he rallies and resolves to press ahead. In lines 10–18 he recapitulates the sequence from somnolence to an arousing—indeed, a frightening—light upon the hills. The sun, for geocentric Dante, is a planetary body (*pianeta*, 17) a star which, because it moves, can figure as a 'guide-before-the-human-guides', that is, before Virgil, Beatrice, and Bernard. Dante's fears are swiftly allayed. He rests, feeling like one who has escaped drowning at sea, then sets himself to walk up the sloping shore: *piaggia* (29) may seem to admit to the main narrative the idea of a threatening sea, from the simile just completed, but the same word occurs again, this time quite clearly with the neutral sense 'slope', at ii. 62. Singleton is surely right to suggest that the biblical Exodus lies behind the entire passage.[18]

It is at this point that Dante is visited by the strange beasts which have so much exercised the ingenuity of commentators: first the beautiful spotted leopard (32–3) then the hungry lion (45), then the famished she-wolf (49). The whole passage is one of dreamlike intensity—especially in its spatial feeling, and in this way Dante is mysteriously forced back into the sunless shadows from which he had emerged. There is a certain affinity with Descartes' famous dream, in which, after he had passed an acquaintance and failed to salute him, a great wind was forcing him towards a chapel (after which he is informed, bafflingly, that a certain person is anxious to give him a melon).[19] It is

---

[18] 'In exitu Israel de Aegypto', in John Freccero (ed.), *Dante: A Collection of Critical Essays* (Englewood Cliffs, NJ: Prentice Hall, 1965), 102–21.

[19] Descartes recorded three important dreams which he had on a single night, 10 Nov. 1619, in a manuscript entitled *Olympica*. This MS is referred to in Adrien Baillet's *Vie de Monsieur Des-Cartes* (1691) and is cited in *Œuvres de Descartes*, ed. Charles Adam and Paul Tannery, 13 vols. (Paris: Léopold Cerf, 1897–1913), x. 186.

surely important that the meaning of the beasts who confront Dante should be, at least for a time, indistinct. The poet might have labelled them but chose not to, subjecting the reader to the disorientation of the dream. Equally, however, there can be no strong reason why we modern heirs of the oneirocritical Freud should, in the long run, refuse to accept the traditional explanation: the beasts signify lechery, pride, and envy.[20]

There, in the shadows to which he has been driven back, Dante finds before him the figure of a person who seems weakened by long silence. Again we must not allow the clarity of the commentary to invade our minds so swiftly that we lose the proper mystery of this. The figure confronting Dante is Virgil; he is faint through long silence because his voice has been eclipsed by death. Dante, the pilgrim, is deemed to intuit all this, in a manner, before he learns the identity of the stranger. Again it is necessary (however unfavourable the critical climate may be to such observations) to stress the empirically cogent character of what is described, the precise manner in which an apparent improbability is suddenly resolved into an entire likelihood. The very celerity of Dante's inference is convincing. I am saying the scandalous thing: it is like real life. I will compound the scandal by adding a real life illustration. Some years ago my daughter, then aged three, fell into a pool; even as I was stepping into the water to pull her out I was aware of an old man on the opposite side of the pool—not only aware of his presence but of the fact that he was inwardly divided, hesitating whether to step in himself—all of which was revealed by slight nuances of posture and bodily motion. Dante is here in a situation of crisis; strain sharpens the eyes.

Then comes a further surprise. Instead of offering to comfort this seemingly weak figure, Dante asks for his pity, thus investing him, before he speaks, with an inexplicable authority. Of course Dante is afraid partly because he thinks he may be looking not at a man but at a ghost:

> '*Miserere* di me', gridai a lui,
> 'qual che tu sii, od ombra od omo certo!'   (i. 65–6)

'*Miserere* me', I cried to him, 'whatever you are, shade or true man!'

---

[20] See Tommaso Casini and S. A. Barbi, *La Divina Commedia di Dante Alighieri* (Florence: G. C. Sansoni, 1923), 7.

Virgil answers, 'Non omo, omo già fui' ('No man, though once I was a man.')

The contrast here drawn between humanity on the one side and ghostly existence on the other, for a moment, propels us back to the Homeric roots of European literature. It has long been observed that at the beginning of the *Iliad* the word *autous*, 'themselves' discloses an implicitly anti-Christian attitude to the world of the dead: 'Sing, goddess, of the wrath of Achilles, the dolorous wrath which hurled down into the house of Hades the spirits (*psuchas*) of so many heroes; but the men themselves (*autous*) he left to be the prey of dogs and birds.' The word *autous* shows a this-worldly ascription of personal reality. That which goes down to the Dark House, that with which Odysseus will converse in the eleventh book of the *Odyssey*, is not the real person but an insubstantial wraith, a 'strengthless head' (xi. 29), the mere echo of a person eager for a draught of blood (xi. 367). Where, meanwhile, are the heroes themselves? *They* lie dead in the field. The corpse is the real person.

This, it will be noticed, is precisely reversed in the figural scheme discerned by Auerbach, a scheme which, we have already seen, began to emerge, with subversive effect, in the sixth book of *Aeneid*. If we, now, in the living flesh, are mere *umbrae futurorum*, shades of a greater reality to come, then the word *autos*, 'himself', will need to be shifted: 'Themselves he sent down to the Dark House, while their evanescent bodies lay in the fields for the dogs to tear.' Startlingly in this first encounter with Virgil, the voice of classical epic, the language assumes not the figural but the ancient, Homeric ontology: 'No man, though once I was one.' The figure Dante meets in the growing light describes himself not as the eschatological fulfilment of the earthly Virgil, but as no man at all, a mere ghost.

The matter is complicated by a theology of intermediacy governing the entire pilgrimage of Dante in the next world. There is a sense in which the Heaven visited by Dante *is not yet itself*, since only at the Last Day will the buried flesh be restored, giving the glorified, spiritual body of 1 Corinthians 25: 43–4. There is therefore a suggestion that, even in the *Paradiso*, still it is a mere *umbra futuri*, 'shadow of the future', which is presented to us. This theology does something to excuse the metallic clarity (so different from the endlessly provisional language of

Langland) with which Dante speaks of things he has never seen (imagine the expression on the face of an angel, reading over his shoulder as he writes).

In *Paradiso*, xiv, when Dante's eyes are dazzled by excess of light the angelic voice of Solomon reaches his ears, expounding the doctrine of the resurrection of the body:

> Come la carne glorïosa e santa
> fia rivestita, la nostra persona
> più grata fia per esser tutta quanta (43–5)

When we are clothed again in the flesh, glorious and sanctified, our personality will be the more acceptable as it is made whole and complete.

Thomas Traherne once wrote, inverting the usual logic of ascetic Christianity, 'You must want like a GOD that you may be Satisfied like GOD'[21]—as if the trouble with the lecher is not that he desires too much but rather that he desires too little. In the words of Dante's Solomon:

> li organi del corpo saran forti
> a tutto ciò che potrà dilettarne (59–60)

The organs of the body will be strong for all that can delight us.

In *Purgatorio*, xv, Virgil explains to Dante that a time will soon come,

> ch'a veder queste cose
> non ti fia grave, ma fieti diletto
> quanto natura a sentir ti dispuose (31–3)

when the sight of these things will not be oppressive to you, but as great a delight as nature has framed you to feel.

It is a theology which gives extraordinary poignancy to Beatrice's reference to her own 'buried flesh', when she lovingly half rebukes Dante for his faithlessness at *Purgatorio*, xxxi. 47–8:

> Sì udirai come in contraria parte
> mover dovieti mia carne sepolta

So shall you hear how my buried flesh should have moved you in the contrary path.

---

[21] *Centuries*, i. 44, in Thomas Traherne, *Centuries, Poems and Thanksgivings*, ed. H. M. Margoliouth, 2 vols. (Oxford: Clarendon Pess, 1958), vol. 1, p. 22.

Since Dante takes into the world of the dead his natural, this-worldly body, by this theology he is more substantial than the beings he meets, though less substantial than what they and he will become. Thus Chiron the centaur becomes aware of an intruder from the world above when he sees that Dante, unlike the damned, has the power to move what he touches (*Inferno*, xii. 80–2). Moreover, *Purgatorio* as a whole is a temporary phase. When sin is burned away, it will cease to be. The Homeric wraith pleads to the living for burial and for blood (*Odyssey*, xi. 72, 96). It might be supposed that in Dante's converse eschatology of ever-growing reality such things could never happen: rather the living will adore the blessed dead. Yet, precisely because *Purgatorio* is process, not completion, its inhabitants *can almost pray to the living*. At *Purgatorio*, vi. 26, Dante speaks of all those shades *che pregar pur ch'altri prieghi*, 'whose sole prayer was that others should pray'. All this indeed was to be cut away at the Reformation. Yet the scholars of Merton College, Oxford, still pray for the soul of Walter de Merton, as if *he* needed *them*.

There is at one point in Auerbach's essay a revealing self-correction: 'Cato is a *figura*, or rather the earthly Cato, who renounced his life for freedom, was a *figura*, and the Cato who appears here in the *Purgatorio* is the revealed or fulfilled figure . . .'.[22] At this point we are not concerned with the complicating factor of an intervening theology of intermediacy but with an altogether simpler underlying problem. If Dante is 'here', in this world, and reality is 'there', Dante will be obliged to draw on this world to impart a feeling of reality to his picture of the next. He has no other material to hand. That which according to his philosophy is truly real will, as it were, be fuelled, in practice, by the less real. Auerbach has collided with one bizarre but inescapable conclusion of his account, namely, that if Dante really believes in the notion of *figura*, the *Commedia* cannot—or, at least, ought not to be—figural: the *world* is figured, the poem purports to be a literal account of the fulfilled reality. But everyone knows that the poem, in so far as it is a work of human art, is a series of shadowings forth, in images, of that other world not yet visited—and this provokes, very

---

[22] 'Figura', *Scenes from the Drama of European Literature*, 65–6.

naturally, the impulse to say that Dante's Cato is a *figura*, that is an image implicated in the fabric of reality. There is a sense in which Dante can offer no better images than are offered by this world, to which, after all, he still belongs. There is an analogy here with the problem of projection which we found in Feuerbach (see above, page 11).

I have tried to sketch a strand of thought in Dante which runs contrary to the splendidly simple intuition of Auerbach and makes possible a kind of treaty with the bloodless ghosts of primary epic. We too, however, must be wary of spurious clarity. Dante is perhaps still less resolved and certain in his mind than we have made him appear. If the dead are, by the theology of intermediacy, insubstantial, the landscape they inhabit is strangely hard and definite. For a while we are encouraged to think that a living intruder, such as Dante, can move objects in the other world but is not himself moved by them. Thus Dante does not feel the flakes of fire which torment Brunetto Latini. But this is not consistently maintained: at *Inferno*, xxxiii. 100, he is affected by the terrible cold of deepest Hell. The vision of glorified bodily delight offered by Solomon at *Paradiso*, xiv. 59–60, is countered by the voice in the sweet-smelling wind at *Purgatorio*, xxiv. 150–4:

> Beati cui alluma
> tanto di grazia, che l'amor del gusto
> nel petto lor troppo disir non fuma,
> esuriendo sempre quanto è giusto

Blessed are they who are so lit by grace that love of the tasting does not kindle in the breast too great a desire, hungering always as far as is just.

However often we are told of the immateriality of the damned, we can never forget the burnt face of Brunetto Latini (*Inferno*, xv. 27). Nor can we resist an intuition of 'deepened' reality when Beatrice says to the disoriented, foolishly arrogant Dante, *Ben son, ben son Beatrice*, 'I really am, I really am Beatrice' (*Purgatorio*, xxx. 73). The willed flight of the *Commedia* is as Auerbach described it: not from the given into the easy liberty of symbolic fictions, but into an ever sharper, more brilliant reality. The presence, meanwhile, of conflicting signals in fact frees the poet for quasi-musical modulating effects. Needing a faint pre-echo of his major motif, Dante chooses that Virgil, on his first appearance, should speak from the *pre*-Virgilian world of the wasted dead before his fuller humanity warms before our eyes.

As soon as Dante knows that this is indeed Virgil, he addresses him with love and reverence: *Tu se' lo mio maestro e 'l mio autore*, 'You are my master and my author' (i. 85). When Dante wrote, *maestro* normally meant 'teacher' (usually, a poet of the immediately preceding generation) while *autore* meant 'classical authority'. Virgil is both. We saw how in Virgil the ancient Muse was relegated to a secondary position and that the real Muse might now be the preceding *poet* Homer, though the relation between Virgil and Homer would prove to be one of, so to speak, loving antagonism. Here, we might think, our intuition is made manifest. We have heard nothing of a Muse; instead, at the beginning of *the* central Christian poem, a pagan poet is summoned, to guide Dante forward. The language 'master and author' is suspended between the literary and the theological (he is very close to the phrase, 'author of my being'). Yet the altered logic of the whole design must be kept firmly in view. It is Dante the *pilgrim*, not the poet, the still benighted man, who so addresses Virgil. The poet knows already that Virgil will be permitted to go so far and no further in the journey that lies ahead. He can be no guide to Paradise. It is as if, by projecting his fallen self into the poem, Dante believes that he can bracket off, by a literary *epochē*, the fallen imperfect inspiration of literature, so that in due course, as the pilgrim is rescued and made new, the *Commedia* itself will be formed and made strong by God himself. God is too fundamental to be easily invoked in a proem; rather, since the beginning is the end and the end the beginning, the poem's prayer-for-itself will be implicit in a concluding prayer to God himself. And so indeed it turns out. In the culminating prayer at the end of the *Paradiso*

> non eran da ciò le proprie penne:
> se non che la mia mente fu percossa
> da un fulgore in che sua voglia venne.
> A l'alta fantasia qui mancò possa;
> ma già volgeva il mio disio e'l *velle*,
> sì come rota ch'igualmente è mossa
> l'amor che move il sole e l'altre stelle
> (xxxiii. 139–45)

My own wings would not have been equal to that, had not my mind been struck by a lightning flash, in which its own wish came; here power failed the high imagining, but already my desire and my will were turned like a wheel which turns evenly on its axis, by the love which moves the sun and the other stars.

Here the strange overlapping of selfhood and godhead which we found in the first, Homeric conception of the Muse, is carried to a new power. The 'wings' which fail are classical, like those on which Milton sought to fly above the Aonian Mount (*Paradise Lost*, i. 14–15). This flight is given time to know its own failure before it is transcended by a grace which carries an element of *will*—and this will becomes Dante's. In the last sentence, which issues so wonderfully upon starry space, the love is, to begin with, the love felt by the creature for God, not God's love. It is the love described by Aristotle in his *Metaphysics*—*kinei dē hōs erōmenon*, 'he moves as being loved' (1072b), God begets motion in the universe not by the 'efficient causality' of a steam engine but by the 'final causality' ('end-directed causality') of amorous attraction (it is, for Aristotle, exactly in this non-mechanical manner that a beautiful person at a party may draw others across a room). Yet even as Dante borrows from Aristotle, the idea begins to escape the Aristotelian limitation. The love alluded to by Aristotle is, unambiguously, that felt by the creature. For Dante love is itself a divine mystery; when it occurs in the creature, then God occurs in the Creature, even when—or perhaps especially when—the love is love of God himself. The idea of the created universe as an immense act of mediated, divine self-love is not one from which Dante flinches. At *Paradiso*, xxxiii. 126, he addressed God as one who alone, knowing, 'lovest and smilest on thyself'. Having said this, however, he at once adds, breaking the complacency of introversion, that God's face is painted with *our* likeness (131). Justinian the lawgiver who says, *per voler del primo amor ch'i' sento*, 'by will of the primal love which I feel' (*Paradiso*, vi. 11), is speaking more of God than of himself. God is more than Muse. He is the maker of the book of the Universe and of the book called *Commedia*, which reflects the universe. By this logic Dante must cease to be author and become *nothing more* than the character within the poem. Yet all this, as we have seen, is not directly believable.

Yet again we must reject the spurious clarity of a saving distinction. Dante the pilgrim is not after all utterly distinct from the man who composed this poem (a certain sour-featured Florentine). The love of Virgil can be felt, not only in the pilgrim's words, but in the surrounding poetry. It can be caught in one modest word: *umile*, at i. 106—*Di quella umile Italia*, 'Of that low-lying Italy'. Dante is remembering the first glimpse, little enough in itself but charged with promise, of long-sought Italy in the *Aeneid*, where the sky reddens—a beautiful use of the inchoative form of the verb—and voices are hushed but then freed in a clangour of glottal consonants:

> Imaque rubescebat stellis Aurora fugatis
> cum procul obscuros colles humilemque videmus
> Italiam. Italiam primus conclamat Achates
> Italiam laeto socii clamore salutant

(iii. 521–4)

Now the dawn was reddening and the stars were put to flight when far off we saw dim hills, low-lying Italy. 'Italy!' Achates first cried out; 'Italy!' the crew hail with joyous shout.

The Dante who saw the power in *humilemque* really did love Virgil. The first canto ends with Dante following obediently in the footsteps of Virgil.

It may be thought that we part company here, since the proem must by now be past. But if we follow Dante, we shall be led to, at last, a classical invocation of the Muses: *O Muse, o alto ingegno, or m'aiutate*, 'O Muses, O high genius, now aid me' (ii. 7). Something odd is going on. An *in medias res* narrative opening is *followed by* a classical proemium. Any suspicion that the directness of Canto i is mere medieval *naïveté* untouched by classical precedent is now thoroughly scotched. Boccaccio himself was probably shocked. In his commentary he feels obliged, first to heap up learned analogues and then to allegorize the Muses as daughters of God the Father and Memory.[23] Benvenuto da Imola, writing close to Dante's own time, deals with the difficulty by presuming that what confronts us is really an enormously extended, thoroughly classical proem. It is as if

---

[23] See Ernst Robert Curtius, *European Literature and the Latin Middle Ages*, trans. Willard R. Trask (London: Routledge and Kegan Paul, 1979), 239.

Dante had set out to defeat those myopic readers who were unable to hold more than one canto in the head at once. There is indeed a superficial confusion in Benvenuto's analysis. He says at one point that the proem extends over the first *three* cantos, but then explains that the *proposal* of the work (thinking here, perhaps, of the cancelled Virgilian lines, *Ille ego*, 'That man am I') occupies the first canto, the invocation of the Muse (corresponding to *Musa mihi causas memora*, 'Tell me, Muse, the causes') comes in the second, and that in the third Dante embarks on his *tractatus*, the treatment of his matter, which implies that the proem is completed at the end of the second canto.[24]

Certainly, the Muse is formally invoked in Canto ii. The line has little poetic force and looks more exclamatory than prayerful, but it is there (and Calliope will be invoked at the beginning of *Purgatorio*, and Apollo, the god of poetry, at the beginning of the *Paradiso*). The collapsing of the Muses into a figurative language for interior states which we noted earlier seems to be lightly assumed by Dante in the smooth transition, *Muse . . . ingegno . . . mente*, 'Muses . . . genius . . . mind/memory'. It is true that in his *De Vulgari Eloquentia*, II. iv. 9–10, Dante draws a careful distinction between craft, carefully learned, and genius, but aside from the fact that both craft and genius are subjective to the poet, it is likely that the Muse is in any case involved more with genius than with craft. This is still traceable in the 'affect' of the word 'inspiration'. Singleton in his commentary observes, somewhat in the spirit of Benvenuto, that we may infer from the invocation that the *Commedia* begins here, in the second canto, in which case *Inferno*, I, is properly a separate prologue. We should remember that at one time a proem would itself have been felt as 'a sort of prologue', and that *it* would have been followed by the *in medias res* narrative opening. It is true that if we detach *Inferno*, I, and renumber the succeeding parts we shall find that each of the *cantiche* (*Inferno*, *Purgatorio*, *Paradiso*) has the same number of cantos (33) and that three thirty-threes, plus one prologue-canto, makes in all a hundred, the 'perfect number'.

Dante writes with an awareness of the fact that his work is

[24] *Commentum*, i. 21.

conditioned by other literary works and shows an instinctive understanding of the tensions so created. The 'preliminary spectre' of classical epic is in no sense a constraint. This response is vital, shifting, and, one senses, internationally mysterious, allowing him, for example, to give greater weight to the narrated arrival of Virgil than to the conventionally summoned Muses. It is likely that when Homer employed the *in medias res* narrative opening he enjoyed, and to some extent exploited, a mild degree of pleasurable disorientation in his listeners. Dante also, for deeper reasons, desires a disorientation, as if he would have us echo the initial *Nescio*, 'I know not', of Propertius's response to Virgil's poem—as if he would have us say (unmetrically), *Nescio quid maius nascitur Aeneide*, 'I know-not-what is here being born, greater than the *Aeneid*.'

CHAUCER AND THE 'OVERHEARD OPENING'

It seems inescapable that Dante drew his notion of the subtly thwarted opening from Virgil. Thereafter, it seems, the Middle Ages learned from Dante. There were indeed great poets in England whom Dante, so to speak, never touched, while the corpus of French romance laid down a pattern of rhetorical 'entries' too intricate to be pursued here. The highly sophisticated poet of *Sir Gawain and the Green Knight* begins with a primitive (not primitivist) capitulation of 'the matter of Rome' bringing his listeners up to the point at which the narrative proper begins:

> Sithin the sege and the assaut watz sesed at Troye,
> The borg brittened and brent to brondez and askez,
> The tulk that the trammes of tresoun ther wrogt
> Watz tried for his tricherie, the trewest on erthe.
> Hit watz Ennias the athel and his highe kynde,
> That sithen depreced provinces, and patrounes bicome
> Welnege of al the wele in the west iles.
> Fro riche Romulus to Rome ricchis hym swythe,
> With gret bobbaunce that burge he biges upon fyrst
> And revenes hit his aune nome, as hit now hat.[25]

[25] Text from Malcolm Andrew and Ronald Weldron (ed.), *The Poems of the Pearl Manuscript: Pearl, Cleanness, Patience, Sir Gawain and the Green Knight*, Exeter Medieval Texts and Studies (Exeter: University of Exeter, 1987), 207.

Coleridge once wrote that the difference between a 'sterile' and 'exuberant' mind could be illustrated by the contrast between Mistress Quickly, in *2 Henry IV*, telling a story, and Hamlet doing the same job.[26] The first kind of mind (which in another place he calls 'the uncultivated mind'[27]) simply says everything it knows, however 'impertinent', while the second is able to organize its narrative in terms of 'point', omitting nothing which is essential to the 'intelligibility' of the events recalled. In Wilkie Collins's *The Woman in White*, Walter Hartright, the drawing master, carefully collecting evidence in order to expose the villain of the novel, introduces one of the book's special miniature narratives with words of warning, 'Knowing by experience that the plainest narrative obtainable from persons who are not accustomed to arrange their ideas, is the narrative which goes far enough back at the beginning to avoid all impediments of retrospection in its course . . .' (pt. 2, s. 6). Both these judgements, class-based as they are, are applicable to the opening of *Sir Gawain and the Green Knight*. It may be, indeed, that the extent to which we owe the very notion of 'point' to the Greeks is startling.

With Chaucer, on the other hand, the matter stands differently. Chaucer certainly read Dante and one is tempted to say that he learned from Dante how to do *his* kind of 'thwarted' opening, but it is impossible to be certain of this.

The Book of the Duchess in effect discovers a new mode of *in medias res* opening in that it pitches the reader, not into the middle of a narrative sequence, but into the middle of an informal, gossiping monologue:

> I have gret wonder, be this lyght,
> How that I lyve, for day ne nyght
> I may nat slepe wel nygh noght;
> I have so many an ydel thoght
> Purely for defaute of slep
> That, by my trouthe, I take no kep
> Of nothing, how hyt cometh or gooth

[26] In his Essay on Method, in T. M. Raysor (ed.), *Coleridge's Shakespearean Criticism*, 2 vols. (London: Cantabile, 1936), ii. 345–6.

[27] In his lectures of 1811–12, reported by Collier, in *Coleridge's Shakespearean Criticism*, ii. 134.

and so on and on, for forty-three lines: stock, repetitious maundering, with a high incidence of metrical 'fillers', all about the fact that Chaucer—or whoever is speaking—cannot get a decent night's sleep. The formlessness,[28] the lack of a proper explanatory courtesy, of any sense of *public* address as commonly understood, creates the presumption that we are overhearing rather than hearing, that we have somehow blundered into the middle of something which may, for all we know, have been going on for hours. We are accustomed, since the Romantics, to the notion that the poet should 'load every rift with ore' (or else attempt the still higher concentrations of Modernism). Yet here rift after rift is packed with mere verbiage, with exclamations which mean *less* than they formally proffer. It is remarkable how swiftly the reader intuits, for example, that in the first two lines the speaker is *not* in fear of his life. We can usually assume that poetry has disengaged itself from the language of 'a man speaking to men' (*pace* Wordsworth) by setting a higher standard of reference. A tape-recorder left running in a common room, it is often said, will never yield a body of 'literature'. Chaucer seems to be bent on the undoing of this fundamental distinction.

Yet this is not nature but art. The first signal of a wry consciousness of what is going on is the word 'ydel' in line 4—'I have so many an ydel thoght'—which anticipates with precision the scandalized critical description I have myself just set down.

At line 44 we may think for a moment that the narrative proper is beginning, but we are deceived. Chaucer reaches out, not to a Muse or to his own genius, but to a book, handed to him by a servant whom we cannot see. M. W. Stearns could find no earlier instance in medieval love-visions of this invoking of a book at the outset of the poem.[29] Chaucer then reads the Ovidian tale of Ceyx and Alcione. We are taken through the tale with all the mind-numbing clumsiness of persons who insist on telling one the entire story of films they have seen. But Chaucer is Chaucer, and the theme of sleep is all the while subject to a

---

[28] Piero Boitani finds in all the 'link passages' of the poem 'the apparently chaotic and disconnected quality that characterises the dream as a human psychic activity'. See his *English Medieval Narrative in the Thirteenth and Fourteenth Centuries*, trans. Joan Krakover Hall (Cambridge: Cambridge University Press, 1982), 143.

[29] 'Chaucer Mentions a Book', *Modern Language Notes*, 57 (1942), 28–31.

covert artistic management which successfully engages our attention. And, of course, it is rather a good story. But, even as I concede that *we* are beginning to awake, Chaucer successfully bores himself to sleep (275), and in that sleep comes to the real matter of the poem, the dream-vision. This in its turn is represented, with a marvellous 'crossing of lines', as an awakening, in bed, on a May morning, to the sound of birds. Now the narrative is magical. The ecphrastic play with the images of Hector, Medea, and the rest in the chamber windows (327 f.) no longer reaches us as mere antiquarian lumber. The sound of the horn (346), Chaucer's hurrying out (as Boitani says,[30] it is part of the dream atmosphere that he seems not to get dressed and we wonder for a moment if he is naked), his haste to join the hunt which after a buzz of vivid activity loses the scent and is then itself lost to us, his following the dog among the trees, till at last he sees, from behind, the man in black sitting leaning against the oak (445)—these things indeed embody, but in a new, mysterious mode, the *in medias res* of ancient narrative poetry.

The whole may be seen as a brilliant play on the entire notion of 'point', as set forth by Coleridge on the wool-gathering Mistress Quickly. Chaucer, as it were, makes a point of pointlessness and in doing so crosses a certain line in the development of literary sophistication. At the beginning of this book I spoke of Virgil's voice rising from silence. At the beginning of *The Book of the Duchess* the voice of European poetry *descends*, to the common tenor of the boringly demotic. Yet, as we realize that we are being practised upon, the effect is exciting. Chaucer has in effect driven a wedge into the relatively stable identity of the reader or listener. For this is pseudo-intimate discourse. Chaucer treats us as if we were tolerant old acquaintances, but he knows and we know that this is not the case. We are now in the world of consciously false dialogue with the reader which will allow Sterne, centuries later, to explain how he has left a page blank for the reader to *draw* the Widow Wadman—with perfect knowledge that a reader who actually did so would be a kind of idiot, a Holy Fool of the Literal Sense. Here I must confess to a certain unease. It is likely, we are

---

[30] *English Medieval Narrative*, 144.

told, that Chaucer's society was still fundamentally auditory, that poetry was read aloud, that Chaucer himself would have 'performed' his poem, before some sort of audience. Yet the kind of pseudo-intimacy I have tried to describe seems closely bound up with the queer privacy of solitary reading. We need to remember that the spectacle of a person reading silently would probably have seemed almost indecent to Plato, who was already worried by literacy itself, as an erosion of memory, (*Phaedrus*, 275; the 'Seventh Letter'). In the time of Augustine, the spectacle of Ambrose reading silently was still considered marvellous (*Confessions*, vi. iii. 3). But *The Book of Duchess* explicitly directs us to the world of the solitary reader, by describing the man who reads himself to sleep. Only through this ivory gate can we now reach the dream-vision of the sunlit wood. The novel has been called 'the only genre that pretends to be true'. Behind that pretence lies another: the pretence-not-to-be-public. There is a certain eeriness in the fact that, with the development of printing and large-scale publication, there comes this confidential, insinuating, 'just the two of us' voice. The word 'persona' originally meant 'mask'. Virgil may speak from an epic persona at the beginning of the *Aeneid*, though to say this is to say little more than that the voice is formally 'enlarged'. With Chaucer the term 'persona' becomes a critical necessity: from now on it connotes deception, evasiveness, wit.

It may be said that Chaucer was in all probability reading aloud to friends who were indeed tolerant and easy-going. But this just will not do. Imagine the scene: all are gathered and attentive; the poet has his script in his hand; he then launches into the rambling account of his insomnia—the only sign that he has not in fact turned into a simple bore being the presence of rhyme and metre. No, if we are to suppose performance, we must press instead for a high degree of sophisticated artifice, an almost Pinterian, mannered informality, in which the poet *played* the bore.[31] Even if this is correct, the supposition that the poem is *simultaneously* aimed at a (later) solitary reader—at, say,

---

[31] This line is ably argued by D. S. Brewer, who suggests that at this stage in his career Chaucer was in some ways remotely akin to a court jester. See his essay, 'The Relationship of Chaucer to the English and European Traditions', in D. S. Brewer (ed.), *Chaucer and the Chaucerians: Critical Studies in Middle English Literature* (London: Nelson, 1966), 1–38, esp. 8.

just such an insomniac as the poet—remains powerful: Chaucer, even as he lowers the poetic register, sends his words beyond the circle of listeners, to the unknown 'hypocrite lecteur, mon semblable, mon frère'. *I liber*, 'Go, little book.' Indeed, the picture offered by J. A. Burrow is both subtler and more persuasive: Chaucer was not an oral, 'minstrel poet'; his works may have been read aloud on many occasions but his own habits of reading were solitary; he was therefore partly alienated from the native literary heritage, but instead of purging all the minstral features from his style he, with varying degrees of irony, accommodated them.[32]

Of course it is impossible to say with confidence that no one had done this before. D. S. Brewer has shown how an informal style involving exclamations is found earlier, the most important examples being the early couplet version of *Guy of Warwick, Dégaré and Eglamour,* and observes that Chaucer may have learned the technique of copious verbosity from Guillaume de Machaut.[33] But in the same essay Brewer speaks of the novelty of Chaucer's spaciousness, of a 'new diction' and a 'new direction'.[34] A scrutiny of such direct source-analogues as Froissart's *Paradys d'amours* leaves one more forcibly aware of Chaucer's originality than of his indebtedness. John M. Manley's admirable account in his 1926 British Academy Lecture[35] of Chaucer's relation to earlier rhetorical practice certainly did less than justice to the extreme informality of the English poet's manner. Barbara Nolan's meticulous argument, that Chaucer crucially disengages himself from French precedent through the use of a self-minimizing persona is the subtlest analysis to date.[36] We must add however that in the modest disclaimers so skilfully explicated by Barbara Nolan a new, covertly manipulative authority over the reader is surely asserted.

E. H. Gombrich in a famous essay contrasted the sketch-

---

[32] *Medieval Writers and their Work: Middle English Literature and its Background 1100–1500* (Oxford: Oxford University Press, 1982), 53–5.

[33] Ibid. 7, 22. [34] Ibid. 15, 27, 30.

[35] 'Chaucer and the Rhetoricians', reproduced in R. J. Schoek and J. Taylor, *Chaucer Criticism: The Canterbury Tales*, 2 vols. (Notre Dame: University of Notre-Dame Press, 1961), ii. 268–90.

[36] 'The Art of Expropriation: Chaucer's Narrator in *The Book of the Duchess*', in Donald M. Rose (ed.), *New Perspectives in Chaucer Criticism* (Norman, Okla.: Pilgrim Books, 1981), 203–22.

books of the medieval artist Villard d'Honnecourt with those of Leonardo da Vinci.[37] His point was that even within the informal parameters of a working notebook the medieval drawings were definite, complete in themselves, with no marks of cancellation, no changes of mind. Even when a note was being made of an architectural detail, a tiny segment of some much larger design, the drawing was itself satisfyingly, unproblematically complete. But in Leonardo's work (as we might perhaps have predicted of an artist who advised his peers to stare at blotchy walls in order to become responsive to the *emergence* of form),[38] we find instead pages of brilliant scribbling, of whirling lines in which the hand seems to have been permitted a kind of free association (the analogy with a psychoanalytic unlocking of the Unconscious is close). The interest in the *non finito* (the 'unfinished work'), in the dynamics of artistic creation is now to be incorporated in the public work of art. As a way of dividing the Renaissance from the Middle Ages this seems more promising than most. Yet Chaucer's place in such a scheme (if we may extrapolate from visual to literary art) is, to say the least, baffling. The rambling opening of *The Book of the Duchess* is a verbal scribbling, covering page after page, out of which, as from a strangely unportentous latency (no Virgilian or Dantesque brooding darkness here) the dominant themes may emerge. England is generally reckoned not to have produced a Renaissance literature until the sixteenth century, yet Chaucer, so much earlier than Skelton or Barclay or Hawes, was himself a reader not only of Dante but of Boccaccio, whose 'Renaissance credentials' are strong. When Chaucer makes detailed use of Dante (as in *The House of Fame*) the use is deeply ironic. In the same poem he offers his own version of *Arma virumque cano*, 'Arms and the man I sing', and it is artfully, knowingly oblique (i. 144).

One cannot help noticing, however, that unlike Leonardo's wildest pages which show, at every point, the hand of a draughtsman, Chaucer's ramshackle diction looks, in certain ways, as if it came naturally to an originally artless speaker.

[37] 'Leonardo's Method for Working Out Compositions', in his *Norm and Form* (London: Phaidon, 1966), 58–63.
[38] *Selections From the Notebooks of Leonardo da Vinci*, ed. Irma A. Richter (London: Oxford University Press, 1952), 182.

Indeed, if one turns from highly concentrated lyric poetry such as that of Marvell to Chaucer, one can begin to feel that Chaucer actually could not write thick-woven, brilliant poetry. Did he then contrive to turn defeat into an amazing innovative victory, clowning his way to unexpected sublimities? We may think here of the rhetorical use made by Harold Macmillan in his later years of 'the controlled dodder'.

Perhaps the lesson of Chaucer is that the *Zeitgeist* is an elusive and unreliable thing. The backbone of this book is a canon of narrative beginnings, indeed, the central canon of European literature. This can be said confidently because it is of the essence of such august literary sequences that they are visible to all. The *de jure* authority of the Homer–Virgil–Dante–Milton line may be disputed, but its *de facto* authority cannot be. Yet Chaucer in the English high Middle Ages, when in every city Gothic towers and pinnacles were springing, displays on his sleeve this self-deprecating, poem-deprecating, sub-comical evasiveness. Those who like to think of Chaucer as the father of English poetry have always been embarrassed by his lack of patriarchal grandeur. Even when he dutifully goes through the business of invocation and proemium (as he does, often enough) we sense that he does so in an edgy and unconvinced manner. A sergeant-major's eye would detect 'dumb insolence'. *Troilus and Criseyde* is a story of terrible sadness which refuses to be majestic. Tisiphone and Calliope are invoked, but they are metaphors. Tisiphone in particular is swiftly overtaken by Chaucer's un-Virgilian, un-Dantesque, 'agony aunt' hope that his poem may help persons distressed in their love-lives (i. 20–1). Matthew Arnold notoriously could never get used to what he saw as an intrusive frivolity in Chaucer, a letting down of the side.[39] As it was, Chaucer transformed the canonical 'interventionist' opening in a manner which was fully exploited only after further centuries had passed.

The pressure created by Dante, it will be seen, is in the opposite direction, towards a higher structure. The canonical interventionist opening can itself be felt as a wayward truancy from the majesty of natural genesis, but that brief sense of falling away is swiftly repaired by the supernatural scale of

[39] 'The Study of Poetry', *Essays in Criticism*, 1st Ser.

utterance, by the presence of a divine or archangelic voice prescribing the point of departure. Dante ensures that, in so far as his poem is interventionist, it intervenes in a life which is itself interrupted, savingly, by divine agency. Thus, in a manner, a sacrificial death of the *in medias res* opening, with its assertion of Form against Nature, is enacted. But, as we have seen, there are difficulties.

First, there is the question of allegory. An allegory is a walking metaphor or, in other words, a metaphor which is not allowed to stand still. It is technically difficult to operate a complex, narrative metaphor where the separate moving parts of the 'vehicle' must continue to correspond, through all the twists and turns of the story, to the relevant moving parts in the 'tenor'. It is likely that when Prudentius wrote the (to us leaden) *Psychomachia*, the allegory of the war in the soul seemed breath-takingly adventurous to the first readers—as if a whole new dimension in literature were revealed. Yet metaphor—the fictive substitution of one term for another—continues to constitute the primary datum or *fiat* of allegory. If the *Commedia* is allegorical, the *Commedia* must be (merely?) metaphorical.

In his letter to Can Grande (the authenticity of which has been questioned), Dante gives a polysemous account of the Biblical Exodus, the departure of the Israelites out of Egypt. There are, he explains, four senses: literal, allegorical, moral, and anagogical. The literal sense is the actual journey out of Egypt; the allegorical sense is our Redemption, as wrought by Christ; the moral sense is the passage of the soul from the misery of sin to a state of grace, the anagogical sense is the passage of the soul from terrestrial corruption to heavenly glory. In the *Convivio* (ii. 1), on the other hand, we have a different picture. Here he sharply distinguishes poets' allegory from the allegory used in scriptural exegesis. He then (as in the Can Grande letter) lists four senses for the scriptural allegory but, surprisingly, gives as his example of the second sense, the allegorical, Ovid's *poetical* account of Orpheus charming the trees and rocks. This represents the wise man softening savage hearts by the power of his voice. His example of the moral sense is however thoroughly scriptural—the Evangelist's account of the Transfiguration, which signifies that in the most sacred matters we should take few companions. For the anagogical sense he uses Exodus, giving an account in substantial agreement with the letter to Can Grande. It is not easy to see exactly how these schemes are to be applied to the *Commedia*. Dorothy L. Sayers set out hopefully but soon found that it was not easy to discover the anagogical sense in a work whose literal sense was already 'other-worldly'.[40] Dante's use of scriptural examples may be his way of alerting us to the probability that the *Commedia* is, precisely, *not* 'mere metaphor' but is rather to be placed with the great significant events of historical Scripture, where both vehicle and tenor are part of the fabric of reality (for God allegorizes using not fictions but real people). This would mean that by the distinction offered in the *Convivio* the 'allegory' of the *Commedia* would not be poetic allegory but somehow closely analogous to scriptural exegesis. We have returned, the reader will have noticed, to Auerbach's problem, to *figura*.

One easy way to deal with Dorothy L. Sayers's difficulty is to coin a new word, *catagogical*. Where *anagogical* means 'leading upward', *catagogical* means 'leading downward'. Instead of seeking an implied other-worldly meaning in a narrative which already deals, literally and directly, with Heaven and Hell, we learn instead to discern an implied *this*-worldly reference, hidden behind the transcendent story. It will be found that the *Commedia,* so resistant to anagogical reading, yields at once to this altered approach. All the political readings of the poem are readings of the catagogical sense. If we take the standard textbook case of Exodus, we might suppose a medieval poem, discernibly derived therefrom, which described the progress of the soul to Heaven. Here we could say, using precisely the scheme offered in the *Convivio*, that such a poem would have, as its catagogical sense, the passage of the Israelites out of their Egyptian captivity. It is a curious thought-experiment to perform, because it seems to yield such immediately positive results. One can almost say, 'No need to imagine; the *Commedia* is that poem'. But it is better to say that the Biblical Exodus is an occasional—not the principal—catagogical sense. Meanwhile, the *Inferno* is remarkable as a narrative for its incessant

---

[40] 'The Fourfold Interpretation of the Comedy', in her *Introductory Papers on Dante* (London: Methuen, 1954), 101–26. See also G. C. Hardie's review of Dorothy L. Sayers' *Further Papers on Dante,* in *Italian Studies,* 13 (1958), 114 f.

downward pointers to the familiar world of Florentine politics. The signposts there are all catagogical.

This reconstruing of the scheme offered in the *Convivio* treats the literal sense as a movable element (which, in some degree at least, it obviously is). There was, clearly, a presumption, impeding the author of the Can Grande epistle, that the literal sense must always be in reference to our world. This presumption is overturned in the reconstructed version. We now have a prior array of senses, which are also, metaphysically, ontological 'bands' of possible reality: (*a*) this world, (*b*) the moral world, (*c*) the world beyond the grave. Given an available developed language for each of these bands, the poet can pitch his tent in any of them, and make that the literal sense of his poem. If (*b*) is chosen it will be futile to dig for a buried moral sense, but perfectly sensible to look (*a*) or (*c*). Dante in fact chose, so the argument runs, to make (*c*) the letter of the *Commedia*. This then indeed permits us to seek figurative reference to (*a*), which from our present elevated plane of literal reference is rechristened 'catagogical', or to (*b*).

Although this scheme succeeds to a surprising extent, one senses that it is too clearly schematic for the huge, overspilling poem Dante made. There are, to begin with, certain minor factors which blur the hard outline: we have seen that by the theology of deferral intermittently present in the poem the figures we meet are not unequivocally fulfilled eschatological realities but foreshadowings and this, operating subliminally, can infect our confidently proposed literal-eschatological sense with the semantic obliquity of metaphor. Then there is the fact, for which I argued in my *Two Concepts of Allegory* (1967), that all accounts of the next world by human beings living in this one will be obstinately metaphorical at root, a huge projection of imagery drawn always from the world we all know. The sense that the literal sense *must* be 'this-worldly' has a strong foundation.

These things, however, are no more than blurrings at the outer edge of the subject. In *Two Concepts of Allegory* I conceded that, by the period of the *Commedia*, an autonomous language for Heaven, Hell, and Purgatory has established itself, so that the fact that its terms may originally have been transposed by *metaphora*, 'carrying over', from the given world, becomes mere background history. As a consequence we are able to say that a given poem deals literally with Heaven. Perhaps the neatest way to illustrate the point is by looking at the word 'Heaven' itself. Historically it is a metaphor, because it once meant 'sky'. Now however it would be a mistake—a *lexicographical* mistake—to say that, in its commonest use, it means sky. The exile has now built the city. 'Heaven' now denotes, unequivocally, an other-worldly place, so that in certain eighteenth-century poetic uses of 'heaven' to mean, once more, 'sky' we sense, quite correctly, a renewal of metaphor, working this time in the opposite direction.

What remains fundamental is the division between fictive metaphor and the impulse (manifestly strong in Dante) to regard structures of sign and signified as somehow *in rebus*, as objective. It is the great merit of Auerbach to identify this distinction, through his use of the terms *allegoria* and *figura*. I have tried to cast doubt on the presumption that the literal sense must always be this-worldly. It is important also that we should not be trapped in the allied presumption that the literal sense is *assertive of actuality*, is the truth-telling sense. There is an endemic confusion in our use of the term 'metaphor'. We sometimes use 'metaphorical' as the simple opposite of 'literal'. A literal sentence is then one which eschews metaphor. This usage makes it strictly impossible to ask of the *Roman de la Rose* what is the literal and what is the allegorical sense. Since the *Roman* is an allegory, it is not literal, period. Literary historians in practice know (though they are not always clear-headed on this point) that this usage is crude and falls short of the sophistication shown, for example, by early exegetes of Virgil. We must be allowed to ask of a polysemous work, 'What is the literal, what the symbolic sense?'—that is, to treat 'metaphoric-al' not as a simple opposite of 'literal', but as denoting the coexistence of literal and non-literal. If we apply this to the *Roman de la Rose* we find at once that the literal sense is concerned with a garden and the metaphoric (implied or variously signalled) sense is a love story. Thus the *metaphor* of the garden constitutes the *literal* sense of the poem. It is symptomatic of the confusion in which people live, in an age of endlessly fissiparous semasiologies, that such a sentence will be experienced as baffling. The bafflement is entirely due to a covert invasion of the mind by the absolute opposition of literal and metaphorical which we set on one side. The literal sense really is something which can be shifted at will.

Once this is fully understood, it suddenly becomes glaringly obvious that, so far from there being some inherent connection between the literal sense and truth or actuality, in polysemous literature it is typically the literal strand which is feigned, while the moral or human significance may be deemed to be some sort of reality. Metaphors, we all know, are things which poets make up. Thus, to understand the full force of Auerbach's argument, one must realize that fictive *allegoria*, as distinct from *figura*, has dominated literature. Most often, the surface story is feigned.

Dante, says Auerbach, refuses this agreeable latitude of fiction and instead seeks to fuse his poem with an *objectively* polysemous universe. He saw that the earthly Beatrice, though real, was in relation to the Heavenly Beatrice a mere foreshadowing. The *figura* or metaphor, in that case, is what walked in Florence, and what Dante gives us is the fulfilled super-reality.

The word 'figural' can have two meanings: first 'representing', 'bodying forth' (within an objectivist scheme); second, 'forming part of an objectivist scheme of signifier and signified'. There is no difficulty in calling the *Commedia* 'figural' according to the second sense. But, by the first sense, we almost need to say that the poem is counter-figural, a poem made not of figures but of fulfilments. By parity of reasoning, following the 'catagogical' line, we could say that though Dante does not explicitly present *figurae*, one can, as it were, read off, catagogically, the earthly foreshadowings from the blazing persons of the poem. It is at this point that a sense of an irremediable lack of fit between the grand eschatological project of the *Commedia* and its actual composition becomes inescapable. For with the persons of the *Commedia*, rather more obviously than with the well-established eschatological topography, we cannot help knowing that Dante, whatever the grand scope of his project, had access only to the earthly versions. I write this on the assumption that the *Commedia* is not the record of a veridical mystical experience, that Dante has not been to Heaven.

In which case we have the odd spectacle of a poet, as it were, struggling to disguise a *figura* as its own fulfilment. If this world is a place of mere foreshadowings, as the theory states, and Dante is an inhabitant of this world, then, as we saw earlier, Dante has no other materials to work with (we must now say) but *figurae*. Thus, that which the poet would register as the literal force of his poem is at odds with what we sense pragmatically to be the case. Such quasi-figural poetry, however, may be found to depend for its vitality or even for its very existence on such underlying uncertainties.

If polysemy is entirely and simply a matter of the structure of the objective world, all of us, willy-nilly, are figural speakers every time we open our mouths. If every action is, objectively, morally laden and further charged with implications for the life to come, then 'I posted the letter' (supposing the letter to be wicked) has the moral force 'I descended into sin' and the anagogical sense 'I passed from Heavenly bliss to infernal torment'. A theory which locates polysemy exclusively in the objective world will leave nothing for the poet to do. There must be a fringe of uncertainty, a latitude of varying awareness, so that some may display their greater insight into the real richness of ontology by actively registering the multiple reference of discourse. Such variable registration will inevitably look awfully like—be endlessly confused with—poetic ingenuity, especially since we do not have direct access to the anagogical level. If Virgil had simply incorporated into his reading of Homer the moralizing and allegorical comments of exegetes, there would have been small logical difference, for Virgil (setting aside the idiosyncratic tenderness of the *Aeneid*) between the poems he read and the poem he made. We all know that this cannot be true.

Dante is therefore free, and can make a poem which belongs to him and to no one else (not to Virgil, not to God). Beatrice is the real Beatrice, haloed by love and fiction. She lived in Florence, but never said,

> Come degnasti d'accedere al monte?
> non sapei tu che qui è l'uom felice?
>
> (*Purgatorio*, xxx. 74–5)

How did you ever deign to come to the mountain? Did no one tell you that human beings are happy here?

Dante made that up. Contemporaries of Dante, unchallenged by the harsh binary questions of twentieth-century philosophy, would have moved with fluid assent from things they believed (that Hell lay under their feet, say) to things that might be true (say, that Purgatory is a mountain on the other side of the earth from Jerusalem), and then on to things which probably were not true (that Dante had personally visited every place he mentions).

Thus, while it is of the essence of figural theory that both terms are real and not feigned, Dante must be acknowledged partly to have feigned the structure of the *Commedia*. In the elegant phrase of C. S. Singleton, 'The fiction of the *Comedy* is that it is not fiction.'[41] One could almost be tempted to an abrupt condemnation of the poet: Dante, then, is the great liar. Langland in *Piers Plowman* proclaimed his uncertainties, the imperfection of his knowledge. When Dante the poet exposes the ignorance of Dante the pilgrim he does so confidently from above, from a separate certainty. In *Piers Plowman* poet and pilgrim are one. Nor does Langland ever essay the brazen, minutely detailed lecture tour offered by Dante, secure in the ignorance of his auditors. In this way we might, if we wished, rain blows on the head of Dante. But, for the last time in this chapter, we have again been beguiled by the spurious clarity of a scheme. If we are still able after all our theorizing to read poetry, our strictures will crumble at the memory of Brunetto Latini, of Ulisse, of the encounter with Virgil. We criticize, as he composed, *nel mezzo del cammin*.

---

[41] *Commedia, Elements of Structure, Dante Studies,* i (Cambridge, Mass.: Harvard University Press, 1954), 62.

3

Paradise Lost

RENAISSANCE EGO AND THE REBIRTH OF THE MUSE

Of man's first disobedience, and the fruit
Of that forbidden tree, whose mortal taste
Brought death into the world, and all our woe,
With loss of Eden, till one greater man
Restore us, and regain the blissful seat,
Sing heavenly Muse, that on the secret top
Of Oreb, or of Sinai, didst inspire
That shepherd, who first taught the chosen seed,
In the beginning how the heavens and earth
Rose out of chaos: or if Sion hill
Delight thee more, and Siloa's brook that flowed
Fast by the oracle of God; I thence
Invoke thy aid to my adventurous song,
That with no middle flight intends to soar
Above the Aonian mount, while it pursues
Things unattempted yet in prose or rhyme.
And chiefly thou O Spirit, that dost prefer
Before all temples the upright heart and pure,
Instruct me, for thou know'st; thou from the first
Wast present, and with mighty wings outspread
Dove-like sat'st brooding on the vast abyss
And madest it pregnant: what in me is dark
Illumine, what is low raise and support;
That to the highth of this great argument
I may assert eternal providence,
And justify the ways of God to men.

(i. 1–26)

The Muse is strong again. The blind, seventeenth-century poet-prophet, the endorser of regicide, the hammer of Salmasius, Protestant Milton begins his epic with two enormous

All references to Milton are, unless otherwise specified, to *The Poems of John Milton*, ed. John Carey and Alastair Fowler (London: Longman, 1968).

sentences. It may be said that the Muse is un–Homerically delayed until the sixth line, somewhat as in Virgil (*Musa mihi causas memora*, 'Tell me, O Muse, the causes', comes in line 8 of the *Aeneid*) but in Virgil the delay is a real relegation, since the first main verb of the poem, the first person singular *cano*, 'I sing', is given to the reader immediately in the first line, after which *memora*, 'tell', assumes a subordinate character. In the 'superhuman' sentence structure employed by Milton we are instead made to breathe hard, to feel intensely the need of a main verb, so that when at last it is given, it comes with a saving force. The crucial fact is that the first main verb of Milton's poem is a prayer-ful imperative and not a first person indicative (and this from the notoriously egotistical Milton!). This binds the English poet to Homer, divides him from Virgil. Milton took a certain pride in being 'more a Greek than a Roman'.[1] The young Milton, however, may have given the *laus prima*, 'the foremost praise', to Virgil (*Elegia Prima*, 24), though even there it is not quite certain that he gives a lower place to Homer (the gist of the sentence is that if Ovid had never had to suffer exile, he might have matched Homer, in which case Virgil would never have had the foremost praise, and this, just possibly, could mean 'foremost praise *among the Latins*'. The high opinion of Ovid embarrasses many post-Victorians, but we should learn to respect it, if only because it is a point on which Milton and Shakespeare are agreed. Even if the young Milton really did think Virgil the greatest ancient poet, it was not Virgil but Homer that the older poet, according to his daughter, continually delighted in.[2] At the beginning of *Paradise Lost* Milton is driving his poem back, to the origin of epic.

Milton is here striving to induce what we may call a rebirth—or, if we move from English to French, *renaissance*. We saw earlier that Chaucer is in some ways a Renaissance writer, though born too soon. Milton is in almost every way a Renaissance writer, though born late. The Renaissance was, we

---

[1] Jonathan Richardson, *Explanatory Notes and Remarks on Paradise Lost* (London, 1734), in Helen Darbishire (ed.), *The Early Lives of Milton* (London: Constable, 1932), 216.

[2] See Samuel Johnson, 'The Life of Milton', *Lives of the English Poets*, ed. G. B. Hill, 3 vols. (Oxford: Clarendon Press, 1905), 1. 154. See also Charles Martindale, *John Milton and the Transformation of Epic* (London and Sydney: Croom Helm, 1986), 53.

have been told many times, a self-christening phenomenon, unlike the Middle Ages (for the medieval inhabitants of Europe never suspected that they belonged to an intermediate time of darkness). It is a moment in history at which the conscious assertion of novelty is simultaneously perceived as the rebirth of something very old, the art of the ancient, pre-Christian world. Few artistic revolutions have been as innovative as the Renaissance; none has ever been so profoundly retrospective. In Italy the sense of historical crisis, of a moment of crucial decision, is strong. One turns a corner in Florence and the eye is arrested by a new sort of visual authority, a cleanness and humane apprehensibility in the lines of a building, which seems indeed to say, 'I have been born again.' In England, however, this is simply not the case. The sixteenth century (the period in which we usually seek to place the English 'Renaissance') was a time of happily muddled transition rather than of crisp counter-assertion. Architects, excited by pattern books which taught more about detail than they taught about scale, encrusted their buildings with miniaturized classical motifs, or piled portico on portico in 'towers of the orders' which must, one suspects, always have looked more dotty than dignified ('dotty' was Dame Helen Gardner's word for them, and I do not see how it can be bettered). Spenser and Shakespeare cannot despise the Gothic past as your true, committed Renaissance artist must. The dominance of the nude in Italian painting of the cinquecento has too often blinded people to the proper austerity of Renaissance art, which is opposed to the proliferation of sensuous detail and rigidly governed by mathematical relationships.[3] Michelangelo's nudes, disposed majestically in indeterminate environments, were conceived in reaction against the glittering, eye-delighting, crowded pictures of Gentile da Fabriano.

Did England, then, have a renaissance at all? In a way it had two, the first being that asserted by the Tudor humanists, More, Erasmus, and their circle. This one however, did not 'take', or to put it another way, the child was delivered but still-born. The reason was nothing to do with any lack of vigour or imagination in the writers but is entirely technical. More's

---

[3] See E. H. Gombrich, *Meditations on a Hobby Horse* (London: Phaidon, 1963), 17.

circle wrote for the most part in Latin. The therefore operated, to begin with, at a narrowly technical level. In due course the revision they effected in the educational programme was to bear a rich literary harvest, but, writing as they did, they could have no such sudden impact on the nation's ear as the great Italian artist had on the eye. The second English renaissance was Milton himself who really did make an immense gesture of abstention, a turning away from the richness of the immediate literary past and a reaching out to the severer structures of classical antiquity.

Milton's position was frighteningly difficult. Where Michelangelo could view his predecessors with some justice as 'little men', Milton followed Shakespeare, who could do anything better than everyone else. Great artists are best nourished by a surrounding inchoative incompetence; transcendent genius, contrary to popular belief, is not a quickener of art in others; it is a killer. As Milton himself wrote, addressing the shade of Shakespeare, 'Thou . . . dost make us marble with too much conceiving' ('On Shakespeare', 13–14). It is a strange picture: Perseus half in love with Medusa. The partly reluctant repression of Shakespearean language in *Comus*, in which the lord of Masque was himself unseated, was followed by a programmatic classicism powerfully joined with an intensified egoism. At this point perhaps we meet with that in the Renaissance which is *pure* innovation, for Renaissance egoism, unlike the feeling-saturated subjectivism of Virgil or the moral self-subversion of Dante, is quasi-heroic in character; if it has any links with the past they will be exceedingly remote—with the formal vaunt of the archaic warrior, the *beotword*. There is only one adequate analogy in English literature to the *terribilità* of Michelangelo, and it is the towering self-projection into English poetry of John Milton. Nevertheless, at the birth of the *only* English Renaissance epic, Milton reaches back, as a Renaissance writer must, to the classical origins of the genre.

The power of the retroactive impulse in Milton is immense. There is a sense in which he can be said to have essayed a vast cancellation, an undoing of the work of Dante and even of Virgil, but the matter is complex and we must proceed step by step.

We need first to remember that Virgil himself consciously

turned his back on the literary practice of his own day and founded his epic on Homer. To this degree, then, Virgil was 'a Renaissance poet before the Renaissance'. C. S. Lewis, who hated formalist classicism, wrote, 'Before they ceased talking of a rebirth, it became evident that they had really built a tomb.'[4] In this humour, he liked to pillory 'classicized' versions of Virgil. Thus Dryden's 'She turned and made appear / Her neck refulgent' for *avertens rosea cervice refulsit* (*Aeneid*, i. 402) is condemned and Douglas's 'Hir nek schane like unto the rois in May' is preferred. Lewis rightly notes that the rose has been dropped entirely by Dryden; moreover, '*refulsit* cannot possibly have had for a Roman ear the "classical" quality which "refulgent" has for an English. It must have felt much more like "schane".'[5] The point is a strong one, but not as strong, perhaps, as Lewis thought. *Refulsit* (that is *fulsit* with the addition of the prefix *re-*) seems in fact not to be the ordinary Latin word, but rather a poeticism. What meanwhile of Virgil's Greek quantitative metre (native Latin poetry was accentual, depending on the stress rather than the length in time of the syllables)? Although the hexameter was by this time strongly established, every line must still have been, metrically at least, 'pleasurably alien' to a Roman ear, and the cultural authority of Greece was such that it makes sense to speak even here of a separably 'classical' effect. But Virgil indeed is never formalist as, say, Fronto was to be in the second century AD. Such formal docility is never allowed to invade the matter of his poem. This continues to be the distinctively Virgilian fusion of a quest for historical origin with a propulsion towards a future, equally historic consummation. Then Dante, through the device of the expanded *nekuia*, integrated classical epic with the medieval *visio* and, so to speak, propelled the Virgilian historical propulsion yet further, into the transhistorical, theological dimension, to a moral and eschatological summation. The story of the Virgilian and Dantean transformations of Greek epic is a story in which the god central to (sung) poetry, the Muse, is replaced by a human voice, a private person who will go seeking, like a pilgrim, a God who is outside poetry, outside the world. All of this is thrown into

---

[4] *English Literature in the Sixteenth Century, Excluding Drama* (Oxford: Clarendon Press, 1954), 21.　　　　　　　　　　　　　　　　[5] Ibid. 84.

reverse in Milton's exordium, with the restored imperative, 'Sing'.

'Rebirth': 'Renaissance'; 'rebirth': 'regeneration'—Milton, the humanist heir of Homer, is also a Protestant Christian. This in its turn involves an erasure of ego of quite another kind, the result not of classical example but of real divine preemption. The essence of seventeenth-century Protestantism, far more evident in the Thirty-Nine Articles than is suspected by the great mass of Anglicans who contrive never to read them, is the persisting Calvinist thesis that we can of ourselves do nothing good, that no one ever got to Heaven by merit, that before we are born we are predestined either to glory or eternal damnation, that 'good works' undertaken independently of God's initiating grace have the nature of sin. Milton resisted the Calvinist denial of free will but the Protestant impulse to erase oneself as a moral agent, to empty oneself in order to make room for the action of God, never left him. That is why in the exordium to *Paradise Lost* the Muse, which we might be inclined to dismiss as a mere convention, once invoked does not step modestly aside but instead grows louder, more clamorous, appearing in changing but ever more potent forms until (at line 17) she is confessedly identical with the Holy Spirit, through whom we are made anew. Here at the beginning or birth of *Paradise Lost*, a poem which deals with the origin of our moral existence, the renaissance of Homeric epic fuses with the regeneration of the poet himself, fitting him to perform the great task proposed.

This strange strengthening of the Muse under the poet's hand seems to happen proleptically, almost as if Milton himself were surprised by a power greater than expected. 'Heavenly Muse' (6) could mean, and could have been left with the meaning, 'Muse dealing with Heavenly matters', but the same sentence entwines the Muse herself with biblical story so that the stronger meaning overlaps the earlier modest one: *this* Muse is whoever or whatever it was that granted Moses the vision of the burning bush and gave him the tablets of the law (Exodus, ch. 3; Deuteronomy, chs. 4, 10; Exodus, chs. 19, 20). Except for the one forward reference to the end of time ('Till one greater man | Restore us', 4–5) the hammer descends, over and over again, this way and that, on the idea of inception: *'first* disobedience' (1), *'brought* death *into the world'* (3), *'first* taught the chosen *seed*' (8), '*In the beginning*' (9), '*rose out of chaos*' (10). We have beginnings strangely nested in beginnings. 'First taught' refers to the first enlightenment of the Jews, when their understanding was brought out of darkness; the news which initiates that enlightenment is news of the beginning of the created world itself. Virgil ended the first book of the *Aeneid* (740–6) with the bard Iopas and his song of creation, reaching out, we sense, from his *in medias res* classical narrative mode towards a profoundly different mode, a glimpsed genesis. But it may be that we should be thinking of Lucretius rather than of Virgil. Charles Martindale observes that there is the *De Rerum Natura* (especially at 50 f.) a 'drive towards primacy' almost as strong as that which we find in *Paradise Lost*, and that, paradoxically, this has to find expression within a materialist philosophy according to which the physical world has no beginning in time.[6] Lucretius therefore fastens imaginatively upon the structural primacy of atoms (*rerum primordia*, 55) and the intellectual primacy of Epicurus (*primum Graius homo*, 66). In Milton the reaching out to a primal origin is brilliantly integrated in the exordium. We still have the ecphrastic nuance of narrative within narrative, but behind the sophisticated enjoyment of complex formal patterns is a growing sense that somehow all these beginnings are one beginning, that the seeming fissiparation is an illusion. The strongly enjambed style which tends to emphasize fluidity rather than intricate antiphonal correspondence encourages this intuition of unity. In ordinary English the phrase 'in the beginning' ought (since it follows 'first taught' and precedes 'how') to modify the verb 'taught' rather than 'rose'; that is to say, it ought to be telling us when it was that Moses did his teaching, but the thunderous echo of the first words of Genesis, followed immediately by the creation story, causes the adverbial phrase to tip forward, as if on a rocker, and join itself to 'rose out of chaos'. Once more the initial grammatical interpretation is overtaken by a larger significance, by a yet more primal beginning.

A. W. Verity thought that there were, so to speak, two Muses at the beginning of *Paradise Lost*, the first presiding over lines 1–16, the second (now fully Christianized) over lines

---

[6] In a letter to the author.

17–26.[7] Stevie Davies and William B. Hunter have argued that we are given not a duality but a threefold development, moving through the persons of the Trinity: the Father from lines 6 to 10, the Son from 10 to 16 ('Siloa's brook' is a reference to Christ's ministry, and there is a sense of mediation which is appropriate to the Son, 'our only mediator'—though this sense is abruptly broken by the Renaissance arrogance of 'no middle flight'), and the Holy Spirit from 17 to 22 (the reference here is to 1 Corinthians 3: 16, the human body as temple of the Spirit).[8]

It is possible that Verity, Davies, and Hunter may all be right. It may be said in favour of Verity's division of the lines that from 1 to 16 the classical 'signals' are strong: 'Muse', 'flight', 'Aonian mount'; after 16 a distinctively Christian humility succeeds. To be sure, the Aonian mount is, precisely, scorned by the sentence, which tells us that the poem will deal with higher matter, but there is a sense in which poetry, like Freud's Unconscious, 'knows not "not" ': the mere occurrence of a classical name, even when negated, will register. In any case, however, the negation itself in this case smacks more of Renaissance 'overreaching' than of Christian humility. The culture in which Milton grew up offered the imagination two profoundly opposed views of human nature: according to Calvinist Protestantism, human beings can do no good of themselves, are totally depraved; according to the Renaissance Hermetists human beings can do anything, can become god: 'Believe that nothing is impossible for you . . . Raise yourself above all time, become eternity.'[9] Thus, even as Milton ostensibly separates himself from the Classical haunt of the Muses, his voice begins to take on the accent of some Marlovian Icarus-figure, or even of Ovid's Phaethon. The word 'adventurous, in line 13 betrays much. It is an unregenerate, banner-waving word, evoking the Arthurian, chivalric epic Milton decided *not* to write (*Mansus*, 81, and *Epitaphium Damonis*, 162–8) and even, perhaps, Dante's 'proto-Renaissance' Ulisse, who, so unlike Homer's unwilling traveller, Odysseus, actually

---

[7] *Paradise Lost*, 2 vols. (Cambridge: Cambridge University Press, 1905), ii. 686.

[8] 'Milton's Urania: "The Meaning, not the name I call" ', *SEL* 28:1 (1988), 95–111.

[9] *Corpus Hermeticum*, xi. 20, ed. A. D. Nock, trans. A. J. Festugière, 4 vols. (Paris: Les Belles Lettres, 1960), i. 155.

longs to break out into unknown seas (*Inferno*, xxvi. 112–20).
It may be observed, however, that here it is the song not the
poet which is to fly up, with 'a Muse of fire, that would ascend',
somehow mediating between arrogant self-assertion and a plea
for help.

There is throughout the exordium a polyphony of self and
not-self. That the not-self is finally God becomes inescapable by
line 17 (hence our sense of a certain justice in Verity's division of
the lines) but it is important to understand that in richly musical
poetry of this kind both strains, classical and Christian, are
running all the time, though with varying relations of dominance. 'Rose out of chaos' is classical (look, for example, at the
opening of Ovid's *Metamorphoses*), and might have carried, for
some Renaissance readers, a further association with poetic
inception, because Thebes rose into towers at the sound of
Amphion's lute (see also *Paradise Lost*, i. 711). Yet the classical
Muse is actually preceded by a 'heavenly' Muse—but a
heavenly Muse which does not assume its full Christian
character until the whole sentence has unfolded. At the very end
of the entire sequence, after the Muse has become God and
Milton has abridged the arc of his soaring flight to seek, in
hushed humility, the aid of the Holy Spirit, so that the wings are
no longer the wings of poetry but are rather the wings of the
Dove who descended from Heaven—after all this, the language
of exalted achievement—'to the highth of this great
argument'—is allowed to return, and the poet employs, with a
more than Virgilian heroic energy, the first person singular
(emphases mine):

> *I* may *assert* eternal providence,
> And justify the ways of God to men   (25–6)

Even now our analysis is still too coarse-grained. I found
humility in the address to the Holy Spirit, yet even here one can
detect a persisting pride (now, perhaps, spiritual pride) in the
lodging of the claim 'upright heart and pure'. The Icarian
upward-moving motif is not quite expunged, for 'upright'
could, easily and naturally, have been 'lowly'; Milton chooses
to stand up when he might have knelt. But then when Milton,
in propria persona, 'asserts', what he asserts is providence,
'pro-vidence', God, as that which runs ahead of the merely

human, seeing our actions before we perform them. It is almost impossible to analyse these things without destroying their proper balance.

The world knows that at the end of the exordium Milton performs a dangerous arrogation. From this promise of justification, this almost embarrassing offer of advocacy to God, a theological violence will follow from which English literature and English Christianity will never recover. Milton does not plead for service, he proffers it. L. A. Cormican may seek to assure us that 'justify' implies spiritual rather than rational understanding,[10] but in fact 'justify' is pivotal in meaning, like so many other things in the exordium. Just as the word 'argument' is beginning to move from 'theme' or 'summary of contents' towards 'logical demonstration' so 'justify' is dynamically charged, beginning to move from a spiritual quiescence to the perilous arena of a rationalist theology, from 'show forth the mysterious justice of' to 'prove, in debate, the rightness of the claim'. Behind it lies, perhaps, the hint of an even more startling subversion. 'Justify', after all, is a favourite word of Protestant preachers, but in their usage it is always God who justifies man. With friends like this, need God seek out enemies? He who would offer thus to plead God's case may indeed find that he is of the Devil's party without knowing it. John Milton steps forth: Milton *agonistes, protagonistes, antagonistes.* The transcending music of 'providence' is still there, still audible, but 'argument', 'assert', and 'justify' are the loudest words in these climactic lines.

It would seem that we must qualify our claim that Milton reverts to archaic, pre-Virgilian purity, since the opening Homeric prayer-imperative is after all overtaken in the end by a colossal assertion of self. Yet the revival of the Muse, its recovery of full, supernatural status, is no illusion. Even *qua* Muse (before the Holy Spirit is named) the invoked deity is stronger than in Virgil. It is time to turn to Milton's blindness.

The slow death of the Muse began with the rise of literacy. The Muse invoked at the beginning of the *Iliad* and the *Odyssey* is a power experientially familiar to those who compose

[10] 'Milton's Religious Verse', in Boris Ford (ed.), *From Donne to Marvell*, Pelican Guide to English Literature, iii (Harmondsworth: Penguin Books, 1956), 175.

without pen and paper, who know that at the start of a work which is also a public performance, the lungs must be cleared and then filled by a breath, a voice not wholly one's own (that is, not clearly subject to ego-control). Milton's blindness reunited him with the preliterate father of epic. As Aeneas descended among the shades to find his father, so Milton was hurled into a darkness in which he could touch hands with the Maker of the first European poem. In his sixteenth sonnet, on his blindness, Milton had launched a bitter, Jobian complaint against the God who first gave him talent and then deprived him of the means of increasing it: 'Doth God exact day-labour, light denied?' The question here, in the epic, receives a strange, an enormous answer. By his blindness Milton is not separated from the company of poets; rather he had become Homer, the *fons et origo* of all poets. Legend said, as if somehow trying mythically to convey to later consciousness the preliterate character of archaic epic, that Homer, also called Maeonides, was actually blind:

> So were I equalled with them in renown,
> Blind Thamyris, and blind Maeonides   (iii. 34–5)

It is odd that Milton calls upon Thamyris and not Demodocus. In the *Iliad* (ii. 594) we are told how the Muses blinded Thamyris and took away his gift of song; they blinded him both outwardly and inwardly. In the *Odyssey* (viii. 64) on the other hand we are told how the Muse loved Demodocus and gave him good for evil: blindness and sweet song. The answer, perhaps, is that because Demodocus is a character in the poem and not a mythic being, he is unsuitable for invocation.

We are accustomed to think of *Paradise Lost* as a learned and therefore a laboured poem. But the labour all happened years before, when Milton still had eyes for reading. The early biographers[11] of Milton, Aubrey, Edward Phillips, and Jonathan Richardson, suggest that at times the work was strangely easy for him (the surprising word 'easy' is used by Milton himself at ix. 24, 'Easy my unpremeditated verse'). Whole blocks or paragraphs of verse would swim up into his

---

[11] Helen Darbishire (ed.), *The Early Lives of Milton* (London: Constable, 1932), 13, 73, 291.

consciousness. Notice that twentieth-century 'up'. We have seen already how hard it is to choose between ancient models, in which poetry is given by inspiration from on high, and modern, in which poetry rises from below, from an infra-consciousness. Blindness has sharpened Milton's sense that his poem has two sources, self and not-self. When we come to Book iii we shall find that Albion's bard, who cannot read over what he has written (though he may hear it read) is constrained to a second invocation: this time it is to light, and light becomes God.

Homer's *Iliad* steps almost directly from its opening invocation to the midway narrative of the quarrel between Agamemnon and Achilles. The transition is mediated by just two sentences, in which the divine setting of the dispute is swiftly set before us: 'Who then among the gods set these two quarreling? It was the son of Leto and Zeus, for he, angered by the king, sent a terrible sickness upon the army and the people were dying, because Agamemnon had insulted Chryses, Apollo's priest' (i. 8–12). In the *Odyssey* we have instead a proleptic reference to the eating of the Sun's oxen (the event itself is described at *Odyssey*, xii. 341 f.). That this episode should be given such prominence in what appears to present itself as the 'argument' of the poem, taken together with the fact that Odysseus' final vengeance upon the suitors is simply not mentioned at all, has led some scholars to suppose that the proem of the *Odyssey* has been thriftily redeployed by the poet;[12] he has used a proem which belonged originally to another, less fantastic 'return story'. Immediately after the reference to the oxen of the Sun we are plunged *in medias res*, confronted with Odysseus on his way home from Troy, detained against his will by the amorous Calypso. Thereafter, however, the opening-out of the narrative in the *Odyssey* proves strangely complex, in a way which suggests local artistic freedom rather than the following (or the laying down) of some iron law of genre. For the poet rapidly abandons the inert stalemate of Odysseus for the more potentially dynamic stalemate of Telemachus, Odysseus' son, adolescent and uncertain how to deal with the intemperate suitors of his mother.

---

[12] See Alfred Heubeck, Stephanie West, and J. B. Hainsworth, *A Commentary on Homer's Odyssey*, i. (Oxford: Clarendon Press, 1988), 67–9.

Even before we come to any massive recapitulatory 'flashbacks' the *Odyssey* has two concurrent stories, each beginning from a kind of frustration (so different from the unimpeded combativeness of Agamemnon and Achilles). The separate journeys of Telemachus (who goes looking for his father) and Odysseus (who is always trying to get home) to reach, that is, the place from which Telemachus set out, do not intersect, do not, though we half expect it, culminate in a meeting of father and son far from Ithaca. Instead, Telemachus' journey is a circle, ending where it began, while Odysseus' is a line.

Quintilian said of Homer, *In paucissimis versibus utriusque operis ingressu legem proemiorum non dico servavit, sed constituit*, 'In a very few lines at the entrance to either work, he—I will not say obeyed—he set up the law of proems' (*Institutio Oratoria*, x. i. 48). There is a clear kinship between the proems of the *Iliad* and the *Odyssey*, but family resemblance is not the same thing as legislative rule. One senses that whoever made the *Odyssey* could have launched an epic narrative in many different ways. Quintilian's *non servavit*, 'did not obey', suggests that he understood this very well, and further understood how in later centuries a sense of literary law gradually crystallized. We must not overstate the case: the poet of the *Odyssey* was *obliged*, we may say, to use hexameters and to call upon the Muse; I do not know for sure whether he accompanied himself upon a lyre or not, but I would guess that there was a rule—to do so or not to do so. But there is absolutely no general, stylistic sense of metallic, authoritative constriction and intensification; the special masochism of canonical epic is not yet in sight. Quintilian's paradox stands: Homer's very freedom constituted (*constitit*) the servitude of the after-poets.

In his proem to the *Aeneid* Virgil followed the *Iliad*, but he expanded the brief intermediate narrative of divine machination to twenty-six lines (8–33). Milton in his turn follows the Iliadic/Virgilian line in telling (before he proceeds to the narrative proper) how Lucifer fell from Heaven (34–49). We are thus made aware from the start that the central story of the Fall of Man is causally rooted in an earlier fall. The preliminary 'divine event', in this case, not only brings about the human expulsion from happiness; in an eerie way, it pre-echoes it. But then we strike a peculiarity. For the Miltonic transition to

in medias res narrative does not, as we might expect, present the
preliminary stalemate of Adam enisled in Paradise like Odysseus in Ogygia, but rather, in almost seamless connection with
what has gone before, proceeds with the story of Satan. It may
be asked, 'How then do we know that the *in medias res* narrative
has begun?' The break is marked, in minimal fashion, by a
transition from past to present tense:

> but his doom
> Reserved him to more wrath; for now the thought
> Both of lost happiness and lasting pain
> Torments him (53–6)

Milton himself tells us in the prose argument to Book i that the
in medias res narrative indeed begins here: 'Which action passed
over [namely Satan's revolt against God], the poem passes into
the midst of things, presenting Satan with his angels now fallen
into hell.' Yet we are still, it would seem, at the 'Olympian' end
of things, with the quarrels of Heaven rather than with the great
story of earth, of our own first parents.

It is at this point that we may notice one of the first, brilliant
effects of what may be termed Miltonic epic multiplication. For
Milton simultaneously doubles the Fall story (Adam's fall
preceded by Satan's) *and* the *in medias res* opening (for we shall
come to a second *in medias res*—some would say the true
one—at the beginning of Book v, where Adam and Eve are
shown together in Paradise). The central idea of falling, Heaven
ruining from Heaven, has enabled Milton to interweave the
'Olympian' and the terrestrial, for the effect of the prior,
'exalted' narrative was, precisely, to translate Satan bodily from
the heavenly realm, by having him fall too, before the main
narrative begins. In this way Satan is both 'a machining
Olympian' (like envious Juno at the beginning of the *Aeneid*)
and, when he appears 'squat like a toad, close at the ear of Eve'
(iv. 800), a kind of animal. To put the matter another way,
something extraordinary has happened to the strand of divine
dissension. The quarrels of the gods in the *Iliad* have struck
generations of readers as curiously trivial, or even as having, odd
as it may seem, a kind of poignancy arising from the very
triviality (it is as if in the hellish human world of the *Iliad* no
hero can ever leave off for long from the work of killing and

being killed; only the gods have the happy leisure to be childish). In Milton these divine squabbles are turned into a real war, as a result of which Heaven itself is divided in two, giving to the subsequent epic narrative both a super-causality (divine) and a sub-causality (devilish). In due course the war in Heaven will be refought, in the analeptic narrative of Book vi. Lucifer's double identity, in the great background narrative of ruin, at first heavenly then sublunary, is mirrored in Adam and Eve, biologically our blood-relations yet, until they fall, exalted to the level of easy intercourse with angels (they are, I allow, a little nervous over the proper details of hospitality to visiting angels at v. 331–451).

To a classically educated eye this effect of multiplication is everywhere apparent, though it falls far short of the *entrelacement* of Spenserian 'Gothick' epic. Certainly Dryden was mildly shocked by Milton's multiplication of heroes,[13] Satan ousting Adam (to whom we might add God the Son, Eve, Michael, the Father . . .). No one ever had this trouble with the *Aeneid*.

It is not altogether wrong to see in this impulse towards reduplication, an assertion of Gothic counter-classical sensibility. In the early years of this century, Andrew Lang,[14] looking at the curious 'tower of the orders' in Wadham College, Oxford—exactly the kind of architecture which Helen Gardner called 'dotty'—was struck by its likeness to Milton's poem. He was thinking principally of the layered quality of Milton's language, the encrusted Latinisms resembling the double gilding which once covered the carvings on the Wadham tower. The analogy might, however, be pressed a little further. At the beginning of this chapter I spoke of 'piling portico on portico'. While a single segment of the Wadham structure is discernibly classical, looking like the entrance or front of a temple, to pile them up in a tower five temples high is to exhibit a Gothic appetite for elaborated height. In like manner Milton seems to heap up, not just stylistic layers, but whole epic structures. To be sure, we find secondary invocations in classical epic, but Milton's following the great proem to Book i with the huge

[13] Dedication to the *Aeneis*, in John Dryden, *Of Dramatic Poesy and Other Critical Essays*, ed. George Watson, 2 vols. (London: Dent, 1916), ii. 233.
[14] *Oxford* (London: Seeley, Service and Co., 1916), 93–4.

invocation of light in Book iii, and his following that with the extended address to Urania in Book vii, and his following *that* with the appeal to his 'celestial patroness', the heavenly Muse at ix. 21—all this can give us the feeling that Milton is piling *Iliad* on *Iliad*, as the giants at the beginning of time piled Pelion on Ossa.

I have called this echoic impulse Gothic, but its seed can be found in Virgil. Just as Dante's *figurae futurorum* were made possible by the inchoate historical typology of Virgil, so Milton's very different technique of doubled fall owes something to the *Aeneid*. Homer's Odysseus struggled to reach the home he longed for. Dante's Ulisse, as we have seen, conversely hungered to travel beyond the bounds of the known world. But Virgil's Odyssean Aeneas comprehended both of these poles, in the multidimensional *nostos*, 'homecoming' of *Aeneid*, i–vi. For Aeneas, who deems himself homeless when un-Paradised from Troy in Book ii, is, for all his unregenerate backward glances, for all his venturing on unknown seas, really drawing nearer all the time to the home which is *anciently* his—more anciently than Troy had ever been. In *Paradise Lost* the same structure can be traced. Adam and Eve are un-Paradised from Eden as Aeneas was from Troy, are shown by Michael the historic future of Christendom as Aeneas in the Underworld was shown the historic destiny of Rome, and the *felix culpa*, or 'happy fall' whereby their very expulsion from Eden is shown to be an essential stage on the journey to Heavenly Bliss corresponds to the achieved *Imperium*, implied though not presented at the end of the *Aeneid*. Not all readers (especially those who doubt the force of the *felix culpa* doctrine in *Paradise Lost*) are aware of the extent to which it is enforced by pre-Christian, Virgilian analogy. Dante made the *Commedia* by expanding Book vi of the *Aeneid* to fill the available space. Milton made *Paradise Lost* by expanding Book ii (and then, of course, incorporating the rest of the *Aeneid*, the *Iliad*, the *Odyssey* . . .).

> High in front advanced,
> The brandished sword of God before them blazed
> Fierce as a comet;

> Some natural tears they dropped, but wiped them soon;
> The world was all before them, where to choose

Their place of rest, and providence their guide:
They hand in hand, with wandering steps and slow,
Through Eden took their solitary way.

(xii. 632–4, 645–9)

Here in the saddest passage of the poem, many readers have felt
that one line, 'The world was all before them, where to choose',
comes with a strange exhilarating sweetness, like an intake of
fresh air when one has just left an overheated room. This feeling
certainly grows no weaker if one turns to the corresponding
lines of the end of *Aeneid* ii:

iamque iugis summae surgebat Lucifer Idae
ducebatque diem, Danaique obsessa tenebant
limina portarum, nec spes opis ulla dabatur.
cessi et sublato montis genitore petivi   (801–4)

And now above the ridges of Ida's mountain top, the Lightbearer was
rising, the star bringing day, and the Greeks were in possession of the
blockaded city gates, no hope of help to be had. I gave way and,
stooping to lift my father on my back, I made for the hills.

There can be no doubt that in these lines the sad disarray of the
defeated Trojans is invaded by a hope which they themselves do
not apprehend, planted for the reader in the imagery of the star,
the lifted father, and the movement out towards higher ground
at the very end. Aeneas, we know securely from the rest of the
poem, is in fact setting out on a journey which will bring him to
the Great Good Place.

It is characteristic of Virgilian poetry that it should propel the
reader's mind forward in time, to literary analogies of which
Virgil himself could not have known. The star over Ida
inevitably calls up, in post-classical readers, the star that guided
the Wise Men in Luke's Gospel. More eerily, if we read the
Latin we cannot help encountering the fact that the name of
Virgil's good star is Lucifer and this, in Milton, is the name of
Satan. Here, some might feel, we have simply run into an
unmeaning contradiction, the very opposite of fruitful analogy,
yet for those who like following clues in labyrinths there is a
thread to be followed even here. Early Gnostic commentators
on Genesis, such as the Ophites, being constitutionally unable
to think of knowledge as evil, saw the Serpent as the good agent
in Eden, precisely because he led Adam and Eve to the Tree of

Knowledge, against the tyrannical will of the oppressor Yahweh, and so was indeed the light-bearer.[15] C. S. Lewis was quite wrong when he considered Blake's championing of Satan a mere Romantic *préjudice de siècle*.[16] It is certainly pre-Miltonic, since it is almost as old as Gnosticism itself and was fiercely 'reheated' by the Ranters, in Milton's own century.

Christopher Hill has shown that Milton was aware of these developments, as he was aware of the older sources. He notes that in *The Reason of Church Government* (1641) Milton dared to compare the much-denounced, Ranter-like 'Familists' with the early Christians.[17] Andrew J. Welburn writes, 'The Ranters were fairly consistent Gnostics. They regarded the Old Testament God as a Demiurge—a "God-Devil".'[18] Hill acknowledges that, in the end, Milton was too far committed to his project of justification to accept a Gnostic solution; he could never go along with Winstanley, Erbery, and other Ranters who claimed that the God worshipped by most Christians was a wicked God, but Hill does believe that *Paradise Lost* was conceived in tense dialogue with such views.[19] The old doctrine that such ideas were simply unavailable to Milton is no longer tenable. Moreover, if we allow that the *argument* of justification failed under the poet's hand, the tension may be supposed further exacerbated, though still, indeed, never resolved by a

[15] One obvious channel by which older Gnostic ideas may have reached Milton is Augustine, who, e.g., describes the Ophite heresy at *De Haeresibus*, 1. xvii, in J.-P. Migne (ed.), *Patrologiae Cursus Completus (Patrologia Latina)*, xlii (1865), 26. The Ophite doctrine is very close to that advanced in *Poimandres* (or *Pimander*), the immensely influential first tractate of what is now known as the *Corpus Hermeticum*, attributed to the immemorially ancient Hermes Trismegistus but really composed between the first and fourth centuries AD. The *Corpus* is available in an edition by A. D. Nock, trans. A. J. Festugière, 4 vols. (Paris: Les Belles Lettres, 1960). Also important are the *Apocrypha of John* (written before 180 AD), Irenaeus's *Adversus Omnes Haereses*, i. 30, and Origen, *Contra Celsum*, vi. 24 f. J. M. Evans observes that the Ophites must have been an important and forceful group, given the number and vigour of the refutations which they attracted: see his *Paradise Lost and the Genesis Tradition* (Oxford: Clarendon Press, 1987), esp. p. 23, and R. M. Grant, *Gnosticism: An Anthology* (London: Collins, 1961), 52–9, 89–92, 104–15.

[16] *Preface to Paradise Lost* (London: Oxford University Press, 1960), 94.

[17] *The World Turned Upside Down: Radical Ideas during the English Revolution* (London: Temple Smith, 1972), 320. See *The Complete Prose Works of John Milton*, ed. Douglas Bush et al., 8 vols. (New Haven: Yale University Press, 1953–82), i. 788.

[18] *The Truth of Imagination: An Introduction to Visionary Poetry* (London: Macmillan, 1989), 218.   [19] *The World Turned Upside Down*, 324–5.

simple capitulation to Gnosticism. Milton puts the orthodox view, that the knowledge gained was merely negative, with great force, in the words of Adam at ix. 1070–1:

> since our eyes
> Opened we find indeed, and find we know
> Both good and evil, good lost, and evil got

If, however, the logic of the *felix culpa* is pressed hard, to the point of detail (as indeed it never is in the dominant Christian tradition) the serpent Lucifer must be an agent of reclamation. There is a whiff of Gnosticism in the argument of *Areopagitica* written years before *Paradise Lost*:

> perhaps this is that doom that *Adam* fell into of knowing good and evil, that is to say of knowing good by evil. . . . What wisdom can there be to choose, what continence to forbear without the knowledge of evil?[20]

Milton is referring, it will be said, to the state of Adam and Eve *before* the Fall: God created them free, from the beginning. But the argument as he states it contains a dangerous, propulsive implication (smelling, indeed, of heresy): that the freedom became real only when they were no longer 'cloistered' in perfect security. It is curious that the word 'heretic' once meant, in its first, Greek use, 'person having the power to choose' (see the *Magna Moralia*, traditionally attributed to Aristotle, i. 21). In *Aeropagitica*, a couple of pages after the passage about Adam, Milton hesitates, fascinatingly, on the word 'heresies', affirming that heresies are not seldom truer than their confutations.[21] Years later, in *On Civil Power* (1659) he showed that he fully understood the etymological history of the term: 'It is no word of evil note, meaning only the choise or following of any opinion.'[22] Milton is here almost a seventeenth-century Structuralist, arguing that knowledge is always by relation and differentiation. Nothing can be known atomically, alone. He who knows only good cannot know good. Adam and Eve can have become aware of the sweet music of Eden only when it ceased. The effect of the argument is to imply a *naturalist* version of the *felix culpa* according to which Adam and Eve are

---

[20] *The Complete Prose Works*, ii (1959), 514.   [21] Ibid. 518.
[22] Ibid. vii (1980), 247.

immediately promoted by authentic knowledge, by admission to
an arena of real, strenuous moral life (for in the even warmth of
Eden, before the Serpent came, no one could ever be brave, no
one could ever pity) and need not wait for admission to Heaven
to complete the demonstration of God's goodness. The angel
seems to incline to the naturalist version with the words, 'a
Paradise *within thee*, happier far', at xii. 587 (my italics).
Christopher Hill remarks that this line is rooted in contemporary Ranterism, with its strenuously 'this-worldly', psychological
application of terms like 'Heaven' and 'Hell'. He writes, 'The
Family of Love and the Grindletonians had taught that
prelapsarian perfection could be attained in this life. But before
the 1640s such ideas had been kept underground. Now nothing
could be suppressed.'[23] To be sure, the 'Gnostic' argument of
Areopagitica, itself uncertainly advanced, is placed by the poet of
Paradise Lost in the mouth of Satan and of Eve (ix. 756–7, 335).
Milton, some may say, is telling us very clearly what to think of
this argument (even though Eve is unfallen when she advances
it . . .).

GENESIS AND THE BEGINNING OF *PARADISE LOST*

It is clear that Milton's is what we may call a 'negotiated
opening'. It chooses to be proudly interventionist, and under-
lines the decision by doing it twice. At the same time, however,
Milton, like Virgil and unlike Homer, continually and strenuously reaches towards genesis, towards a natural beginning.
That is why the word 'first' (*primus*) appears in the first lines of
both *Paradise Lost* and the *Aeneid*, but not at the *very* beginning
of the *Iliad* or the *Odyssey* (in the *Iliad*, we must allow, it does
come through at line 6, but it is relatively unemphasized, in a
subordinate clause: 'when first the quarrel broke out . . .'). The
primacy (and ultimacy) sought by Virgil is fundamentally
historical, for all that one can smell in it some straining towards
a Hebraic genesis. In Milton it is confessedly cosmic. The
Virgilian invention of the Great National Subject of epic has
become the Great Universal Subject, not just the story of all
Romans, but the story of us all. In an unbelieving age we have

[23] *The World Turned Upside Down*, 133.

to some extent lost this sense of reference to ourselves, but for Johnson in the eighteenth century, it was still strong. The start of our existence as fallen creatures—as what we now are—is itself a huge natural *principium*, publicly available as a known beginning, before Milton wrote his poem. The inception of Achilles' wrath (unlike, say, the start of the Trojan War) is not that sort of thing. But because the beginning of fallen existence was itself located within a sequence of cosmic agencies, Milton is able, technically, to present it as an *in medias res* opening.

The negotiations set up by Milton between the twin poles of 'naturalism' and 'interventionism' are, as we have seen, surprisingly complex, creating a new, distinctively literary species of analogy to polyphonic counterpoint. Behind the beginning of fallen existence lies the beginning of the created world. It is important to remember, further, that Genesis itself is preceded by the Generator, God. Since God is himself fullness of being, there is a theological sense in which the Creation itself is intelligible only as diminution, or mitigation of perfection. St Augustine sought to resolve the ancient problem of evil—the problem, that is, of reconciling the existence of an imperfect world with an all-good, all-powerful Creator—by arguing that imperfection is inherent in creation: for if God had created perfection unlimited, he would merely have reasserted his own already infinite existence and no separate creation would have taken place (in a way, the argument is an early application of the principle of the identity of indiscernibles); therefore, if we are to have a creation at all we must have that which is not God, and that which is not God will be (variously) less than God, imperfect: *non essent omnia, aequalia si essent*, 'All things would never have been, had all things been equal.'[24] The first making was therefore a kind of subtraction. *A fortiori*, a still darker impulse of negation grips, from the start, the story told by Milton. The first disobedience is the black obverse of creation, the beginning of death ('brought death into the world and all our woe', i. 3). From this lower darkness primary creation can seem after all to blaze with unqualified radiance. The first teaching of Moses (18) was of this blazing creation (10)—and so

---

[24] Augustine, *De Diversis Quaestionibus*, lxxxiii, q. 41, in J.-P. Migne (ed.), *Patrologiae Cursus Completus (Patrologia Latina)*, xl. 27.

the poem can at least be joined to the bright creation through the invocation of the dovelike, intervenient Holy Spirit, whose wings covered the abyss at the beginning of time just as now they touch, protectively, the poet setting out on his epic enterprise.

Virgil, we saw, contrived somehow to move, in the first book of the *Aeneid*, from the majestic proem to the creation song of Iopas, but the transition is not musically organized; it does not, so to speak, understand itself, artistically. Milton's dazzling interweaving of intervention and origin is, on the contrary, a triumph of complex, orchestrated art.

It may be surprising to some that the notion of origin, which may be thought peculiarly to propose itself as unitary (there can be only one real Origin) should be subjected to the Miltonic multiplication, yet it is so. In Book ix, when the narrative recounts in minute detail the beginning of sin, we again find a curious shimmering of the Primal Act, a system of echoes and pre-echoes. If we ask, 'When did imperfection first enter Paradise?' the answer is not easy. Was it when Satan entered Paradise and insinuated his wickedness into the unconscious mind of Eve, toad-like at her ear as she slept (iv. 800 f.)? All this, note, is made possible by the reduplicated fall, Lucifer's fall going before Eve's. Or did imperfection enter when Eve insisted on going apart in the garden by herself, asserting as she did so, as we saw, the potentially heroic postlapsarian morality of Milton's own *Areopagitica* (ix. 335)? Or was it already there, more obscurely but with strange imaginative power, when the plants in the garden began to get out of hand (ix. 202–3)? Of course, the answer to all these questions is 'Not yet' for the real fall comes, with immense power, at ix. 781. But the sense of a whole series of foreshadowings of the 'primal act' is inescapable. We are even told that Satan got into Eve's heart before the moment of the fall:

> Into the heart of Eve his words made way (ix. 550)

At this point, most interestingly, Milton plants in the reader's mind a sense of analogy, linking Satan's enterprise with the poet's, by letting fall the word 'proem' in the preceding line ('So glozed the tempter, and his proem tuned'). Indeed Satan is poet-like in that he causes Eve to fall through her sympathizing

imagination, for at ix. 575–601 he tells, not the true story of his
own fall through pride, but a richly fictitious, almost Keatsian
tale of a tempted fall (the tree 'loaden with fruit', the 'savoury
odour blown', 'the teats | Of ewe or goat dropping with milk at
even', 'the sharp desire I had | Of tasting'). Because the fall is
only duplicated and is not triplicated, there was no fallen
creature on hand to act as tempter to Lucifer. Eve's subjection to
the spell of Satan's tale is a tragic, darkened version of the
Narcissus story, the hard Ovidian light invaded by the
threatening shades of grief and sin. Satan must present an altered
mirror of her present situation. Therefore he must feign a prior
temptation story. But the tempter in his story is not separately
visible, but only the honey-sweet means of tempting. It would
be a mistake, however, to assume that this tempting object
might simply be equated with the prospect of exalted status
which so vexed Lucifer at the time of the first fall. The fruit so
lovingly described by Satan is obviously *designed* to tempt, and
design, as Paley would say, implies a (hidden) designer. In
Satan's story, then, it remains true that we have a distinct and
powerful temptation motif such as *could not* have been present at
the first fall. And if we cannot see the tempter, why, that suits
Satan's purpose very well. Let him be as invisible to Eve as the
blind poet is to the reader.

One uneasy thought persists: if we say that the fruit in Satan's
tale is *designed* to tempt, must we not say the same of the real
tree in Eden? And we know who planted that. Or are we to
think it never smelled so to Adam and Eve? Eve fails to
recognize the tree from Satan's description and has to be led to
its foot before she realizes that they have been talking about the
forbidden tree. Did Satan then, poet-like, *invest* the tree with its
alluring fragrance? Milton's century will become in due course
the century of the philosophical doctrine of Primary and
Secondary Qualities, in the light (or darkness) of which it will
be argued that all fragrance, all colour, all sweetness, as distinct
from mathematically measurable qualities like length and
breadth, are feigned, not perceived by human subjects. Milton,
to be sure, will issue severe reminders that the Fall is still to
come, for example, 'To whom thus Eve *yet sinless*' at 659. Why
are reminders needed if the poetry has not in fact begun to tell us
something else?

Here too the polyphonic art of Milton is operating with great power but one senses that Book ix differs from Book i in that the multiplication no longer springs joyously from a poetic or mythic source. A very different pressure arising from logical difficulties inherent in theodicy ('justification of God') may be at work. Augustine notoriously pointed out in *The City of God* (xiv. 13) that our first parents must have been secretly corrupted, before the eating of the apple, 'for the evil act had not been done had not an evil will preceded it'. That is, if Adam and Eve are to err *culpably*, it is insufficient to explain their error as wholly due to an impulsion from outside—from a previously fallen creature. They must, in some vivid way, say 'Yes' to what is offered. But perfect creatures, *however free their will*, will not say yes. Spontaneously they will reject the vile proposal. Augustine's intuition that the origin of evil eludes the mechanism of aetiological myth has been rebutted again and again. But it continues to nag at the mind. Indeed the twentieth century is not exempt from these problems. Sigmund Freud in *Civilisation and its Discontents* and in *Totem and Tabu* offered his own aetiological myth of the origin of guilt, and it is open to precisely analogous objections. It is possible that Milton found, when he came to tell the story in detail, that he could not see how perfect people would say yes to Satan, so that the only course open to him was to introduce a kind of narrative tremor: 'It is possible that this Eve should fall for, look, she strayed a little before (straying is not falling: please do not notice that it is not perfection either); Eve did not admit Satan in Book iv, her unconscious did that (a woman is, and is not, her own unconscious).' Thus the brilliant multiplication of falls in Book ix may spring in part from an impulse to cheat or bemuse the logical faculty. A perfect Eve who is made to move through a moral Limbo of imaginative analogies to sin can more plausibly be presented as capable, when the time comes, of falling culpably. She can fall because she already has and yet she has not.

I have suggested that there is an inherent tension between the Greek interventionist opening and the Natural Beginning, which, for all its Virgilian credentials, I have associated with Hebraic culture and with Gothic. I have further suggested, apropos of epic elaboration, that the labyrinthine *Faerie Queene* is in some sense a 'Renaissance Gothic epic'. Yet *The Faerie Queene* gives us, after the proem, one of the most abrupt *in medias res* openings, the knight on his great horse in mid-quest, spurring over the plain. Because Spenser is Spenser and loves imaginatively alienated emblematic figures which are 'eterne in mutabilitie' (III. vi. 47), the scene at the beginning of *The Faerie Queene* offers us a peculiar mixture of vigorous motion and metaphoric stillness. Notoriously the knight spurring his horse is followed by a lady mounted on an ass and she in turn is followed by 'a lazy, lagging Dwarf' (I. i. 6). Such a group quite clearly would break up and become widely separated in two minutes. It is as if they are painted on a board and it, not they, is being carried along before our eyes. Yet the opening remains violently interventionist.

Moreover, the more one reads *The Faerie Queene* the more aware one becomes of Homeric affinities, almost always with the magical *Odyssey*, seldom the austere *Iliad*. Book II especially is alive with Odyssean detail. The highly distinctive spatial conception of the projected *Faerie Queene* may be seen as a Renaissance Gothic elaboration of the Odyssean scheme, yet it is explicitly noticed by few. The linear journey home of Odysseus is, we saw, countered in the early part of the epic by the circular outward journey made by Telemachus in search of his father. In the projected *Faerie Queene* Arthur was conceived as making a linear journey from far away, drawn by a dream of Gloriana, terminating at the Court of the Queen herself (see I. ix. 6–20). Meanwhile the various questing knights— Telemachus times *x*—set out from the Court on circular journeys, through which Arthur moves as he draws nearer and nearer.

Milton revered Spenser and would indeed have wished us to compare *Paradise Lost* with *The Faerie Queene*. It is interesting, however, to compare the opening of Milton's epic with that of Cowley's *Davideis* also, published in 1656, twelve years before *Paradise Lost*. Cowley begins with a strong, first person, 'I sing' but then at line 13 invokes Christ, after which by an odd logic of his own he dedicates his Muse to Christ:

> Lo, with *pure hands* thy heavenly *Fire* to take,
> My well-changed Muse I a chast *Vestal* make!

From earths vain joys and loves soft witchcraft free,
I consecrate my *Magdalen* to Thee![25]

No real Muse is present, so much is clear. The deity invoked is
unequivocally external to the poetry. The 'Muse' when she
appears is wholly metaphorical and can be translated, without
remainder, into 'poetry'. That is why, instead of being invoked
herself, she is instead 'consecrated' to a divine end. Cultural
memory of the fact that the Muse was once a pagan divinity
gives, as it were, an echo of urgency (an urgency wholly
'polite', in no way theological) to the consecration. Hence the
general air of lugubrious, baroque humour.

The metaphor, certainly, is pregnant. Poetry is a redeemable
whore, a Magdalen who may be brought to the feet of Christ.
What is wholly absent is the Miltonic strengthening-from-
within, the Muse becoming God himself, living as the Holy
Spirit in the throat, lungs, and brain of the singer. This
exaltation of the Muse is joined by Milton to his own blindness
in the invocation of Book iii:

> Hail, holy Light, offspring of heaven first-born,
> Or of the eternal co-eternal beam
> May I express thee unblamed? since God is light,
> And never but in unapproached light
> Dwelt from eternity, dwelt then in thee,
> Bright effluence of bright essence increate.
> Or hear'st thou rather pure ethereal stream,
> Whose fountain who shall tell? Before the sun,
> Before the heavens thou wert, and at the voice
> Of God, as with a mantle didst invest
> The rising world of waters dark and deep,
> Won from the void and formless infinite.
> Thee I revisit now with bolder wing,
> Escaped the Stygian pool, though long detained
> In that obscure sojourn, while in my flight
> Through utter and through middle darkness borne
> With other notes than to the Orphean lyre
> I sung of Chaos and eternal Night,
> Taught by the heavenly Muse to venture down

[25] *The Works of Mr Abraham Cowley*, 6th edn. (London: Henry Herringman,
1680), 4.

The dark descent, and up to reascend,
Though hard and rare: thee I revisit safe,
And feel thy sovereign vital lamp; but thou
Revisit'st not these eyes, that roll in vain
To find thy piercing ray, and find no dawn;
So thick a drop serene hath quenched their orbs,
Or dim suffusion veiled. Yet not the more
Cease I to wander where the Muses haunt
Clear spring, or shady grove, or sunny hill,
Smit with the love of sacred song; but chief
Thee Sion and the flowery brooks beneath
That wash thy hallowed feet, and warbling flow,
Nightly I visit: nor sometimes forget
Those other two equalled with me in fate,
So were I equalled with them in renown,
Blind Thamyris, and blind Maeonides,
And Tiresias and Phineus prophets old.
Then feed on thoughts, that voluntary move
Harmonious numbers; as the wakeful bird
Sings darkling, and in shadiest covert hid
Tunes her noctural note. Thus with the year
Seasons return, but not to me returns
Day, or the sweet approach of even or morn,
Or sight of vernal bloom, or summer's rose,
Or flocks, or herds, or human face divine;
But cloud in stead, and ever-during dark
Surrounds me, from the cheerful ways of men
Cut off, and for the book of knowledge fair
Presented with a universal blank
Of nature's works to me expunged and razed,
And wisdom at one entrance quite shut out.
So much the rather thou Celestial Light
Shine inward, and the mind through all her powers
Irradiate, there plant eyes, all mist from thence
Purge and disperse, that I may see and tell
Of things invisible to mortal sight.

(iii. 1–55)

This invocation marks the upward movement in the poem from
Hell towards Heaven. Again, the presentation is polyphonic.
Again we have the claim-lodging word 'first' in the first line,
'first-born'. It is likely that 'Or' in line 2 is Latin *aut* rather than
vel; that is, it marks a transition to a real alternative state of

affairs rather than to an alternative expression for the same phenomenon. In which case the first line means, 'Hail, holy Light, the first thing made by Heaven'. Here light is conceived as a kind of pre-creation, that is, an early creation ahead of the rest, but for all that still something created and therefore not identical with the creator. This having been said, 'Or' introduces the counter-thought, which is precisely that light is not any sort of creature but *is* identical with the Creator. Light created and light creating become one. If we set aside for the moment the technical question of Milton's Arianism, we shall see that it is impossible to exclude the intuition that God may be invoked from the start. Arianism or no Arianism, the first-born offspring looks like Christ, the Light of the World. Logic-choppers who say Christ cannot have been *first*, since God had no other children by this direct mode of fissiparation, may be referred to Colossians 1: 15, 18 and Revelation 1: 5. Meanwhile I am sure that it is the essence of light, rather than the human physiognomy of Christ, which is foremost in Milton's mind. He has found his way, in a bookless darkness, to the proem uttered by God himself, 'Let there be light.' Because word and deed are one in God this poet-like utterance is instantly translated into natural fact. This, the exordium of creation, is therefore like nothing in Greek literature. That is why it is such a shock when we meet it in *On the Sublime*, the treatise of the first century AD attributed to Longinus.

The lawgiver of the Jews, no ordinary man—for he understood and expressed God's power in accordance with its worth—writes at the beginning of his *Laws*: 'God said—' now what?— '"Let there be light", and there was light; "Let there be earth" and there was earth'. (ix. 9)[26]

This sentence, which is indeed sandwiched oddly between two Homeric examples, has been suspected since the eighteenth century of being an interpolation: 'Greeks do not think this way; this must be some Byzantine intruder.' Yet the entire treatise is concerned with *the sublime*. More than anything else in the work this passage conveys the new, alternative aesthetic, an aesthetic

[26] The translation is that of D. A. Russell, in D. A. Russell and M. Winterbottom (eds.), *Ancient Literary Criticism: The Principal Texts in New Translations* (Oxford: Clarendon Press, 1972), 470.

not of balance and apprehensibility but of that which escapes our apprehension, threatens to overwhelm us. This was the aesthetic which Algarotti, in the eighteenth century, saw as especially the property of Milton—*mostruosità* combined with *sublimità*, an extravagant, gigantesque sublimity.[27] 'Let there be light' figures, beyond all the Homeric specimens, in the theory of the sublime as it grew in subsequent centuries.[28]

Nevertheless, even as we choose the '*aut . . . aut*' path of objective alternatives, creature or creator, we sense that in the case of light the division may be in some way objectively transcended. Milton is now driving his poem back, harder than he ever did in the invocation to Book i, to a beginning which is before Genesis: 'Before the sun | Before the heavens thou wert' (8–9). In neo-Platonic theology light must be prior to all *particular* created things since those things are generated from its differentiation.[29] At the same time the poet's reference to himself is sustained, but now in a manner more sharply intimate, more physical than before. As one surveys commentaries on these lines, the sense grows that the endless parsing and construing of distinct philosophical traditions, the division of spirit from matter, metaphor from letter, is somehow ill-conceived, since the poetry itself is pressing in precisely the contrary direction, towards a mysterious, never-completed fusion of these things. Light is real light, as is given off by the sun. But then it overspills. Creative power both divine and literary, eyesight, insight, poetic vision, knowledge, the light that pre-existed the creation of things, the Holy Spirit, the Son, God the Father: all these seem to be on the point of becoming, within some as yet unapprehended ontology, one thing. Alastair Fowler catches this quality in a note which bad Miltonists might describe as vague, but which is really unusually precise. Of line 23, 'Revisit'st not these eyes', he writes, 'Certainly now referring to physical light. But there is

---

[27] Francesco Algarotti, 'Lettere sopra vari argomenti di letteratura scritte da un inglese ad un Veneziano', in his *Opere*, ed. E. Bonora, 2 vols. (Milan, Naples: Riccardo Ricciardi, 1969–71), ii. 708.

[28] See S. H. Monk, *Th Sublime: A Study of Critical Theories in XVIII-Century England* (Ann Arbor: University of Michigan Press, 1960).

[29] See Alastair Fowler's note *ad. loc.* in *The Poems of John Milton*, eds. Carey and Fowler (London: Longman, 1980, corr. 2nd imp. of 1968 edn.), 559.

no change of address: the celestial light of Truth or Wisdom was thought of as purer and brighter, but not categorically different from physical light.'[30] It is probably true that no one in the seventeenth century, including Isaac Newton, was quite sure, in the way we are sure, that light is a physical thing, in the sense in which ordinary objects like sticks and stones are physical. Milton pursued the question of the material character of all creation with more than ordinary obstinacy, but the poetry makes it clear that he shared in the dynamic uncertainty of the age. We need also to remember that while our minds run habitually on the axis: concrete particulars/abstraction, theirs ran just as frequently on the somewhat different axis: impermeable 'things of earth'/subtle spirits.

The Miltonic vision is unstable. Even the proclamatory 'God is light' of line 3 seems to be partly retracted by 'dwelt then in thee' at line 5, where the inhabitant must presumably be other than the habitation; yet the sentence returns us at the end to 'bright essence increate', where 'increate' does not mean 'created internally' but rather 'not created'. There is only one Being which was not created.

The presumptuous analogy between divine and poetic creation is essayed once more, in imagery of rising and falling. It was a *vocal* act of God which caused the waters to rise up and be dressed in a garment of light (9–11). This world of waters, which remains fluid, unshaped, more akin to potentiality than to differentiated actuality, is itself described as being heroically won from formlessness (12). Milton likewise has risen on the wings of poetry from the Stygian pool (that is the infernal subject matter of Books i and ii). Here we find one of the finest 'altered echoes' in the whole of Milton. Virgil's Aeneas is told by the Sibyl that it is easy to enter the world of the dead, *sed revocare gradum superasque evadere ad auras,* | *hoc opus, hic labor est* (vi. 128–9) 'but to recall one's step and escape to the winds above, this is hard, this is toil'. In fact the narrative of *Aeneid* vi strangely reverses this picture; Aeneas enters the world of the dead only after great labour but at the end of the book he flits through the gate of ivory with ease, like a false dream. Yet somehow the Sibyl's words are not clearly falsified or erased by

[30] Ibid. 561–2.

the story which follows them. For Milton, clearly, they carry an authority, in which bitterness and hope are mingled. For he, Milton, *has* climbed again up the hard, steep path out of darkness, but he can see no light. At this point the distinction (as opposed to the incipient fusion) of different meanings of *light* is allowed to appear, and the effect is harrowing—even shocking. The harmonious blending of luminescences breaks down as the poet discovers, in the simplest and most direct manner, that he cannot see. One sort of light, for sure, has *not* been given. There is a hint here of the agonized complaint of the octet in Sonnet xvi, 'When I consider how my light is spent'. For Milton has dared great deeds. The usual upward-aspiring motion of the Marlovian overreacher is, dizzyingly, turned upside-down, for Milton was taught by the Muse who dwells on high (19) 'to venture down the dark descent' (19–20), to sing a song, not of Orphean bright divinities (17) but of Chaos and eternal Night (18). Poetically he has engaged negation and darkness and now he is rewarded, not with the 'sovereign vital lamp' (22) of day (felt but not seen), but with a yet more torturing privation, a deeper darkness, peculiarly his.

At line 25 we reach the point of maximum physical specificity with medical detail: cataract, *gutta serena*. But then, from this apparently unanswerable, concrete despair the poetry moves laterally into the alternative world of imaginary enjoyments, literary pleasures. Here the Muses are named and are for the moment entirely figurative, like Cowley's, signifying, quite simply, poetry. But the poetry he loves is, we learn, the poetry of the Bible ('Sion', 30); the flowery river can become a river of sacred truth, something ontologically stronger than Milton's own specific blindness. But then once more he turns aside, as if recognizing that the essence of his poem is after all not light but darkness, and seeks the very different comfort of kinship with the great blind pagans. This, however, is the 'Renaissance eclectic' Milton, not the exclusive Puritan; he is here more interested in echoes and similarities than in a harsh contrasting of pagan with Christian.

Within this movement we find yet again that we are redirected from the notion of imagination to the idea of veridical vision, from Homer the poet to Tiresias the prophet. It is the paradox which haunted Sophocles: 'I close my eyes and see.'[31] This sombre grandeur is succeeded by the strangely gentle image of the poet as nightingale, the wakeful bird who 'sings darkling'. Such vigilant awareness, the poet suggests, may be essentially involved with night, since the sweetest singer among birds is nocturnal. Somehow Milton's thought is becoming more plaintive. It is as if he is seeking some alternative conception, for the moment, to the stark, Greek idea of the blind seer.

Sophocles in *Oedipus Rex* linked physical sight with ignorance and blindness with knowledge. The sightless Tiresias knew from the start; Oedipus destroyed his eyes at the moment of learning the truth. Meanwhile all is watched by Apollo, the great Eye that sees all (*Trachiniae*, 102). Leonardo da Vinci once wrote in a notebook 'the sun has never seen any shadow'.[32] He is thinking, like a good pupil of Alberti, about the lines of perspectival vision and has become suddenly aware that if the eye were simultaneously the *one source* of light, it will see nothing but surfaces evenly illuminated by itself. Such vision implies a certain strange ignorance in the all-seeing sun, an ignorance of darkness. It is as if the sun, Apollo, any god who is never humiliated or crucified, can know nothing of what it is to be human, to sing darkling.

It is a thought of potential power, deeply relevant to the central story of *Paradise Lost*. The paradox whereby man was cast *out* into *darkness* because he ate of the tree of *knowledge* is one with which Renaissance Christians wrestled endlessly. Sir John Davies in his poem *Nosce Teipsum* (1599) saw the knowledge acquired in Eden as, precisely, a knowledge of darkness, and therefore of error, privation, negation:

> *Battes* they became, that *Eagles* were before.[33]

Eagles can gaze upon the sun, bats are fitted only for the dark.

---

[31] Fragment 702, in *Sophocles*, ed. Lewis Campbell, 2 vols. (Oxford: Clarendon Press, 1889), ii. 548.

[32] *Selections from the Notebooks of Leonardo da Vinci*, ed. with commentaries by Irma A. Richter (London: Oxford University Press, 1952), 52.

[33] *The Poems of Sir John Davies*, ed. Robert Krueger (Oxford: Clarendon Press, 1975), 7.

Davies thinks of darkness as simply bad. He can be sure that his reader will not wish to identify, for example, with a bat. But change your image of the nocturnal creature from bat to a nightingale pouring out its soul, half in love perhaps with easeful death, and everything begins to feel different. The notion that Adam and Eve, as they became acquainted with shadows, grew in humanity, has occurred to more than one reader. 'Pity would be no more, if we did not make somebody poor.'[34] 'Strange blessings ne'er in Paradise | Fall from these beclouded skies'.[35]

At this point in *Paradise Lost* the thought is allowed to fade. Tiresias might have led Milton to the Platonic eye of the soul (*Republic*, 533d) and the poet could then have made a connection between his own private distress and what I have called the naturalist version of the *felix culpa* doctrine. Remember that the central, supernaturalist version of the doctrine is that the Fall was happy because it led through Christ's redemption to heavenly bliss; the naturalist version is that the Fall was happy because it led to authentic moral life, in which virtue turned real as it was made subject to the test of suffering. But Milton lets the image go. The nightingale motif dies away into a very ordinary and therefore very moving grief: 'but not to me returns . . .' (41). Out of this confused human distress comes the final *volta*, or turning to Light, not this time as the proud possession of the poet-seer but as the object of a famished desire, something to be prayed for. But Milton is Milton still: the words, 'that I may see and tell | Of things invisible to mortal sight' (54–5) begin, because of the way in which they are unhurriedly disposed across the division between two lines, to assume before the phrase is closed the status of an accomplished feat. Even when at prayer Milton can sound proud. Kneeling, indeed, did not come easily to him.

There is one more extended invocation in *Paradise Lost*, at the beginning of Book vii (the one at the beginning of Book ix is in an altogether lower key):

---

[34] William Blake, 'The Human Abstract', in *The Poems of William Blake*, ed. W. H. Stevenson and D. V. Erdman (London: Longmans, 1972), 216.

[35] Edwin Muir, 'One Foot in Eden', in *The New Oxford Book of English Verse*, ed. Helen Gardner (London: Oxford University Press, 1972), 868.

Descend from heaven Urania, by that name
If rightly thou art called, whose voice divine
Following, above the Olympian hill I soar,
Above the flight of Pegasean wing.
The meaning, not the name I call; for thou
Nor of the Muses nine, nor on the top
Of old Olympus dwell'st, but heavenly born.
Before the hills appeared, or fountain flowed,
Thou with eternal Wisdom didst converse,
Wisdom thy sister, and with her didst play
In presence of the almighty Father, pleased
With thy celestial song. Up led by thee
Into the heaven of heavens I have presumed,
An earthly guest, and drawn empyreal air,
Thy tempering; with like safety guided down
Return me to my native element:
Lest from this flying steed unreined, (as once
Bellerophon, though from a lower clime)
Dismounted, on the Aleian field I fall
Erroneous there to wander and forlorn.
Half yet remains unsung, but narrower bound
Within the visible diurnal sphere;
Standing on earth, not rapt above the pole,
More safe I sing with mortal voice, unchanged
To hoarse or mute, though fallen on evil days,
On evil days though fallen, and evil tongues;
In darkness, and with dangers compassed round,
And solitude; yet not alone, while thou
Visit'st my slumbers nightly, or when morn
Purples the east: still govern thou my song,
Urania, and fit audience find, though few,
But drive far off the barbarous dissonance
Of Bacchus and his revellers, the race
Of that wild rout that tore the Thracian bard
In Rhodope, where woods and rocks had ears
To rapture, till the savage clamour drowned
Both harp and voice; nor could the Muse defend
Her son. So fail not thou, who thee implores:
For thou art heavenly, she an empty dream.

(vii. 1–39)

The first word, 'Descend', sets the tone, Milton now turns with
a certain relief to the lower matter of human history (to be

retailed, of course, by the angel Raphael). There is again some pressure upon the classical Muse to become more than herself, but this time the process does not terminate unequivocally in God. 'Urania', as Lily B. Campbell showed,[36] had been annexed for Christian poetry before Milton wrote these lines. Milton himself enjoyed the pleasures of literal translation and formal substitution. Thus 'happy-making sight' ('On Time', 18) is obtained from *beatifica visio* ('beatific vision'). Here, contrariwise, *Urania* (Greek *ouranie*) simply translates the 'heavenly Muse' of i. 6 and iii. 19 (and *Nativity Ode*, 15).

Urania is, however, one of the nine Muses named by Hesiod (*Theogony*, 77 f.) and was in antiquity associated with astronomy. It appears, however, that the firm allocation of separate Muses to specific arts and sciences was a relatively late development. Pausanias says (IX. xxix. 1 f.) that originally there were three Muses: Melete ('Meditation'), Mneme ('Memory') and Aoede ('Song'). Cicero[37] speaks of four original (*primae*) Muses, daughters of Zeus, Melete, Thelxinoe ('heart-delighting'), and (most excitingly for the writer of this book) Arche ('Beginning'). Homer, at *Odyssey*, xxiv. 60, speaks of nine Muses but does not give their names. It really almost seems as if Milton (assisted no doubt by earlier specimens of self-consciously Christian poetry) happens by translation on Urania, but is then made uneasy by the fact that Urania has been codified in advance, by an unchristian antiquity. At first he hesitates, with a curious prosy explicitness, over the appropriateness of the name and then says, 'The meaning not the name I call' (5).

We may suppose that Milton is here toying with the view that the ancient world was peopled with 'lisping Christians', the idea that ancient sages were unconsciously able to adumbrate sacred truths. This is the world of Bacon's *De Sapientia Veterum* (1609)—Prometheus signifying Providence and the like—or of Comes (Natale Conti) or of *Ovide Moralisé*. In the present case this posture of interpretation is charged with a distinctively Miltonic personal urgency, which rather conveys, 'What *I* mean

[36] 'The Christian Muse', *The Harvard Library Bulletin*, 8 (1935), 29–70.
[37] *De Natura Deorum*, iii. 54, in the edn. by A. S. Pease, 2 vols. (Cambridge, Mass.: Harvard University Press, 1955–8), ii. 1100. M. van den Bruwaene prefers the reading 'Chione' in place of 'Thelxinoe'; see his edn. of *De Natura Deorum*, Collection Latomus, vol. cvii (Brussels: Latomus, 1970), Book iii, pp. 96–7.

by Urania'. One's first instinct is that Milton's conception of the significance is figural, as we have come to understand that term in relation to Dante. That is to say, the 'significance' in this case will not be some abstraction but will be a spiritual individual, having greater reality than merely historical persons and therefore *far* greater reality than ancient mythology, conceived as a purely pagan system of fictions. But what we are given is, so to speak, an *evanescent figura*. We have, as in the other invocations, a drive towards pre-creation primacy, 'Before the hills appeared' (8), and we are told that the being signified by 'Urania' was sister to eternal Wisdom, and that her song, before history began, was pleasing to the Father. The commentators are in some disarray. Influenced, as in a way they should be, by the Muse → God movement in earlier invocations, they seek to identify Urania's significance with an aspect of the Holy Spirit[38] or else with the divine Logos, Christ.[39] Alastair Fowler, arguing for the latter view, observes that although the wisdom referred to at Proverbs, ch. 8, was commonly identified with Christ, Milton rejects this identification at *De Doctrina Christiana*, bk. 1, ch. 7 (Columbia,[40] xv. 12) thus accounting for the possibility of a conversation *with* wisdom, as a separate companion or interlocutor ('Thou with eternal Wisdom didst converse', 9). But the still unplaced mythological resonances of 'sister' sit ill with this, even if Milton did conceive of Wisdom and Christ as simultaneously present at the creation. There is something pagan about this readiness to multiply the numbers on stage. The fact that the Father is 'pleased' by Urania's *song* suggests that she is still some sort of Muse, associated with poetry (as if poetry and philosophy are allegorically accorded an equal primordial status). We are aware as we read that Milton is engaged with one of the running controversies of Protestantism: whether poetry—even divine poetry—*especially* divine poetry—is ever pleasing to God. At the same time there is a notable absence of the proclamatory identification with God so powerfully presented in the two earlier invocations ('Dove-like sat'st brooding', i. 21, and 'since God is light', iii. 3). It is now enough for

---

[38] H. F. Fletcher, *Milton's Rabbinical Reading* (Urbana, Ill.: University of Illionis, 1930), 112. [39] Fowler, *Poems of John Milton*, 775.
[40] *The Works of John Milton*, gen. ed. Frank Allen Paterson, 18 vols. and 2 vol. index (New York: Columbia University Press, 1931–40).

Milton that his Muse be Christian: heavenly, intimately acquainted from eternity with the Godhead.

The calling down of Urania is followed by an ascending movement which will itself be brought low again, in its turn. In lines 2–3, 'whose voice divine | Following, above the Olympian hill I soar', gives us the now familiar breakthrough of Miltonic pride, the humility of 'Following' virtually erased by the triumphant confidence of 'soar'. Again, there is some uncertainty in the writing as to whether such ascents are like the flight of Icarus, doomed to the proper punishment of presumption. The word 'presumed' is there in line 43 but seems somehow unashamed, as if the possible offence is comprehensively dealt with by the mere fact of confession. At first it may seem that 'Pegasean wing' has been carefully chosen instead of 'Icarian wing', since the flight of Pegasus, the winged horse, was gloriously successful. Hesiod tells (*Theogony,* 28 f.) how he rose to the dwelling place of the immortal gods and became the bearer of thunder and lightning for Zeus. But the myth is not unequivocally optimistic. Though Bellerephon (with whom Milton compares himself at line 18) was able through his mastery of Pegasus to defeat the Chimera, Milton also knows—and tells us—the sadder story given in Comes' *Mythologiae,* ix. 4,[41] of how Bellerephon came to earth in the Aleian Field, the 'Field of Error'. At first Milton writes as if this falling into an erroneous vagrancy of spirit is some future evil to be feared, something to be prayed away, but as his sentence unfolds (too late now!) the future evil becomes a present reality: the phrase 'Though fallen on evil days' (25) is immediately, with the numbness of something very close to despair, subjected to a chiastic repetition, 'On evil days though fallen' (26). It is as if the grateful opportunity to return to earthly concerns, to *come down,* has been transformed, first into the feared termination in confusion of a glorious flight and then into the real social and political humiliation of John Milton, the defeated Republican. But again, as in Book iii the sweetest singer was the bird that sang by night, so here Urania comes most surely to him at night, inspiring his dreams or mingling with his thoughts at first waking (29).

---

[41] Comes (Natale Conti), *Mythologiae* (Patavii: Tozzius, 1616), 499–500.

The sense that Milton is somehow locked, throughout the invocation, in a specifically literary anxiety, or at least in an anxiety about the Christian acceptability of literature, is further enforced when the Bacchanals in turbulent rout break the grave procession of the lines, at line 32. It is a marvellous passage. The Dionysiac clamour conveys the richness of unregenerate poetry which Milton always fears might invade, but he is able to pluck from mythology a story showing how this orgiastic energy was in fact the enemy of poetry. This dissonant clamour drowned the harmonies of Orpheus, before the Thracian women tore him to pieces. It seems likely that behind the fear of unregenerate song lies a deeper fear, of an unmanning sexual intensity. Milton has written before out of this fear, with even greater power:

> What could the muse herself that Orpheus bore,
> The muse herself for her enchanting son
> Whom universal nature did lament,
> When by the rout that made the hideous roar,
> His gory visage down the stream was sent,
> Down the swift Hebrus to the Lesbian shore
>
> (*Lycidas*, 58–63)

The preposition 'down', metrically emphasized, has enormous force in these lines; here, as in *Paradise Lost*, the general notion of descent into darkness stands in the background of the entire poem, for *Paradise Lost* is an epic elegy. The word 'tore' (vii. 34) propels our minds back to the ancient Bacchic *sparagmos* (think of the dismembering of Pentheus in the *Bacchae* of Euripides). At the same time its measured monosyllabic release into the line conveys very exactly the Ovidian quality of all this, the queer combination of splendour, sexuality, and violation. The same verb has the same effect in Shakespeare, in another, still finer Ovidian passage:

> Else would I tear the cave where Echo lies
> And make her airy tongue more hoarse than mine
>
> (*Romeo and Juliet*, ii. ii. 162–3)

The old Muse could do nothing for Orpheus, for she was insubstantial. The new Muse, Milton devoutly hopes, will not fail.

The whole passage, and in particular the relevance of sexual fear to the latter part of *Paradise Lost*, remains puzzling. Is Milton already afraid of his own soon-to-be essayed treatment of prelapsarian sexuality? The thought in some degree 'makes sense' of the present passage, but I cannot say that I believe it.

I have in general contrasted the universalism of Milton with the pretypological imagination of Virgil and the elaborate figural structures of Dante. I have conceded, however, that 'the meaning not the name' at the beginning of *Paradise Lost*, vii, connotes an 'evanescent figura'. There was forward typological reference in 'till one greater man' (i. 4), though the faintly odd way of referring to Christ (in which some have detected Arianism) worked against the upward direction of the typology by heroizing, and therefore humanizing Christ. In Books xi and xii the angel Michael offers an account of what for Adam is future history though for us it is past. This must count as an example of what I here called catagogic poetry (see above, p. 68) since it involves a *downward* reference from the still Paradisal scheme to the order of history. But the angelic narrative is not lovingly integrated, as Virgil's forward references are integrated, with the main narrative; Milton does not move easily in a world of typological echoes and in this regard his art is, when set beside Virgil's, primitive.

There remains one further respect in which the Miltonic universalism must be qualified, and this is the most important. I have said, following Addison and Johnson, that *Paradise Lost* is the story of us all, but Milton makes it clear that he is writing not for all, but for an elect people. It is possible that the scope of this election is narrowed as the work proceeds. When Milton likens himself to Moses in the proem to Book i, it is clear that, as commonly in Puritan discourse, the English are seen as analogous to the Jews of the Old Testament, as God's chosen people.[42] In Book vii, on the other hand, when he speaks of 'fit audience . . . though few' (31) we understand that in an England where Milton has found himself isolated and beleaguered 'the chosen' may be very few. The notion of a sacred people is of course strongly present in the Virgilian conception of the high

---

[42] See David Daiches, 'The Opening of *Paradise Lost*', in Frank Kermode (ed.), *The Living Milton* (London: Routledge and Kegan Paul, 1960), 55–69, esp. 59.

destiny of the Latin race, but this, when Virgil composed, was in large measure a thesis of the poem itself, while for Milton it is a cultural datum from outside, grounded pre-emptively in the Bible, so that any question of immediate imaginative alliance with more freely moving poetry is excluded. Then the narrowing of this destiny in the proem to Book vii so that we even begin to hear a note of sour, personal grousing, places it paradoxically at a *sub*-historical (personal) level. The taint indeed is one from which Dante himself is not free. Many readers have felt that the *Inferno* is as much a gallery of personal grudges as a noble spectacle of history *sub specie aeternitatis* ('Dante put his enemies in hell . . .'). But no one feels that Virgil's analogies are basely personal in this way. Such typology as we find in Milton is variously inept, less than wholly successful. The careful imitation at the beginning of *Paradise Regained* of the Donatian 'Ille ego' opening to the *Aeneid* is poorly executed. The great Miltonic word, meanwhile, is 'all': 'all our woe', 'The world was all before them' (i. 3; xii. 646). His poetic achievement, likewise, is one of comprehensiveness. He more than anyone else found a way to fuse the arbitrary intervention of the human poet with the necessary beginning of all humanity, all poetry. Moreover in doing so he brought back the Muse from the dead.

4

The Prelude: Ille ego qui quondam . . .

THE RETROACTIVE POEM

> Oh, yet a few short years of useful life,
> And all will be complete—thy race be run,
> Thy monument of glory will be raised.
> Then, though too weak to tread the ways of truth,
> This age fall back to old idolatry,
> Though men return to servitude as fast
> As the tide ebbs, to ignominy and shame
> By nations sink together, we shall still
> Find solace in the knowledge which we have,
> Blessed with true happiness if we may be
> United helpers forward of a day
> Of firmer trust, joint labourers in the work—
> Should Providence such grace to us vouchsafe—
> Of their redemption, surely yet to come.
> Prophets of Nature we to them will speak
> A lasting inspiration sanctified
> By reason and by truth; what we have loved
> Others will love, and we may teach them how:
> Instruct them how the mind of man becomes
> A thousand times more beautiful than the earth
> On which he dwells, above this frame of things,
> (Which, 'mid all revolutions in the hopes
> And fears of men, doth still remain unchanged)
> In beauty exalted, as it is itself
> Of substance and of fabric more divine.
>
> (*Prelude*, xiii. 428–52).

Each chapter of this book, so far, has begun with the poet's own opening. This one begins instead with his conclusion. Yet the change is far less violent than one might expect, because *this* conclusion has a strange way of sounding like a proem:

All references to W. Wordsworth, *The Prelude*, are, unless otherwise noted, to the 1805 version.

Prophets of Nature, we to them will speak
A lasting inspiration   (443–4)

Even as, at the very end of the poem, this proemial sentence is
uttered, the poet's mind reaches back yet further, to the idea of
inspiration, the source of proems when European literature was
in its infancy. The poet calls upon his friend (as if the Muse had
now assumed, a little incongruously, the rotund, pallid physiognomy of Samuel Taylor Coleridge) to help him in the great
work that lies *ahead*. One might suppose for a moment that this
limp, parsonical language refers to some work of social
amelioration—'fieldwork', as we say in the twentieth century.
But it is not so. All these references to the imminent future
enterprise—'will be complete', 'will be raised', 'shall still find',
'helpless forward', 'will speak'—are to an utterance and not to
some mode of practical agency. Wordsworth is talking about a
poem. *The Prelude* ends in the future tense because it is exactly
what its name tells us: all proem, all exordium. Therefore even
when one quotes the conclusion one is still quoting from an
opening. The poet is still clearing his throat, preparing to sing.

Wordsworth himself indeed never knew that his poem was to
be called *The Prelude* (*praeludium* exactly translates the Greek
prooimion, 'proem'). The title was given by his widow. But
Wordsworth himself, writing to Sir George Beaumont on 3 June
1805, having just completed the work, describes it as 'a sort of
portico'[1] to his great projected work, 'The Recluse'. In the same
letter he glimpses the possibility, of 'a narrative poem of the
Epic kind', beyond 'The Recluse'. Some three months earlier he
told De Quincey that *The Prelude* was to be succeeded by 'a
larger work and more important work to which it is
tributary'.[2] Evidently, two metaphors of prologue, the one
classical, architectonic ('portico'), the other natural (for when
Wordsworth wrote 'tributary' he was probably thinking of a
lesser river flowing into a greater) coexisted in his mind at this
time.

The world knows that 'The Recluse' was never finished,
though we have 'Part First. Book First', 'Home at Grasmere',

---

[1] *The Letters of William and Dorothy Wordsworth*, ed. E. de Selincourt, *The Early
Years, 1787–1805*, rev. Chester L. Shaver (Oxford: Clarendon Press, 1967), 594.
[2] Ibid. 454.

and *The Excursion*. De Selincourt observed that all that came of
Wordsworth's original plan 'apart from one Book, was a
Prelude to the main theme and an Excursion from it.'³ If it is not
exactly a digression, *The Excursion* is alarmingly like (once
more!) a proem. Wordsworth himself describes the last hundred
lines or so of 'Home at Grasmere' which reappear in the prose
preface of *The Excursion* as 'a kind of *Prospectus* of the design and
scope of this whole poem'.⁴ To be still writing one's prologue at
this stage may be thought to show a tendency to deferral which
is almost pathological. Wordsworth himself, a sentence earlier,
explains that the proposal of a system was not his intention, but
that it was 'more animating' to him to follow a different course.

The word 'animating' one surmises is not lightly used. It still
carries, just discernibly, reference to the inspiring Muse, derived
from the time when *anima* meant 'breath'. There are signs that
the title of the proposed work, 'The Recluse', itself betrays an
impulse towards curtailment, reduction to the subjective
source, a flinching from the major, objective project. Because
by this date the Muse has been changed into—or replaced
by—the Friend addressed, and because the friend in this case has
a palpable, historically attested existence independent of the
poet, the account we must give of the original inspiration of *The
Prelude*–'Recluse' is an untidily pragmatic affair. There are signs
that Coleridge in some fashion projected upon his friend his
own dream of writing a universal poem, hoped for a work
which would move out from the Romantic subject into the
public sphere.

Then the plan laid out, and I believe, partly suggested by me, was that
Wordsworth should assume the station of a man in mental repose, one
whose principles were made up, and so prepared to deliver upon
authority a system of philosophy. He was to treat man as man—a
subject of eye, ear, touch, and taste, in contact with external nature,
and informing the senses from the mind, and not compounding a mind
out of the senses; then he was to describe the pastoral and other states
of society, assuming something of the Juvenalian spirit as he
approached the high civilisation of cities and towns, and opening a

³ *The Poetical Works of William Wordsworth*, ed. E. de Selincourt and Helen
Darbishire, 5 vols. (Oxford: Clarendon Press, 1940–9), v. 368.
⁴ Wordsworth's preface to the 1814 edition of *The Excursion*, in Wordsworth,
Poems, ed. John O. Hayden, 2 vols. (Harmondsworth: Penguin Books, 1977), ii. 37.

melancholy picture of the present state of degeneracy and vice; thence
he was to infer and reveal the proof of, and necessity for, the whole
state of man and society being subject to, and illustrative of, a
redemptive process in operation, showing how this idea reconciled all
the anomalies, and promised future glory and restoration. Something
of this sort was, I think, agreed upon. It is, in substance, what I have all
my life been doing in my system of philosophy.[5]

One is tempted to say that Coleridge himself could never
have completed the desired work because he just was not well
enough organized, did not have the staying power. When,
however, Wordsworth finds (even as the words pour forth) that
he too is mysteriously arrested, at the subjective level, we sense
that this time it is Romantic subjectivism itself which stands
guard, athwart the entrance. Certainly the words 'Man, Nature
and society' stood for a time in Wordsworth's mind as properly
describing the argument of the great poem, and in a letter to
James Losh (11 March 1798) they appear as a possible title, an
alternative to 'The Recluse'.[6] In the 1814 preface, however, the
design seems, with strange suddenness, to be curtailed and reduced from a public to a private reference, even as he sets it forth:
he begins with 'a determination to compose a philosophical poem,
containing views of Man, Nature and Society' but then says that it
is 'to be entitled The Recluse; as having for its principal subject
the sensations and opinions of a poet living in retirement'.[7] The
universal 'view' is, as it were, loyally commemorated, but the
principal subject is now Wordsworth himself. The explanation
of the word 'recluse', 'living in retirement', is unexcitingly
factual. It is very far, of course, from being the whole story.
Wordsworth's imagination is itself *epistemologically recluded*.
Man as 'a subject of eye, ear, touch, and taste, in contact with
external nature' remains the alpha and omega of *The Prelude*.
The latter end of his commonwealth *does nothing but* remember
its beginning. The perennial, *usque ad finem* formal exordium of

---

[5] 21 July 1832, *The Table Talk and Omniana of Samuel Taylor Coleridge* (London:
Oxford University Press, 1917), 188–9. See also Coleridge's letter to Wordsworth
of 30 May 1815, about the ways in which *The Excursion* disappointed his
expectations, in *Collected Letters of Samuel Taylor Coleridge*, ed. E. L. Griggs, 6 vols.
(Oxford: Clarendon Press, 1956–71), iv. 572–6.

[6] See 'Home at Grasmere', 754 (*Poetical Works*, v. 338) and *Letters: of William and
Dorothy Wordsworth, The Early Years*, 214.

[7] *Poetical Works*, ed. Selincourt and Darbishire, v (1949), 2.

The Prelude reflects an epistemology which is now circum-scribed by origins, haunted by solipsistic fear.

Meanwhile, if the Muse is not 'the Friend', but rather 'Whatever is the source of his poetry', we have another way of understanding why it is that *The Prelude* should be 'all proem'. The work is arrested at the level of the *initiating experience*. This, the experience, can grow in the mind, but nothing else can. Political reference will be reduced as it were to the figure it made in the original experience. Thus once more we can find a certain justification for our sense that the poem is one protracted prayer to the Muse.

Certain qualifications, however, are urgently required. I suggested that the appearance of future tenses, referring at the very end of *The Prelude* to projected designs, marked the work as proemial to the very end. In one way, however, the future tenses can be construed as showing that this is not a proem in the full rigour of the term—for the natural tense of the proem—whether in the Homeric imperative or the Virgilian first person singular—is the present: 'Sing, Muse', 'I sing'.

In fact the reader intuits all this, very swiftly. The work proposed my be described as imminent, but the future tenses somehow work in a contrary direction, suggesting an ever-growing distance between the poet and his design. If such a thing were possible, we might speak here of a *valedictory proem*, a work implicitly bidding farewell to its own firm promise.

Meanwhile, the notion of a great future action opening at the *end* of the poem is, if not Homeric, certainly Virgilian and therefore thoroughly classical. Milton's epic ends in exactly this way. Yet, when all this is said, Wordsworth's reference *is* to his own major, literary project. Since, 'the subject of eye, ear, touch, and taste' is the Aeneas of the poem's journey, it follows that a reference to the hero's future must be in this case a reference to Wordsworth's future—though that could, conceiv-ably, have been a non-literary future. And so the notion of the proem returns to haunt us.

Indeed, if the Virgilian analogy is pursued, it too will take us in a contradictory direction; we cannot but be drawn away from the *historically* inchoative ending of the *Aeneid*, back to the 'proem before the proem', the mysterious personal introduction preserved by Donatus:

Ille ego qui quondam gracili modulatus avena
Carmen et egressus silvis vicina coegi

That man am I, who having once played his tune upon a slender reed, emerging from the woods compelled the neighbouring fields

The whole of *The Prelude* is contained in that strange collision of pronouns: *Ille ego*, 'That person' (far away) 'I' (here): that child Wordsworth who, when Skiddaw's height was 'bronzed with a deep radiance, stood alone | Beneath the sky' (i. 300–1) and the mature poet, now writing in his cell of privacy.

Virgil, as we saw, subjectivized Homeric epic. This made it easy for commentators in the ages which followed to detect allegorical resonances in the *Aeneid*. We are perhaps too easily contemptuous of Fulgentius's reading of the poem as an allegory of the life of a man. Even his notorious exegesis of the song of Iopas early in the poem, as corresponding to the nurse's lullaby,[8] may spring from an intuition of latency in Virgil's manner of writing which is leagues ahead of any interpretation which confines itself, briskly, to the letter. A modern commentator might say, 'The primal song of Iopas, dealing with the childhood of the world, affords a brief, strangely quiescent version of the theme of origins, appropriate to this stage of the epic narrative in which Aeneas remains locked within an essentially immature understanding.' In other words: the story signifies infancy, Fulgentius has not acquired the civil art of the prudently placed 'perhaps'. He knows no other way to convey his intuition than through the structure of allegory. This may look metallically cold to us but was, I surmise, excitingly mysterious in the sixth century AD. The sense grew among readers of Virgil that the *Aeneid* was not just resonant with the general idea of spiritual, human growth but was in some way a projection of Virgil's own, personal experience of dispossession and restoration. This, as we saw, found expression in certain passages of the *Appendix Vergiliana*. Indeed, these very lines (*Ille ego qui quondam . . .*) may be not so much the source as the product of the readers' desire to find the poet in this poem.

---

[8] *Fabii Planciadis Fulgentii V. C. Opera*, ed. R. Helm (Leipzig: Teubner, 1898), 93. See also *Fulgentius the Mythographer*, trans. with introductions by L. G. Whitbread (Columbus: Ohio State University Press, 1971), 126.

When a few pages ago I said that Wordsworth was the Aeneas of his poem, the emphasis lay on the stark contrast between ancient martial epic and subjective Romanticism; yet the early readers of the *Aeneid* had precisely this intuition: that Virgil was his own Aeneas, that Aeneas was Virgil. If this thought is allowed to grow, the future tenses of Wordsworth's 'exordial conclusion' may permit a different construction. They are there (and this must be the last of our 'transformations') not because the passage is 'post-proemial' but because it is '*pre*-proemial'. When Dante expanded the episode of 'the Dead' to fill his poem, the feat of formal reorganization seemed spectacular enough. Yet Wordsworth seems in a way to have built the entire structure of this strange poetic *Künstlerroman* not from the true proem of the *Aeneid* (*Arma virumque cano . . .*) but from the preceding *dubia*. Even now we have not cut back far enough, for it could be said that in these Latin lines this poet describes his *emergence* into public, martial epic, an emergence which in Wordsworth's case was never accomplished. Wordsworth remains at the level of *silvis*, in the retired forests of privacy, and never reaches *egressus*, the word which marks Virgil's stepping forth.

M. H. Abrams, in a brilliant essay, noted that *The Prelude* does in fact possess a developing narrative structure,[9] having three stages: early mental growth, followed by a shattering despair, followed in turn by a renewed vision, strengthened by the suffering through which the poet has passed. The process, Abrams points out, is one of justification—a justifying of pain.[10] We are only a hairsbreadth away from the notion of theodicy—which would of course translate us in a trice to *Paradise Lost*. Wordsworth's phraseology,

> In the end
> All gratulant, if rightly understood   (xiii. 384–5)

actually evokes not Milton but (somewhat surprisingly) the

---

[9] This essay first appeared in his *Natural Supernaturalism: Tradition and Revolution in Romantic Literature* (New York: W. W. Norton, 1971). I refer here to the rev. version of the essay in Wordsworth, *The Prelude, 1799, 1805, 1850*, ed. Jonathan Wordsworth, M. H. Abrams, and Stephen Gill (New York: W. W. Norton, 1979), 585–97.

[10] Ibid. 589.

grand, highly polished eighteenth-century emulation of *Paradise Lost*, Pope's *Essay on Man*, written, as he said, 'to vindicate the ways of God to Man':

> God sends not ill: if rightly understood   (i. 16)

But of course *Paradise Lost* (iv. 113) remains the terminus of the allusion.

Abrams further observes that the whole story of *The Prelude* is the story of a homecoming. Once again the roots of Wordsworth's poem, not just in classical proem but in the larger classical epic structure, are deep. The *Odyssey* is what the ancients called a *nostos*, a journey home. Indeed Wordsworth's redaction, in *The Prelude*, of this classical *nostos* may be said to have given the term a distinctively modern nuance: nostalgia is something distinct from the ordinary homesickness of Odysseus. Abrams himself acknowledges this Miltonic connection when he writes that the vale described in *Home at Grasmere* is a recovered Eden, in which 'Wordsworth and Dorothy, "a solitary pair' (255) are somewhat incongruously the Adam and Eve'.[11]

Thus, while Odysseus's journey is linear, Wordsworth's is cyclical. He ends in his beginning. Abrams points out that *The Prelude* even ends with precisely the same walk as that with which it began, the walk to Grasmere.[12] Again it may be said that the journey of Aeneas terminates in a homecoming, but it is the whole point of the *Aeneid* that the home the hero attains is unfamiliar to him. For Aeneas there is no Wordsworthian special sweetness of recognition. This progenitor of his line, Dardanus, was a Roman. Therefore the journey made by the House of Dardanus may be cyclical, but the journey of Aeneas is linear, as was the journey of Odysseus. In like manner, it may be said that *Paradise Lost* culminates in the idea of a *felix culpa*, 'fortunate fall' and that *Paradise Regained* is therefore already inscribed in the conclusion of *Paradise Lost*. But even if we accept (in order to come as close as we can to the pattern of *The Prelude*) what we earlier termed the naturalist version of the *felix*

---

[11] Ibid. 595.
[12] See John Finch, 'Wordsworth's Two-Handed Engine', in *Bicentenary Wordsworth Studies*, ed. Jonathan Wordsworth (Ithaca, NY: Cornell University Press, 1970), 1–14, for corroborative evidence.

culpa, the 'Paradise within thee, happier far' of xii. 587, this is never simply identified by Milton with the original garden, somewhere in Eden. That, they unequivocally leave. It remains, then, for Wordsworth, proceeding, as he says, by 'motions retrograde' (ix. 8) to write the true reversal of Milton's tragic story. In 1832 Wordsworth introduced the backward-looking traveller (1850, ix. 9 f.), so eerily anticipated in the pseudo-Virgilian *Dirae* (see above pp. 19–21).

Here, however, I must confess what may be a personal prejudice in my own reading of Wordsworth. To me, the childhood vision is manifestly the potent thing and I mistrust the profession of confidence in the renewed vision through suffering which comes later. Phrases like 'for such loss, I *would believe* | Abundant recompense' (*Tintern Abbey*, 87–8, my italics) are more eloquent of desperate need than of bliss secured. Childhood vision naturally imposes a strongly retroactive scheme; it pulls the poet back towards the past. Thus Henry Vaughan wrote, in the seventeenth century,

> O how I long to travel back
> And tread again that ancient track.[13]

The ancient Greeks, unlike Christians, usually conceived immortality as 'double-ended': an immortal, for them, is not only someone who will live for ever but also someone who has lived forever. When Plato argues for immortality in the *Meno* and the *Phaedo* he assumes that he must make a case for both a retrospective and a prospective infinity. Christians on the other hand are by and large willing to believe that human beings begin at a certain point in time and then go on for ever. Wordsworth in the 'Immortality Ode' is notoriously 'More Greek than the Greeks' in that, through an eccentric revision of the Platonic doctrine of *anamnesis* (recollection of the eternal Ideas) he represents the soul as proceeding from eternity but moving towards death:

> The soul that rises with us, our life's Star,
> Hath had elsewhere its setting,
> And cometh from afar:

---

[13] 'The Retreat', 21–2, in Henry Vaughan, *The Complete Poems*, ed. Alan Rudrum (Harmondsworth: Penguin, 1983, rev. repr. of 1976 edn.), 173.

Not in entire forgetfulness,
And not in utter nakedness,
But trailing clouds of glory do we come
From God, who is our home:
Heaven lies about us in our infancy!
Shades of the prison-house begin to close
Upon the growing Boy,
But He beholds the light, and whence it flows,
He sees it in his joy;
The Youth, who daily farther from the East
Must travel, still is Nature's Priest,
And by the vision splendid
Is on his way attended;
At length the Man perceives it die away,
And fade into the light of common day.[14]

The strange idea of an *accompanying* soul (a little like the Latin *genius*) once likened to a star, might naturally have led us to an imagined, infinite future. But what happens in the stanza is in fact quite different. The subject is further and further separated from the star, which is itself allowed to *die* into the light of common day. For an imagination so constituted there is only one road which offers happiness, and that is the road back. The factors which differentiated the mature happiness from the childhood bliss are a mere tissue of Christian Stoic moralizings. W. H. Auden once observed that the world is divided into those who locate happiness in the past (Eden, Arcadia) and those who locate it in the future (the new Jerusalem, the Communist State).[15] There can be no serious doubt as to which of these is Wordsworth's party.

Geoffrey Hartman has argued with great subtlety that *The Prelude* is made out of Wordsworth's failure to become an epic, publicly prophetic poet.[16] Wordsworth was led by nature not to

---

[14] 'Ode', Later known as 'Ode: Intimations of Immortality From Recollections of Early Childhood', 59–76, text from *William Wordsworth* ('The Oxford Authors'), ed. Stephen Gill (Oxford: Oxford University Press, 1984), 299.

[15] 'Horae Canonicae: Vespers', in W. H. Auden, *Collected Shorter Poems, 1927–57* (London: Faber and Faber, 1966), 333–5. Cf. Auden's essay, 'Dingley Dell and the Fleet', in his *The Dyer's Hand* (London: Faber and Faber, 1956), 407–28. Cf. also Laurence Lerner, *The Uses of Nostalgia: Studies in Pastoral Poetry* (London: Chatto and Windus, 1972), 66–7.

[16] 'A Poet's Progress: Wordsworth and the *Via Naturaliter Negativa*', *Modern Philology*, 59 (1962), 214–24.

an objective vision but to a mistrust of sense and of reality. There is a metaphysical difficulty in Hartman's conception which arises from the fact that the imaginative posture he ascribes to Wordsworth is both anti-natural in its assumption of transcendence and yet still (as compared with the older Christian mystics) circumscribed by a continued deference to nature. One is tempted to say that Hartman cannot have it both ways: the Nature who prescribes transcendence must herself be supernatural or, at the very least, trans-natural; she can no longer be wholly immanent. *Naturaliter negativa*, 'naturally negative' (Hartman's phrase) is a contradiction in terms. Yet in the very contradiction there is a certain fidelity to the real character of Wordsworth's writing. For something which is hiding behind particular landscapes, particular encounters, produces in Wordsworth *feelings* of *unreality*; the *sensation that sensation is not to be trusted* sounds contradictory but in fact may not be so. Hartman sees Wordsworth's poetry as essentially *nourished* by this intuition of unreality. This seems to me very nearly but not quite true.

Certainly Wordsworth discovers in the real opening of *The Prelude* that he cannot address 'present good' (1850, i. 100) and that the matter of his poetry must always be subject to the poignant obliquity of memory or else filtered through an interior *sensibility*, whose temperature (to borrow an image from Keats[17]) Wordsworth is for ever taking, an anxious physician to his own state of imaginative health. But it is never, in my view, absence alone which is separately relished by Wordsworth. Even in lines like 'Fallings from us, vanishings' ('Immortality Ode', 146) which in the strange, teetering grammar of that poem seems at first to be offered as that among Nature's gifts for which the poet is most truly grateful, is shot through, dialectically, with a sense of diminishing substance, and of the poet's own falling away. In the very next sentence Wordsworth seems in any case to reverse the order of values, as the 'shadowy recollections' gradually brighten, as they are focused, into 'the fountain light of all our day' (154). For

---

[17] For Keats and 'the pleasure thermometer' see his letter to John Taylor, 30 Jan. 1818, in *The Letters of John Keats*, ed. H. E. Rollins, 2 vols. (Cambridge, Mass.: Harvard University Press, 1958), i. 218.

Hartman, Wordsworth becomes the visionary of absence; for me, he is always the visionary of a once-presence.

In the narrative of *The Prelude* Wordsworth travels in Europe almost as far perhaps as Odysseus sailed, yet we sense that he goes nowhere. Because the account is always filtered by sensibility, always psychologized, we feel that Wordsworth and we have together witnessed some kind of moving picture of the Alpine waterfalls, that the poet has always in fact been confined, within his own skull, relegated to subjective responses. One thing alone mitigates this solitude: the original unity of the child Wordsworth with nature. Even if one becomes convinced, instinctively, that the childhood vision was never truly present, so that if *per impossibile* one were to travel back one would discover that it fled before one like a rainbow, always in the next valley—a thing of which I am by no means certain—the dialectic of substance and absence remains in place. Wordsworth's poetry is quickened, not by absence *simpliciter*—but by the tragic unavailability of a conceivably veridical glory.

The reader will observe that here Hartman and I are *together* amicably setting aside the 'recovered vision' of maturity. But Hartman's Wordsworth is propelled into negation while mine is endlessly led back (like Alice in the Garden of Live Flowers) to the point from which he began. Hartman himself actually allows that the greatest poetry *takes its origin* from the memory of given experiences to which the poet is often 'pedantically faithful'.[18] Hartman seems to regard the retrograde impulse in Wordsworth as (in Puritan language) a real backsliding, from his proper deconstructive calling. It is, he says, 'our problem' with Wordsworth (though just before, with his habitual generosity of mind, he described it, less censoriously, as 'his secret').[19]

What, then, of the 'mature vision'? If I mistrust it as a dubious assertion of will over truth, Hartman sees it as an assertion of imagination, this being almost the *opposite* of sensation—something 'unborrowed from the eye' (*Tintern Abbey*, 83). For me, on the contrary, that which is strong in the recovered vision is that which is one with the early experience:

---

[18] 'Poet's Progress', 217.
[19] Ibid.

> I had felt
> Too forcibly, too early in my life
> Visitings of imaginative power.   (xi. 252)

The word 'imaginative' is there, to help Hartman; 'visitings' helps me.

That is why Abrams was right to see in *The Prelude* a *return* to the Garden. For Hartman the imagination (perhaps because of his own will to discard perception) terminates in darkness: '. . . the Imagination expressed as a power distinct from Nature opens his eyes by putting them out'.[20] Both images, Abrams's garden and Hartman's blinding, direct us to Milton.

Wordsworth himself invokes *Paradise Lost*. The Miltonic vaunt, 'things unattempted yet in prose or rhyme', is genteelly echoed in Wordsworth's hope of joining those who are enabled 'to perceive | Something unseen before' (xii. 304–5). The describing of himself as 'a chosen son' and 'a dedicated spirit' (iii. 82, iv. 344) are more powerfully Miltonic. Like Moses, with whom Milton identified himself at *Paradise Lost* (i. 7), Wordsworth is vouchsafed vision on the top of a mountain (xiii. 1–119). It is a measure of his weight in the canonical line that we can without absurdity add Snowdon to Oreb and Sinai.

There is truth in Hartman's interpretation and there is truth in Abrams's. Hartman is saying that poetic imagination, itself a gift of nature, has blinded Wordsworth to the sensory world. It seems to me true that articulate, poetic consciousness, at least, has destroyed his childhood vision. We may thus reach a negotiated agreement that some sort of blinding has taken place. Because of this blinding Wordsworth experienced something very like Milton's urgent need for inspiration. Therefore Wordsworth becomes one more poet of the modern age to seek a way of reviving the Muse, but the attempt is not made explicit in the Miltonic manner. Using the classical language we can say that Wordsworth's Muse, like Hesiod's is the daughter of Memory. In this way the Garden and the Muse are one. *The Prelude* has indeed an external Muse (though he is never named as such) in Coleridge. But it also has an internal Muse—and *she* is the true divinity, *The Prelude* is inspired—breathed in—by the vision of the child Wordsworth.

[20] Ibid. 224.

Book i of *The Prelude* actually begins with these words:

Oh there is blessing in this gentle breeze,
That blows from the green fields and from the clouds
And from the sky; it beats against my cheek,
And seems half conscious of the joy it gives.
O welcome messenger! O welcome friend!
A captive greets thee, coming from a house
Of bondage, from yon city's walls set free,
A prison where he hath been long immured.   (1–8)

We are far removed, it would seem, from traditional epic phraseology. The poet may in a manner have plunged *in medias res*, but of all the poets we have so far considered it is Chaucer, with his *in medias sententias* opening who comes closest to Wordsworth. *The Book of the Duchess*, as we saw, opens with the poet musing aloud about his own insomnia and the reader is made to feel that he has suddenly been made privy to a discourse which may have been going on for some time. Wordsworth's initial 'Oh' is strangely—perhaps deliberately—weak. There was clearly a moment of literary fashion around the end of the eighteenth century which favoured the use of such conversational expletive openings (compare Coleridge's 'Well!' at the beginning of 'Dejection').

If Wordsworth ostensibly neglects classical form, he has a way, nevertheless, of going behind that form in order to make use of *its* source. The poet who despised the conventional Dryads of eighteenth-century pastoral was acutely aware of the spirits who inhabit woods. So here the poet who declares his independence of precedent in the phrasing of his exordium may nevertheless be reaching back to the genesis of inspiration. For he addresses a *wind*: a *spiritus*, an *anima*. Moreover, in the marvellous, hesitant epithet, 'half conscious' the wind is made to co-operate in the sentience of the poet. The appearance in the 1850 *Prelude* of the pronouns 'it . . . it . . . its' in place of 'he . . . he . . . his', in reference to the wind, seems to be due to interference from Christopher Wordsworth, the poet's clerical nephew. The Bishop's anxiety to alter the words in instructive; he has scented (correctly) animism. The *conscius aether* ('conscious air') of Virgil (*Aeneid*, iv. 168) has become, through a further subjectivization of the Pathetic Fallacy, an accomplice in the composition of the poem, and yet, even as this extra sophistication is achieved, we move closer perhaps to the experience of the ancient singer-poet, as he inhaled deeply, before his finger moved to touch the strings of his lyre. Wordsworth *addresses* the wind, which is seen as a messenger (in Greek an *angelos*). 'Welcome' is, strictly, an imperative verb, quite as much as Homer's 'Sing'. In the Donatian proem Virgil describes himself as moving out of the pastoral woods to the bristling spears of warlike epic; within his poem the Latin race itself moves from an Arcadian to a civic existence, from Eden towards the new Jerusalem.

For Virgil Arcadia is linked with pre-sexual childhood. The bluff Whig historian Macaulay was haunted[21] by the lines:

> Saepibus in nostris parvam te roscida mala
> (dux ego vester eram) vidi cum matre legentem.
> alter ab undecimo tum me iam abstulerat annus,
> iam fragilis poteram a terra contingere ramos:
> ut vidi, ut perii, ut me malus abstulit error!
>
> *(Eclogue* viii. 37–41)

When you were small I saw you in our orchard picking dew-wet apples with your mother (I showed you the way). My eleventh—indeed my twelfth—year had already come upon me, and I could now reach the frail branches from the ground. As I saw you, I perished. Sin carried me off.

Here the child-love encounter is not, as in Dante, the source of redemption. Rather, it is strangely Miltonic. Fallen sexuality enters Paradise with the picking of an apple.

Some hundreds of years later the pastoral poet Mantuan wrote some verses which tell how a certain peasant picked an apple and gave it to his city-dwelling master. The master, enticed by the sweetness of the fruit (like Eve!) transplanted the tree to the city. But the tree withered and died.[22] The story was conventionally interpreted as showing the futility of immoderate greed.[23] Yet one senses the presence of a larger, or at least a

---

[21] See Sir George Otto Trevelyan, *The Life and Letters of Lord Macaulay*, 2 vols. (London: Oxford University Press, 1935), i. 343–4.

[22] *Apologus alter ad eundem*, Mantuan (Baptista Spagnuoli), *Primus (secundus, tertius) Operum B. Mantuani*, (Paris: Praelo Ascensiano, 1513), fo. 194. v.

[23] Mantuan offers this interpretation in the last two lines of the poem. Cf. William Bullokar, *Aesop's Fables in True Orthography* (London: Edmund Bolliphant, 1585), 80–1. I owe the references to Mantuan and to Bullokar to Dr Estelle Haan.

more literary significance. Apples, temptation, death, all
present in *Eclogue* viii, with a general reference to innocence,
seem here to have been joined to the town–country antithesis,
which lies behind all pastoral poetry. It is as if the myth of a lost
Eden, always echoic of lost Arcadia, is here permitted to assume
a form which more exactly expresses the real fear: that the
transposition of vision from the artless world to the artificial
entails death: that pastoral *art* kills the thing it loves.

In *Paradise Lost* Adam and Eve were forced out of the green,
happy garden. At the beginning of *The Prelude* this sequence is
swiftly reversed in Wordsworth's brief picture of himself,
suddenly freed from an oppressive city, delivered from maturity
to childhood, from a finite, death-bound future to a potentially
infinite origin. yet, all the while, we sense that something is
wrong. In the lines which follow Miltonic echoes begin to
crowd in—all from the end, not from the opening of *Paradise
Lost*.

> The world was all before them, where to choose
> Their place of rest, and providence their guide:
> They hand in hand with wandering steps and slow,
> Through Eden took their solitary way.
>
> (xii. 646–9)

In Wordsworth:

> The earth is all before me—with a heart
> Joyous, nor sacred at its own liberty,
> I look about, and should the guide I chuse
> Be nothing better than a wandering cloud
> I cannot miss my way. (i. 15–19)

In Milton the vagrant, hesitant steps of Adam and Eve, now
up-Paradised, are really watched over and guided by Providence, which will indeed lead humanity to a great Further
Good. In Wordsworth Providence slips away unnoticed. The
poet is strangely free to choose his own guide, which may be
something as errant as a stray cloud. Because Wordsworth is not
un-Paradised but re-em-Paradised (however briefly) freedom
and devout security can seem for the moment to be one. For,
even without Providence, however random his steps, we are to
think that he cannot lose his way. We are to surmise that Nature
(who knows no futurity) is watching over him, and that in

Paradise all paths are, equally, the right path. While Dante began his poem in the dark wood of fallen existence where the path was lost, Wordsworth *si ritrovo*, 'came to himself', in a bright landscape where it was impossible to get lost. Nevertheless (again it must be said) all is not quite well.

Dante's recurrent example of a great figural allegory, in both the *Convivio* and the Can Grande letter, is the Biblical account of the departure of the Israelites out of Egypt. This example should already have been plucking at the sleeve of the mind because of the guiding cloud in Wordsworth's lines. I have so far stressed the errancy of Wordsworth's cloud, but it is important to remember that the exodus of the Israelites was led by a pillar of cloud, in the Bible. Yet Wordsworth will not allow this thought to grow; '*Nothing better than* a wandering cloud' forbids any confident ascription of divine authority to this guide. We sense that, if nevertheless it cannot mislead, that is precisely because it is natural (or 'of Nature'). In another poem, which belongs to the period 1804–7, Wordsworth can liken *himself* to this 'guide' ('I wandered lonely as a cloud . . .'). As Richard J. Onorato says, Wordsworth becomes momentarily 'an oracle to himself'.[24] In fact the sense of divine immanence is not pursued to the point of inert identity, but remains, dynamically, a matter of affinity. Nevertheless, Onorato's inference is not without encouragement from the text.

The first hint that this liberty is a recovery of something the poet has had before comes in line 19, 'I breathe *again* . . .'. The lines continue,

> Trances of thought and mountings of the mind
> Come fast upon me. It is shaken off,
> As by miraculous gift 'tis shaken off,
> That burthen of my own unnatural self,
> The heavy weight of many a weary day (i. 20–4)

'Trances of thought and mountings of the mind' can in a Wordsworthian context look very like the working of memory (*mémoire involontaire?*—but there is no 'trigger' to set memory in motion, as there is in Proust). Wordsworth's memory wells up 'momently' (Coleridge's word). The reader is unsure whether

[24] *The Character of the Poet: Wordsworth in the Prelude* (Princeton: Princeton University Press, 1971), 102.

this sudden action within the poet is or is not a gift from the animating wind.

The poet then turns again to the fact that he can go down any path at all. This is not felt as a rebuttal but rather as a confirmation of 'I cannot miss my way' (19). As we saw, Paradise and freedom are not opposed, as in Milton, but are somehow fused. Yet—still—one cannot quite trust this happiness. On the one hand, the poet is almost too grateful: such gratitude strongly suggests the rarity, and perhaps the unreliability, of this joy vouchsafed; on the other hand, one senses at the same time that, in a thoroughly practical fashion, this casting about for a path to follow corresponds to *a real difficulty in getting started on the poem.*

Certainly the poem seems somehow to be stuck. The Wordsworthian 'hemming and hawing', half infuriating, half endearing—'Nay more, if I may trust myself' and the like—continues. The wind becomes two winds, an external, natural 'breath of heaven' and a corresponding mild creative breeze which is 'felt within' (41–3). The language grows complex and powerful at 46–7,

> A tempest, a redundant energy,
> Vexing its own creation.

'Redundant' may suggest sea-waves, but notice that, if that is the case, the waves are flowing back. The poem will not move forward, it is a vexed creation, a difficult birth. Yet the latent energy is clearly there—and perhaps it is growing stronger.

The religious notions: 'consecration', 'heaven', and 'the holy life of music and of the verse' (40, 41, 54) seem to be a matter partly of pious aspiration, partly of lived, creative experience. It is notable that Wordsworth later felt obliged to dilute the last of these, offering in the 1850 version a picturesque, 'distanced' version:

> not wanting punctual service high,
> Matins and vespers, of harmonious verse! (44–5)

By then he knew that the 'prowess in an honourable field' promised, as following the break-up of the long continued frost in the 1805 version, was not to be. The poet in 1850 knew that 'The Recluse' would never be written.

At line 55 the rug is pulled from under our feet, albeit in an almost unnoticeable fashion. It is done by means of a quietly intruded past tense, 'did'.

> Thus far, O friend, did I, not used to make
> A present joy the matter of my song,
> Pour out that day my soul in measured strains   (55–7)

The effect of this is to put everything that has gone before in inverted commas, yet no reader can be conscious of this when he begins *The Prelude* (for editors never in fact put the inverted commas in). The situation is a little like that which we find in Milton's *Lycidas*. There, 'Thus sang the uncouth swain', at line 186, retrospectively frames the entire preceding poem, turns it into a dramatic utterance, delivered at some time in the poem's past; yet this information comes so late that the retroactive convulsion required in the reader's understanding can barely be achieved. Wordsworth *says* that it is not his custom to deal with *present* joy and in a curious manner the authorial strategy confirms this. For we find that this visitation of the animating wind, this temporary and provisional presence which alone can set the poem in motion, is itself located in the past. Even in his invocation a welcoming of the breath of poetry proves to be something to which he looks *back*. The narrative tells us indeed that *then* he was equal to a poetry of present bliss, but we also know, pragmatically, that the experience must really have been pre-poetical—that Wordsworth was not actually scribbling away as the wind began to blow in his face. Even if the words came 'that day', 'spontaneously' (57, 61), there was, we know, an interval. The wind is not, after all, exactly like the Muse's breath in an archaic, oral poet. It is a retrospective construction of experience.

Meanwhile the real birth-pangs of the poem continue. The strenuous optimism of Wordsworth begins to assume its familiar, hollow note: 'My own voice cheered me', 'a cheerful confidence in things to come' (64, 67). As Evelyn Waugh's 'lady of leisure' would say, 'Goodness how sad'.[25]

Everything is slipping back. Wordsworth is now launched

---

[25] Cf. 'This is the Sphinx. Goodness how sad,' in 'Cruise', in *Work Suspended and Other Stories* (Harmondsworth: Penguin Books, 1951), 19.

upon a sort of pseudo-narrative. Instead of telling the story of the growth of a poet's mind (itself a subjective curtailment of 'Man, Nature and Society') he instead narrates, in a fussily prolix manner, the inception of his own poem; the poem itself meanwhile waits upon this process. There is much throat-clearing and shooting of cuffs: 'I made a choice . . . nor did I fail', 'assurance of some work . . . forthwith to be begun' (81, 85, 86–7). But all ends in pieces. There was no lack, Wordsworth assures us, of 'Aeolian visitations' (104). Aeolian harps were hung on trees, to be played by the wind. The image was dear to the Romantics because it suggests an artistry which is wholly of nature, since it is the wind which calls forth the harp's music. But here

> The harp
> Was soon defrauded, and the banded host
> Of harmony dispersed in straggling sounds,
> And lastly utter silence   (104–7)

Hartman says, 'The Prelude opens with a success immediately followed by a failure.' I would prefer to say, 'The Prelude opens with a *seeming* celebration of present bliss which is swiftly relegated to the past, after which we learn how, in any case, it terminated in failure.'[26]

Therefore the opening of The Prelude may be more like the opening of the Commedia than we at first thought. Dante cannot find the right path in the dark but is found by God. In Wordsworth not finding the right path is certainly presented, at first, as joyous freedom, in bright sunlight, not darkness. But the brightness proves to be delusive, and the motif of searching for a path increasingly betrays a real, inward desperation, and Wordsworth is saved by the intervention of his dead, childhood self—the truly creative Wordsworth. Dante also is saved by a dead poet—called by him 'that stream' (*quella fonte, Inferno*, i. 79)—by Virgil.

The Prelude starts then, with a false dawn, a non-beginning. Yet the verse grinds remorselessly on, with further, variously implausible promises of amendment: 'To brace myself to some determined aim' (124). One is reminded of the advice some-times given to pupils who say, 'I can't write anything; I'm so

---

[26] 'Poet's Progress', 214.

confused': 'You *are* allowed, you know,' the teacher answers, 'to explain the nature of your confusion to the examiners; at least that would start you writing': Somebody, one surmises, must have said this to Wordsworth—or perhaps he, of all men, did not need to be told.

But then we have the flat truth of 'But I have been discouraged' (134). Behind all this stands the pattern of Puritan autobiography in which God is not expected to communicate with the subject except at rare intervals. The existence of this prior mode makes it possible for Wordsworth to do what he does. Protestant assurance of salvation becomes in Wordsworth the long-withheld, occasionally granted power of inspiration (though Wordsworth, all the while, is producing line after line of poetry):

> gleams of light
> Flash often from the east, then disappear,
> And mock me with a sky that ripens not
> Into a steady morning.   (134–7)

Milton is, of course, the poet who bridges the transition:

> Seasons return but not to me returns (*Paradise Lost*, iii. 41)

> And that one talent which is death to hide,
> Lodged with me useless   (Sonnet 16)

Here 'talent', the divinely entrusted gift which the receiver is expected to increase, takes on the meaning, for all posterity, of 'artistic gift'. Curiously there may be a half-allusion to Milton's sonnet in Wordsworth's 'false steward' who 'renders nothing back' at line 270.

So Wordsworth continues, casting about for his subject in this direction or that. Instead of the high Miltonic calling, 'things unattempted yet' (*Paradise Lost*, i. 16) we meet the weakly concessive word, 'settle' (almost as in 'settle for'):

> I settle on some British theme, some old
> Romantic tale by Milton left unsung   (179–80)

The groves of chivalry, Mithridates, Sertorius, Dominique de Gourges, Gustavus Vasa, Wallace, and—most desperate of all—'some philosophic song' (230) follow in lugubrious procession—all poems never written, never to be written.

Not only is this a narrative of failure, but, to an embarrassing
degree, the failure is enacted before our eyes. The poem, as it
recounts its inability to kindle, seems to be dying on the page.
*But then Wordsworth remembers the stream, that flowed behind his
father's house:*

> Was it for this
> That one, the fairest of all rivers, loved
> To blend his murmers with my nurse's song,
> And from his alder shades and rocky falls,
> And from his fords and shallows, sent a voice
> That flowed along my dreams? (271–6)

With water comes life. The poetry begins to sing in our ears.
The very prepositions—especially 'along'—are vital. The work
itself is surprised by joy, taken unawares, this time not by a false
present but by a real origin. We have found at last the authentic
Muse; as in *Lycidas*, not wind but water is the bearer of
imaginative renewal. The transitional phrase, 'Was it for this?' is
superb. Instead of a strenuous, implausible optimism we have a
wondering incomprehension: the river flowing along my
dreams *cannot* have been leading towards, as its proper issue,
this ramshackle, literary disarray. This time the sheer goodness
of the remembered stream is not a product of will but is on the
contrary so manifestly and simply itself as to proclaim its
incompatibility with all that has gone before. Then, after this
brief moment of direct evocation, the poem flows with the
stream. We are admitted to the long glories of *The Prelude*:

> Oh, many a time have I, a five years child,
> A naked boy, in one delightful rill,
> A little mill-race severed from his stream,
> Made one long bathing of a summer's day,
> Basked in the sun, and plunged, and basked again,
> Alternate, all a summer's day, or coursed
> Over the sandy fields, leaping through groves
> Of yellow grunsel; or, when crag and hill,
> The woods, and distant Skiddaw's lofty height,
> Were bronzed with a deep radiance, stood alone
> Beneath the sky, as if I had been born
> On Indian plains, and from my mother's hut
> Had run abroad in wantonness to sport,
> A naked savage, in the thunder-shower. (291–304)

Perhaps the strangest thing of all is that all the groping towards the true source of poetry, all the tedious to-ings and fro-ings, were *added later* by the poet. For the 'two-part *Prelude*' of 1799 actually began with the words, 'Was it for this . . .?' Was Wordsworth propelled backwards into his preliminary meanderings by a simple, formal requirement: to connect the half-line, 'Was it for this', to some (any) preceding matter, to complete the metre? Or are the lines the oddly inflated product of a formal anxiety, of a sense that a thirteen-book poem (as distinct from a two-book poem) must have an elaborate introduction? Or did Wordsworth come to feel that the reader must be made to suffer, as he had suffered, the full, protracted travail of the poem's inception?

THE MUSE AND THE DEAD SELF

Is the inspiration of *The Prelude* internal or external to the poet? The question has become almost impossible to answer. The river leads us to the blazing image of the boy Wordsworth, the 'naked savage, in the thunder-shower'. Once again we are almost forced to say that Wordsworth's Muse turns out to be his own childhood self, which is as much as to say, his dead self. The child is father to the poem . . .

> So wide appears
> The vacancy between me and those days
> Which yet have such self-presence in my mind
> That musing on them, often do I seem
> Two consciousnesses, conscious of myself
> And of some other being   (ii. 28–32)

In the 1850 version Wordsworth gave an upper case 'B' to 'being'. The line thus altered will suggest to some readers the idea of God—as a kind of Berkeleian guarantor, whose ever-watchful presence might serve to heal all solipsistic fears concerning the continuous reality of the external world. Even if we accept this interpretation it would be wrong, I suspect, to use it as a retrospective gloss on the 1805 version. There 'being' with a lower case 'b' naturally suggests the conscious existence of another human subject. Moreover, the sentence preceding this point directs us to the idea of an interior division in

Wordsworth himself. The locus of fertilizing memory is now someone other than the poet, and yet its name is William Wordsworth.[27]

In *Lycidas* Milton mourns Edward King. But, by an undistributed middle common in the operations of the imagination, Edward King becomes first the Poet and then, somehow, Milton himself. At the very end of the poem he becomes, most mysteriously of all, the genius of the shore. *Genius* in Latin can be a tutelary spirit accompanying a person through life or a spirit of place (*genius loci*)—or else some inborn talent which is yet thought of as a gift (each term as we come to it—'talent', 'gift'—exhibits the same problematic tension between the autonomous and the extrinsic). In *Lycidas* the extreme assimilation to the poets' egoistic genius is diffused at the end, when the spirit is left haunting the shore.

Wordsworth's poem, 'There Was a Boy', is a much simpler elegy than *Lycidas*:

> There was a Boy; ye knew him well, ye cliffs
> And islands of Winander!—Many a time
> At evening, when the earliest stars began
> To move along the edges of the hills,
> Rising or setting, would he stand alone,
> Beneath the trees, or by the glimmering lake;
> And there, with fingers interwoven, both hands
> Pressed closely palm to palm and to his mouth
> Uplifted, he as through an instrument,
> Blew mimic hootings to the silent owls   (1–10)

This boy, Wordsworth tells us, died before he was twelve. The poem ends with the poet standing in the churchyard, looking at his grave. But we can tell, as soon as we come to the interlaced fingers—so clearly an *experience*, remembered from the inside—that the boy is Wordsworth. The biographical scholars' quest for the 'dead Hawkshead school friend' is wholly misconceived. The earliest manuscript drafts of this poem are written in the first person.

[27] It is difficult to be sure when the upper case 'B' first appeared. Stephen Gill, in a letter, suggests that it was in or around the year 1817, but adds that there is a possibility that it can be found as a reading in one of the alternative fair-copy manuscripts of 1805–6 (photographs not yet available in the Cornell Wordsworth series).

The poem was written in 1798 and appears in the earliest manuscripts of the two-part *Prelude*. Wordsworth then published the lines as a separate poem in the second (1800) edition of *Lyrical Ballads*. Thereafter the lines reappear in Book V of *The Prelude* (389 f.) Lines such as

> Then, sometimes in that silence, while he hung
> Listening, a gentle shock of mild surprise
> Has carried far into his heart the voice
> Of mountain torrents; or the visible scene
> Would enter unawares into his mind
> With all its solemn imagery, its rocks,
> Its woods, and that uncertain heaven received
> Into the bosom of the steady lake   (18–25)

are evidently continuous with passages descriptive of Wordsworth's own boyhood, so that it is slightly disconcerting to discover that in *The Prelude* too the boy is made to die. One suspects that there is a greater truth in this fictitious death than in the pretence elsewhere offered in Wordsworth's poetry of a successfully recovered vision. The old self is gone for ever, though its ghost inspires the poem. *O temps, suspends ton vol!*

All of this is curiously pre-echoed in Gray's *Elegy written in a Country Churchyard* (it may be that the *Elegy* is deliberately evoked in the opening of *The Prelude* in 'the homebound labourer' (1850, 101)—compare Gray's 'The ploughman homeward plods'). The dead poet of the *Elegy* is a sort of *genius loci*, glimpsed (like Arnold's scholar gypsy a century later) in the landscape:

> For thee who, mindful of the unhonoured dead,
> Dost in these lines their artless tale relate;
> If chance, by lonely Contemplation led,
> Some kindred spirit shall inquire thy fate,
>
> Haply some hoary-headed swain may say,
> Oft have we seen him at the peep of dawn
>   .   .   .   .
> 'One morn I missed him on the customed hill,
> 'Along the heath and near his favourite tree;
> 'Another came, nor yet beside the rill,
> Nor up the hill, nor at the wood was he;

'The next with dirges due in sad array
'Slow through the church-way path we saw him borne.
'Approach and read (for thou can'st read) the lay,
Graved on the stone beneath yon aged thorn.'

THE EPITAPH

Here rests his head upon the lap of earth
A youth to fortune and to fame unknown
Fair Science frowned not on his humble birth
And Melancholy marked him for her own

(93–8, 109–20)[28]

Despite the appearance of eighteenth-century marmoreal clarity the thought is strangely involved. Who or what is addressed by the word 'thee' in the first line quoted? Roger Lonsdale observes that in the four stanzas which form the conclusion of the poem in the Eton manuscript draft the poet clearly addresses himself (as he manifestly does, in all versions, at the beginning), and that there is no reason to suppose that he is referring to anyone else in the published, revised version.[29]

If that is so, we are forced to infer that the poet goes on to imagine a future time at which someone like himself will come to the churchyard and ask about Thomas Gray, whereupon some rustic will obligingly explain how he (Gray) was to be seen

Hard by yon wood, now smiling as in scorn,
Muttering his wayward fancies he would rove   (105–6)

Here, uncannily, Gray exactly anticipates the way rustics described Wordsworth after his death, as muttering to himself as he walked.[30] He then imagines the sympathetic visitor being shown his (Thomas Gray's) tombstone. This elaborate supposition is in itself confusing, yet the experience of reading these lines is more confusing still. By a type of ambiguity which Empson never defined, we intuit that Gray is describing himself

---

[28] In *The Poems of Thomas Gray, William Collins, Oliver Goldsmith*, ed. Roger Lonsdale (London: Longman, 1969), 135–9.

[29] Ibid. 135.

[30] See Emile Legouis, *The Early Life of William Wordsworth, 1770–1798*, trans. J. W. Matthews, with a new introduction by Nicholas Roe (London: Libris, 1988), 372.

and, simultaneously, some other dead poet. By the time we reach the 'epitaph' the ghost seems to be separating itself from Gray. The poet's career was quiet enough, but 'a youth to fortune and to fame unknown' seems to connote an altogether lower degree of obscurity. Nor could anyone say of Gray that fair Science (knowledge) frowned not on his birth. The poet's double is becoming an antitype: ignorance as against his knowledge, nature as against his art, a separated self which has successfully merged with the heaving earth of the churchyard, with the landscape through which the poet moved darkling, but still alienated.

The sympathetic visitor, glassed in, as it were, with literacy, is invited by the rustic to read ('for thou canst read') what is written on the stone. Gray who at the beginning of the poem was left alone with the darkness and the dead now looks forward, with a kind of future-nostalgia, to his own passing, as it will be recounted long afterwards. If one can get behind the obviously very different diction, one can discern here a strong affinity with Wordsworth. This should not be fundamentally surprising in a poet who could write of children playing,

> Still as they run they look behind,
> They hear a voice in every wind,
> And snatch a fearful joy.[31]

Both Gray and Wordsworth (as Hartman saw) are vexed by a latent antagonism between art and nature. For an ancient Stoic no such opposition could appear, because to the Stoic 'nature' means 'That Which Is, considered as an ordered whole'. For the Romantic 'nature' means 'that which exists, before the meddlesome, distorting intellect of men has interfered'. The ancient roots of *this* conception of nature lie not in Stoicism but in pastoral. That is why nature for the Romantic is green. For the Stoic, to follow nature and to follow reason are one and the same thing. For the post-pastoral Romantic they are opposites. According to pastoral usage the proper antithesis of nature is art, and art includes, of course, poetic art. The nostalgia for a natural simplicity or for oneness with nature is perceived by ancient poets as a haunting, poignant absurdity. Therefore, even

---

[31] 'Ode on a Distant Prospect of Eton College', 37–40, in Lonsdale's edn., 58–9.

as they celebrate artlessness, they are careful, through a kind of inverse honesty, to foreground the element of artifice in every line they write. In Virgil's Latin Eclogues, as in the English pastoral of Milton, the shepherds are given learned Greek names. The poet may place himself as an artless figure within the pastoral scene, as Tityrus playing upon an oaten flute, but the stratagem whereby the swain figures as singer or poet (Colin Clout) is touchingly, consciously false.

In this we may see the creation of pathos of distance, as it applies to art. Pastoral was born in Alexandria, perhaps the first western city which was palpably too large. So far from being a form natural to real shepherds, it was made for city-dwellers who remembered, or thought they remembered, a greener, simpler existence. The poet within the poem, the swain, is therefore indeed the double of the poet writing, but he is a double with a difference. He cannot see the irremediably literary, conscious, urban, artful, real poet, who gazes at *him* so hungrily. The sense of literary art as a dark obverse to the world of nature is unknown to Homer. The huge poem which the Muse-led bard enters is itself part of the natural world. With pastoral is born an idea from which we have never since escaped: that the long triumph of verbal art somehow extends the kingdom of death. Virgil, who wrote pastoral before he wrote epic, projects this anxiety into his *Aeneid*, when Aeneas brings an unneeded rule of law to the Arcadian Kingdom of Evander.

Wordsworth in the Preface to *Lyrical Ballads* seems seriously to have hoped for something which all ancient poets knew to be impossible, an inartificial art, a poetry in which Nature might appear, at last, in her own dress. The poet, he affirms, is 'a man speaking to men'.[32] But anxiety swiftly reinvades as soon as the real poetry begins. Wordsworth re-enacts, in an intensely personal mode, the poignant doubling of pastoral. Unparadised from his childhood unity with nature, he can still be energized by what is in essence a cruel trick. Because art is the opposite of nature, *qua* artist he is plunged in solitude. The very separateness of nature can consequently form the now problematic matter of his poetry. Nature is now no longer simply 'the

---

[32] Preface to Lyrical Ballads, in *William Wordsworth*, ed. Gill, 603.

world' within which fictions are framed but rather something on the far side of a glassy wall, such that the state of communications between it and the psyche must itself be the object of an unsleeping solicitude. The trick is worked upon him when he encounters, in a deserted landscape, a solitary figure who seems somehow to answer his own isolation. Figures such as this also are 'doubles-with-a-difference'. Like Wordsworth they move in solitude through the green world; unlike him they are almost unconscious, inarticulate, and so capable of absorption by nature. The old Cumberland beggar, the leech-gatherer, the solitary soldier in Book iv of *The Prelude*, are all on the point of merging with the environment. In each case a sort of masquerade of social morality is dutifully performed by the poet, as due acknowledgement that such existence must be painful, but, equally, in each case we detect a kind of envy in the poet, a desire to feed upon their substance. Some say the solitaries in Wordsworth are like ghosts, but in truth the poet is the ghost. Like the dead in Homer, Wordsworth lacks blood. As in pastoral we have an answering self who *per impossibile* belongs to nature, as Wordsworth the child once really belonged. But it is a trick, because, as the ancients always knew and Wordsworth can never quite learn, no real fusion can ever be achieved. The growth of a *poet's* mind must be a growth into art, out of nature.

Romanticism is a dialectic. Its thesis is 'Defer to nature', its antithesis, '*Imagination* is supreme'. A little thought will show that these are virtual opposites. According to the thesis, the meddling intellect must fall silent; the green world of plants, animals, children, is supreme. But according to the antithesis, in its more extreme forms, mind becomes the maker of everything, a repetition of God's creative act. Often, indeed, this notion is arrested at the level of ethics and aesthetics: physical objects may exist independently but they are dressed in beauty and value by the human imagination (does this mean that God's prior creation was confined to the production of valueless chunks of matter?). At other times the notion is given full epistemological force; the world of objects is itself the product of the (primary) imagination (in which case is there now *nothing* for God to create—unless those same creative imaginations?). In such formulations it might seem that we have lost the root meaning of *imagination*, which always involves a contrast with perception, but that is not the case. As long as the word 'imagination' continued to be used, the idea of fiction, and therefore of an essential unreality, persisted. It is as if the Romantic poet were confronted with a terrible choice between nature and art. If you deify nature, you will revere perception and be distressed by your own articulateness. If you deify imagination, you will hate science and come in due course to hate sensation. Blake was clear that Wordsworth, at least in theory, was a thetic Romantic, while he, Blake, was an antithetical Romantic. Thus he writes, 'Natural Objects always did & now do weaken deaden and Obliterate Imagination in Me.'[33] Blake detested Newtonian science; Wordsworth, notoriously, was unwilling to join in the toast 'Confusion to Newton' at the 'immortal dinner' given by the painter Benjamin Haydon on 28 December 1817.[34]

The opposition stated thus may seem irreconcilable, but of course various partial syntheses or accommodations are possible. The imagination, though distinct from the sensuous perception of ordinary objects, may be reconstrued as (once more) a species of perception—perception, that is, of a transcendent realm (at such times the term begins to 'creak' and to give way to the cognitive word 'vision'). Keats noticed that sensation, in all its intensity, was too good a thing to be left to the scientists (who instantly drained it of all its richness) and therefore fought Newton's party, on occasion, under the flag 'Sensation' rather than 'Imagination'. Elsewhere, in order to affirm imagination and yet at the same time avoid blasphemy against nature, poets stressed the pre-rational sources of

---

[33] Annotations to 'Poems' by William Wordsworth, i. (London, 1815), in *William Blake's Writings*, ed. G. E. Bentley, 2 vols. (Oxford: Clarendon Press, 1978), ii. 1511. Cf. Frank Kermode, explaining Blake's perception of Wordsworth, 'The Wordsworth who matters was a maker of symbols—the Leech Gatherer, the tree "of many one"; these place him among the great artists ("but there is no competition"). The other, mechanistic, Wordsworth was the sane reasonable man who failed to see that natural objects deaden and was constantly abstracting from his vision, having misunderstood his own poetry,' *Romantic Image* (London: Routledge and Kegan Paul, 1961), 101. Even if we decide that Wordsworth ended in imaginative solipsism, we must allow that it is an anguished solipsism. For Blake there was no such anguish, because reality was simply forgotten.

[34] *Correspondence and Table Talk of Benjamin Haydon*, ed. F. W. Haydon, 2 vols. (London: Chatto, 1876), ii. 54–5.

imagination; the shaping spirit is itself a force of nature; poetry must come as naturally as leaves to a tree.[35] The mind may be a waste land, but the unconscious is green and fertile still.

In Coleridge's 'Kubla Khan' the language moves from a poetic of construct (dome, towers, circles) to a poetic of inadvertent powers, waters flung up from the depths. The idea of a river, flowing as it might be from the past, begins to serve as a healing icon of recovered unity. The stream that flowed behind Wordsworth's father's house is just such a river.

The solitaries encountered by Wordsworth may provide a brief recruitment, but the more they merge with nature the further off they are, the greater the distance between them and the watching poet. This does not apply to the child Wordsworth, who is a 'double' of another kind. He, the first of the 'two consciousnesses' (*Prelude*, ii. 31), is more securely linked to the second by the river of memory. As for the rest, each solitary as he appears may be, as it were, a walking poem, but can never be a poet like Wordsworth himself. But if poetry is in fact borne to the mature poet by a natural river, all may yet be well. Wordsworth, turning to the Derwent for inspiration, seems to find that he can derive his poetry from a natural Origin. In ancient epic poetry the Muse assists the *in medias res* opening, but in Wordsworth it is not so. So far in this study we have observed a tension between 'interventionist' openings, made by poets, and natural beginnings, the foundation of Rome, the Fall of Man, Genesis. But we have also seen in Virgil and Dante a gradual subjectivizing of epic: *Literaliter bellum Troianum, allegorice homo . . . allegorice poeta*, 'Literally the Trojan War, allegorically man . . . allegorically the poet'. By the time we reach Wordsworth the drive towards a natural origin can suddenly and amazingly fuse with the source of the poem: the *matter* of *The Prelude* is the growth of the poet's mind (for this poem is quite inescapably about the growth, not of poetic intelligence in general, but of Wordsworth's mind—that is why, for all its astonishing local insights—for example, at ii. 245 f.—as a whole it presents no theory of psychology). In this, Genesis and the *poem's* inception can be one.

[35] See Keats's letter to John Taylor, 27 Feb. 1818, in *The Letters of John Keats*, ed. H. E. Rollins, 2 vols. (Cambridge, Mass.: Harvard University Press, 1958), i. 238–9.

True, the poem begins to be written by a mature Wordsworth at a date long after its real inception in the green, childhood world. But it is the nature of a river to flow from one place to another, and so join the child and the man. The actual present, the here and now of composition, becomes in the circumstances little more than an adventitious, trivial impediment. Wordsworth's quasi-Chaucerian *in medias res* opening, so far from launching us upon the poem proper, proves to be an *ignis fatuus*, a false light, a pseudo-start to be discarded when the true source is found. In Homer the proem is followed by a powerful intervention in the story. In Wordsworth we find the exact opposite. The *in medias res* opening (complete with the false Muse of a '*present*' wind) is an essentially dispensable preliminary, to be followed by a proem. This proem, rooted in memory, is destined to grow and grow until it fills the space of the poem.

I have stressed, as I fancy Wordsworth would have wished me to stress, the quickening force of an originary nature in *The Prelude*. But (and here I am aware of the writings of Geoffrey Hartman) it is clear that Nature so conceived, even if borne to the mature poet on the river of inspiring memory, cannot be the ordinary, given nature with which the rest of us are engaged in daily life. Wordsworth's nature—one can go this far—is essentially non-present, ulterior in character. That is why she appears in brief visitations (trees and fields do not visit us; they are there all the time). It is usual to say that with Romanticism God became Nature. It is important to remember that pantheism can be a two-way street. Nature can begin to look, not just like God, but like *le Dieu caché*. The thought is one on which we should pause.

If one looks in an unphilosophical manner for the most obvious peculiarities of Wordsworth's writing, one has to say something like the following: where for centuries poets had sought *point* in their writing—brilliant analogies and cogent similitudes—Wordsworth seems to despise point. Where previous writers had found vitality in the joys and fears occasioned by common appetites and loves (money, sex, power), Wordsworth's principal anxieties lie elsewhere. He worries about his relation with nature itself, as if he, unlike everyone else, were only half in this world and therefore had prior, special cause for alarm. Others tell how they went to University and were there conducted into a larger, more exciting world. Wordsworth tells how he went to Cambridge and read some books, but he knows—and makes sure we know—that Cambridge is a truancy from the real excitement. All the action is in Cumberland. Society is all but rude, to that delicious solitude. The most active participation will come when the poet gets a chance to go for a walk by himself. Wordsworth is not the poet of love, or death, or war; he is the poet who goes for walks.

The walk seems at first to be a curiously English, parochial thing. One discovers on visits to American universities that one's transatlantic colleagues do not have the concept. It is, to be sure, a general Romantic phenomenon. Even as one begins to write, 'Shakespeare never went for a walk', one remembers that Romeo was seen at dawn, 'early walking' by himself (*Romeo and Juliet*, I. i. 123) and is at once forced to the perception that although 'amorous solitude' is Petrarchan, this swift presentation of Romeo is indeed a proto-Romantic episode of great significance in the history of literary solitude. Milton's *Penseroso* goes for walks and, again, the exception proves the rule, for here too readers exclaim, 'Proto-Romantic!' Most importantly of all, Rousseau wrote a book called *Les Rêveries du promeneur solitaire* (1782). In looking at such rare moments we are, however, attending to faint pre-echoes only.

Meanwhile there is nevertheless something which really is like the Wordsworthian walk and yet wholly and obviously of an earlier age and culture: Protestant peripatetic self-examination. 'I would advise thee', wrote Richard Baxter in the seventeenth century, 'to frequent solitariness'.[36] A little later he adds, 'If thou canst, take *Isaac's* time and place, who went forth into the Field in the Evening to mediate.'[37] Puritan autobiography, such as Bunyan's *Grace Abounding to the Chief of Sinners* (1666), exhibits very clearly the curious spectacle of a life occurring in ordinary historical time yet somehow disconnected from all the usual urgencies. Getting a job, having enough money, falling in love, marrying, seem hardly worth mentioning. Instead Bunyan moves through a darkened world which is

---

[36] *The Saints' Everlasting Rest, or A Treatise of the Blessed State of the Saints in their Enjoyment of God in Glory*, 4th edn. (London: Thomas Underhill and Francis Tyton, 1653), IV. vii. 8, p. 172.
[37] Ibid. IV. xiii. 1, p. 252.

only occasionally irradiated, as it might be, by happening upon a cheering passage in Scripture. Bunyan's 'Castings down and Risings up'[38] at the hand of God are clearly analogous to Wordsworth's at the hand of Nature. If one compares Bunyan's book (old-fashioned in its time) with an Anglican personal testimony like Sir Thomas Browne's *Religio Medici* written a generation earlier, it is notable that Bunyan's is the book which, for all its relative unworldliness, repeatedly fastens upon moments of actuality—spots of time—which sometimes bear a significance somehow beyond analysis. It is not Browne but Bunyan who tells how the tiles on the houses seemed to hate him, or how he gazed at the crows which had settled on the ploughed field, or saw three women in a pool of sunlight, sitting in a doorway.[39] This special combination of moments of sharply perceived actuality, inexplicably unique, charged with hope or fear, is precisely what is done over and over again in an ostensibly more naturalist mode by Wordsworth.

The link with previous Protestant writing is not, indeed, confined to Wordsworth. Coleridge's 'Dejection', with its story of successive alienations and its unsubduably religious vocabulary, is oddly reminiscent of a poem by another English Protestant, George Herbert's 'Affliction (i)'. But it is in Wordsworth that we find the most extended development of spiritual autobiography, into psychic (or psychological) autobiography. Even the meetings with strange, solitary figures can be paralleled, as J. E. V. Crofts found, in seventeenth-century Puritan writing. Ranter Coppe told how he met an old beggar in a field, 'a most strange, deformed man, clad with patcht clouts'.[40] Coppe explains how the Lord, burning within him, set his tongue on flame to speak to the old beggar. There is something irresistibly Wordsworthian about the dialogue which follows (vacuous verbal exchange attended by extraordinary excitement):

---

[38] G. Bunyan, *Grace Abounding to the Chief of Sinners*, ed. R. Sharrock (Oxford: Clarendon Press, 1962), 2.

[39] Ibid. 58–9, 30, 14.

[40] *A Fiery Flying Roll* (London, 1649), ch. 3 in J. E. V. Crofts, *Wordsworth and the Seventeenth Century* (London: Humphrey Milford, 1940), 13. For Wordsworth and Puritanism, see also Geoffrey Hartman, *Wordsworth's Poetry, 1787–1814* (New Haven: Yale University Press, 1964), and Vincent Newey, 'Wordsworth, Bunyan and the Puritan Mind', *ELH* 41 (1974), 212–32.

'How now, friend, art thou poore?'
He answered
'Yea Master, very poore.'
Whereupon my bowels trembled within me, and trembling fell upon
the worm-eaten chest (my Corps, I mean) that I could not hold a joint
still. And my great love within me (who is the great God within that
chest or corps) was burning hot towards him; and made the lock-hole
of the chest (to wit, the mouth of the corps) again to open, thus:
'Art poor?'
'Yea, very poor', said he.

Coppe thinks of giving him twopence, then sixpence, but he
has only a shilling and therefore asks the beggar for sixpence
change. The poor man has no change and Coppe starts to ride
away, but then turns back to tell the man to call for sixpence at
the next town, where it will be left for him. Thereafter Coppe
rides off 'filled with trembling, joy, and amazement'.[41] In some
way the whole passage is a heightened, concentrated version of
Wordsworth's meeting with the discharged soldier in Book iv
of *The Prelude*. Wordsworth, likewise, deals in a small-scale,
stop-gap manner with the economic distress and goes away in
an exalted state (though Wordsworth's state, unlike Coppe's, is
one of inner *peace*) (iv. 504). Crofts observes that both Coppe
with the beggar and Wordsworth with the leech-gatherer repeat
their questions.[42]

I have linked Wordsworth with the in-breathing Muse of
archaic epic, with the *in medias res* opening commended by
Horace, with the lost path of Dante's first Canto. But it is not
Wordsworth's way to register these traditional connections in
the texture of his verse. He does not parade learning but rather
mistrusts the whole business of accreted literary allusion. If he
has recourse to the Muse it will indeed be 'the meaning, not the
name' that he will call up. But there is one literary figure to
whom Wordsworth alludes continually in the cadence of his
enjambed blank verse, and that is Milton. Here literary
genealogy is confessed, and incorporated in the presented poem.
For, long before Wordsworth, Milton joined Protestant spiritual autobiography to vatic self-assertion. Milton after all was
not writing in the dawn of European civilization when, perhaps,

---

[41] Crofts, *Wordsworth and the Seventeenth Century*, 14.
[42] Ibid. 15.

the roles of poet and prophet were undissociated. When he joined them, he had to build bridges in the imagination. *Paradise Lost*, we have seen, is significantly analogous to *The Prelude*. It may be that *Lycidas* is closer still.

Lycidas, like *The Prelude*, begins, so to speak, before its own beginning, with the poet casting about for his poem, for his own voice. In imagery which strangely mingles Spring with Autumn, a 'harsh and crude' unripeness with shattered leaves and brown myrtle—'too soon' with 'too late'—the poet tells us how the time is wrong. Where the other authors of tributes in the volume for Edward King, wrecked at sea, get off to a brisk start with pointful, elegant openings, Milton's voice seems choked (though the language, unlike Wordsworth's, is majestic from the first word). But then the poem flows with the mention of water. The 'watery bier' (12) leads to the 'tear' (14), which leads in turn to the fountains and rills of that youthful time which Milton shared with King (24). Moreover water in which the forerunner-poet, the dead *alter ego*, was drowned becomes the water of poetry itself ('Return Alpheus . . .', 132) and at last of resurrection ('through the dear might of Him who walked the waves', 173). *Paradise Lost*, having begun with words of loss—'brought death into the world, and all our woe'—went on to tell the story of a triumph over that death. I have suggested that the transition from *Paradise Lost* to *The Prelude* is essentially one of deepened subjectivism, involving a still more radical relegation of the poem to the poet who is its source. Yet in *Lycidas*, some fifteen years before the composition of *Paradise Lost*, Milton went surprisingly far in subjectivizing resurrection, making it something that happens to the poet, to John Milton. It will be said that the poet rises again in *Lycidas* only through the strength of Christ, and that Christ is not Nature. All this is true, but Milton keeps alive in the 'orchestration' of the poem a classical strain suggesting not so much redemption as apotheosis:

> Where other groves and other streams along,
> With nectar pure his oozy locks he laves   (174–5)

It is this pagan music which will permit the strange transition to 'genius of the shore' at 183 (for already, in 'other groves and other streams', we are descending from the 'day-star' of 168). In due time the Muses make their appearance in *Lycidas* (15), but (as in Gray, as in Wordsworth) it is the dead self, the Double, who inspires the poem. In both the Puritan poet and the Romantic water is the healing medium of exchange, between life and death.

Coleridge, as he looked at Wordsworth, seems to have been caught between a mild embarrassment at his friend's lack of erudition, and awe before one whom he knew to be a genuine philosophical poet, one whose writing would transform the very categories by which we view the world. In Wordsworth the canonical line begun by Homer is significantly continued not by docile imitation but through a process of profound transformation. After Wordsworth we must move from verse to the novel, that is to a form which is still less anxious to remember its own generic prehistory. The greatest successor of *The Prelude* is not a poem but a novel, and so it begins, very quietly, in prose: 'Longtemps je me suis couché de bonne heure . . . .'.[43]

---

[43] Marcel Proust, *A la recherche du temps perdu*, 1913–27.

5

Tristram Shandy

Drunkenness is always improper, except at the festivals of the God who gave wine; and particularly dangerous, when a man is engaged in the business of marriage; for at such a crisis of their lives a bride and bridegroom ought to have all their wits about them . . . wherefore, also, the drunken man is bad and unsteady in sowing the seed of increase, and is likely to beget offspring who will be unstable and untrustworthy, and cannot be expected to walk straight either in body or mind . . . For the beginning, like a god, . . . preserves all.

Plato, *Laws*, 775e[1]

TELLING VERSUS EXPLAINING

I wish either my father or my mother, or indeed both of them, as they were in duty both equally bound to it, had minded what they were about when they begot me; had they duly consider'd how much depended upon what they were then doing;—that not only the production of a rational Being was concern'd in it, but that possibly the happy formation and temperature of his body, perhaps his genius and the very cast of his mind;—and, for aught they knew to the contrary, even the fortunes of his whole house might take their turn from the humours and dispositions which were then uppermost:—Had they duly weighed and considered all this, and proceeded accordingly,—I am verily persuaded I should have made a quite different figure in the world, from that, in which the reader is likely to see me.—Believe me, good folks, this is not so inconsiderable a thing as many of you may think it;—you have all, I dare say, heard of the animal spirits, as how they are transfused from father to son, &c. &c.—and a great deal to that purpose:—Well, you may take my word, that nine parts in ten of a man's sense or his nonsense, his successes and miscarriages in this

All references to *Tristram Shandy* are to the edition by Melvyn New, 3 vols. (Gainesville, Fla.: University Presses of Florida, 1978–84).

[1] Translated by Benjamin Jowett except for the last sentence, where I have substituted my own, more literal version.

world depend upon their motions and activity, and the different tracks and trains you put them into; so that when they are once set a-going, whether right or wrong, 'tis not a halfpenny matter,—away they go cluttering like hey-go-mad; and by treading the same steps over and over again, they presently make a road of it, as plain and as smooth as a garden-walk, which, when they are once used to, the Devil himself sometimes shall not be able to drive them off it.

Pray, my dear, quoth my mother, have you not forgot to wind up the clock?—Good G—! cried my father, making an exclamation, but taking care to moderate his voice at the same time,—Did ever woman, since the creation of the world, interrupt a man with such a silly question? Pray, what was your father saying?—Nothing. (I. i; New, i. 1–2)

We are now in the world of the novel, though far indeed from Proust's *A la recherche*. We have moved back in time from Wordsworth to Sterne. Hence a play of sheer intelligence is permitted which would be unthinkable in a major Romantic poem. Indeed I take this to be the most brilliant opening ever written. That is a bold statement, so perhaps I should add that the word 'brilliant' was chosen with pusillanimous care. I do not say, for example, that it is the *best* opening, the one having the highest literary merit. The opening of Conrad's *Nostromo* or the great, emblematic London fog at the beginning of *Bleak House* are both, in my judgement, superior to the beginning of *Tristram Shandy* in imaginative power, though inferior in— say—scintillation.

In these opening pages Walter Shandy, Tristram's father, is matrimonially engaged with Mrs Shandy at the moment when the first words of dialogue are given. The Shandys, we learn, have sexual intercourse once a month; the family clock, likewise, is wound once a month. The effect of this concurrence on Mrs Shandy (who is a little like Pavlov's dog) is that she cannot think of clock-winding without thinking of sex, and vice versa. Hence her inopportune question which interrupts not a speech by Mr Shandy but the act of procreation itself. Her question 'puts him off', as we say, at the moment of climax, with the result that his emission of spermatozoa is weakened. By the biological theory of the day a weakened emission meant a weakened child. Little Tristram, unlucky from the start, sets out in life, biologically speaking, on half-rations.

At a certain point in *Alice in Wonderland* the White Rabbit asks where he is to begin; ' "Begin at the beginning", the King said, very gravely, "and go on to the end: then stop." '[2] Sterne, notoriously, overgoes the ordinary primacy of birth by driving on, past the doors of the womb (and out again) to the crucial moment of conception. As he does so, his persona, Tristram, gravely announces that he is following the precept of Horace and beginning *ab ovo*, 'from the egg'. It is the nature of Sterne to put the reader on his or her scholarly mettle. We need, therefore, the *ipsissima verba* of Horace (the passage will be found to include the famous phrase, to which we have recurred so often, *in medias res*):

> Nec sic incipies ut scriptor cyclicus olim:
> 'fortunam Priami cantabo et nobile bellum.'
> quid dignum tanto feret hic promissor hiatu?
> parturient montes, nascetur ridiculus mus.
> quanto rectius hic qui nil molitur inepte:
> 'dic mihi, Musa, virum captae post tempora Troiae
> qui mores hominum multorum vidit et urbis'.
> non fumum ex fulgore, sed ex fumo dare lucem
> cogitat, ut speciosa dehinc miracula promat,
> Antiphaten Schyllamque et cum Cyclope Charybdin.
> Nec reditum Diomedis ab interitu Meleagri,
> nec gemino bellum Troianum orditur ab ovo:
> semper ad eventum festinat et in medias res
> non secus ac notas auditorem rapit, et quae
> desperat tractata nitescere posse, relinquit . . .
>
> (*Ars Poetica*, 136–50)[3]

These lines were elegantly translated into English verse by Philip Francis in 1750, only a few years before *Tristram Shandy* began to appear, but better for our purposes is the more ruggedly literal version by Ben Jonson:

> Nor so begin, as did that circler late,
> 'I sing a noble war, and Priam's fate.'
> What doth this promiser such gaping worth
> Afford? The mountains travailed, and brought forth
> A scorned mouse! O, how much better this,
> Who naught essays unaptly, or amiss?

---

[2] *Alice's Adventures in Wonderland,* ch. 12, in *The Complete Works of Lewis Carroll* (London: Nonesuch, 1939), 114.

[3] The text is that of the Oxford Text, ed. E. C. Wickham and H. W. Garrod (Oxford: Clarendon Press, 1901).

Speak to me, muse, the man, who after Troy was sacked,
Saw many towns, and men, and could their manners tract.
He thinks not, how to give you smoke from light,
But light from smoke; that he may draw his bright
Wonders forth after: as Antiphates,
Scylla, Charybdis, Polypheme, with these.
Nor from the brand, with which the life did burn
Of Meleager, brings he the return
Of Diomede; not Troy's sad war begins
From the two eggs, that did disclose the twins.
He ever hastens to the end, and so
(As if he knew it) raps his hearer to
The middle of his matter: letting go
What he despairs, being handled, might not show.[4]

We need to elaborate our earlier analysis (see pp. 26–7 above). Horace is contrasting the opening used by the ignoble 'Cyclic Poet' ('circler') with that of Homer's *Odyssey*. The phrase *ab ovo*, 'from the egg', appears in Jonson's version as 'From the two eggs', because of the presence of *gemino*, 'twinned' in the Latin. Helen, whose fatal beauty sent all those Greeks to their deaths around the walls of Troy, was hatched from one of the paired eggs provided by Leda after her cygneous coupling with Zeus (the other contained the twins Castor and Pollux). Horace takes pains to emphasize artistic order as distinct from the merely serial order of nature, commending the Homeric example. Just as Aristotle in the *Poetics* condemns the writer who thinks he can attain artistic unity merely by retailing 'everything that happened to Theseus' (1451ᵃ20), so Horace is fascinated by the *separateness* of poetic and biological sequence. *Tristram Shandy* is, on Tristram's part at least, a wilful act of reasserted innocence; the floating island of artistic narrative is to be joined to the sea-bed of natural sequence. Sterne, meanwhile, is conscious both of the philosophically doomed character of Tristram's enterprise and of the spectacular absence of august, ancient authority. That is why he makes Tristram cite authority with, so to speak, an *exactness of error* which is rarely met with. Tristram gets his Horace *precisely* wrong:

[4] Ben Jonson, *The Complete Poems*, ed. George Parfitt (Harmondsworth: Penguin, 1975), 359.

I know there are readers in the world, as well as many other good people in it, who are no readers at all,—who find themselves ill at ease, unless they are let into the whole secret from first to last, of everything which concerns you.

It is in pure compliance with this humour of theirs, and from a backwardness in my nature to disappoint any one soul living, that I have been so very particular already. As my life and opinions are likely to make some noise in the world, and, if I conjecture right, will take in all ranks, professions and denominations of men whatever,—be no less read than the *Pilgrim's Progress* itself—and, in the end, prove the very thing which Montaigne dreaded his essays should turn out, that is, a book for a parlour window; I find it necessary to consult every one a little in his turn; and therefore must beg pardon for going on a little further in the same way: For which cause, right glad I am, that I have begun the history of myself in the way I have done; and that I am able to go on having everything in it, as *Horace* says, *ab ovo*. (I. iv; New, i. 5)

Of course he immediately adds, with an admirable air of judicious concession, that this may not be *quite* what Horace had in mind. Notice that it is the ideal of exhausting the subject, of completeness, which dominates Tristram's thought (he pretends of course that it is the result of the reader's—not his—insistence).

The grand design is clear. Horace is taken, inversely, at his word. It is entirely possible that the *ovo*, 'egg', triggered in Sterne's mind the marvellous idea of beginning not with a birth but with the insemination of an egg. This is a book which really will begin at the beginning and march steadily forward, as the King of Hearts commands. Not for Tristram the ignoble confusion (Horace's 'smoke') of an *in medias res* opening—one which hurries the half-comprehending reader 'into the midst of things'.

But, if Tristram abhors the Horatian violence, what are we to say of Sterne? If ever there was an opening which bewilders the reader by plunging him into a situation which he does not at first understand, it is that of *Tristram Shandy*. In Horace's words, we have an abundance of *fumus*, of smoke, in our eyes, before the *fulgor*, the lightning-flash of understanding breaks upon our minds.

Sterne has contrived an opening which is *ab ovo* and *in medias res* at the same time. The trick is done, technically, by mismatching the major sequence of events (that which would appear in a summary) with the detailed mode of presentation. A summary of *Tristram Shandy* begins in a thoroughly intelligible manner: 'Tristram is conceived.' But the *reader* is dropped into a situation and a conversation which he does not understand for some moments. There are, after all, different ways of beginning *in medias res*. There is the epic mode, which is primarily a matter of action in the public world, and there is the mode which increasingly found favour among novelists, in which the reader finds himself in the middle of a conversation, or even someone else's private reverie. Spenser in the sixteenth century begins his great allegorical epic in a thoroughly Horatian fashion, with St George on his great horse already in mid-quest. Yet, as we have seen, Chaucer two centuries before opens both *The House of Fame* and *The Book of the Duchess* in a manner which can feel startlingly modern. In either poem the poet seems to be rather overheard than heard by the reader; we seem to have come, almost by chance, within earshot of a soliloquy which might have been going on for some time—not so much *in medias res* as *in medias sententias*, 'into the midst' not of 'things' but of opinions. Remember here how even before the first chapter of *Tristram Shandy* we are given the epigraph from Epictetus: 'Human beings are harried, not so much by things as by opinions concerning things': Thus Sterne's opening unites an ostensibly naturalist logic—closing the gap between writing and reality, orienting he map—with a violent disorientation of the reader at the level of discourse. The confusion is assisted, moreover, by a certain complicity of nature. For to concentrate one's attention on conception rather than birth is to be confronted with *pre-existing* persons and relationships. Meanwhile, the natural beginning of the infant Tristram was itself quite objectively spoiled by a spoken interruption. Sterne carefully explains that the spermatozoa inside Walter Shandy are themselves *homunculi*, microscopic human forms, now bewildered by lack of guidance from the 'animal spirits' (who bear messages from 'the world above'). We may imagine the *homunculus* momentarily dazed, so to speak, by the Horatian smoke.

We must allow that, long before Sterne, Rabelais's great book begins not with the birth but with the conception of Gargantua.

There is even some play with the tension between Renaissance fireworks and plodding, exhaustive biblical genealogy (the genealogy itself is actually given at the beginning of the second book, when Pantagruel's birth is described). But the robust coupling of Grangousier with Gargamelle is very different from the sad-hilarious impaired connection of Mr and Mrs Shandy (I am not persuaded, by the way, by the suggestion that Walter is not the father of Tristram[5]). The glittering multiplicity of microcosm and macrocosm and the equivocation on the Horatian formula are wholly absent from the passage in Rabelais.

The opening of *Tristram Shandy* is certainly self-referential, but there is one form of self-reference which, perhaps surprisingly, is not pressed. I mean reference to the physical character of the text as book. Later in *Tristram Shandy* there is, of course, a good deal of this in the way of black, blank, and marbled pages, rows of asterisks and the like. But we have only to compare the beginning of *Tristram Shandy* with that of, say, Pope's *Dunciad* or Swift's *Tale of a Tub* to see that, in this respect at least, Sterne's entry is remarkably unobtrusive. Where they, a generation before, put up a fanfare of bibliolatry, an elaborate pseudo-apparatus of prefatory apologias, epistles dedicatory, booksellers' prescripts, advertisements, testimonies, prolegomena, periocha, Sterne instead slips into the reader's mind, as it were, by the back door—*in medium librum* ('into the midst of the book')?

I suspect that there is a moral in this change of tack. Twentieth-century criticism is obsessed with self-reference. But it is almost true to say that Sterne was writing at a time when self-reference was old hat. The really fashionable thing was the novel, which must have seemed an agent of *nature*, driving before it in rout the ghostly armies of false wit, just as today formalism senses that it has nature on the run. It is commonplace to speak of *Tristram Shandy* as an explosion or send-up of the linear novel (an essentially self-referring model of explanation) despite the mild historical difficulty that Sterne was writing at a period at which Thackeray, George Eliot, and

---

[5] The argument is based on a puzzle in the number of months which elapse between the episode described in I. i and the birth of Tristram. See Melvyn New's edn., iii. 52.

Henry James had not yet happened, but Rabelais, Cervantes, and Swift *had* (the old problem of the eccentrics outnumbering the normals). It is really more fruitful, I suspect, to see *Tristram Shandy* not as an explosion of the narrative mode *from within*, but as dramatizing an act of invasion *from outside*. In this novel the serial order of *narration* is continually invaded by the order of *explanation*.

While narration naturally moves forward in time—'and then, and then, and then'—explanation naturally moves backwards: 'You can't understand Z unless you understand Y, and you can't understand Y unless you understand X.' The suggestion that Sterne exposes an inherent impossibility in narrative is misconceived. It may be said that stories can in fact extend themselves indefinitely in either direction. But in practice this has presented few difficulties. Tale-tellers usually get under way easily enough. 'Once upon a time there was a woman called Helen, who was curious about ways of launching ships. One day . . .'. There is no problem. It is further true that analepsis or 'flashback' is a narrative device with a very long history. As soon, however, as the actual narration of the analepsis is begun, the movement is once more forward. It is not just that chronology itself is naturally thus; narration also naturally follows the same order. Difficulty enters with the impulse towards *completeness* of understanding (remember here the words 'whole secret' and 'everything which concerns you' in the second Sterne passage cited). So Sterne becomes the novelist of the dash, of the uncompleted narrative sentence.

I think, replied my Uncle Toby, taking his pipe from his mouth and striking the head of it two or three times upon the nail of his left thumb, as he began his sentence—I think, says he:—But to enter rightly into my Uncle Toby's sentiments upon this matter, you must be made to enter first a little into his character, the out-lines of which I shall just give you, and then the dialogue between him and my father will go on as well again. (I. xxi; New, i. 70–1)

Technology has taken a long time to catch up with Sterne. Some years ago some of us, struck by the effect of perception through lenses on eighteenth-century novelists struggled briefly to discover cinematic qualities in *Tristram Shandy*. The enterprise was less than fruitful. Today, however, we are all buying video machines; we can accelerate, reverse, or freeze the action at will. Suddenly the analogy with Sterne's technique is perfect. It will be a long time before Toby can knock the ash from his pipe and resume his conversation. Meanwhile we are hurled, not only backwards in time to Toby's wound at the siege of Namur, but also laterally, into the synchronically relevant theory of hobby-horses.

Of the two modes, the forward-pressing narrative mode and the retrograde explanatory mode, it is the second which looks at first sight more respectable, more rational. Yet it is the explanatory mode which can be shown to contain an *inner* absurdity (as distinct from the absurdity arising from a deliberate mismatch of two modes). Here I remember a lecture on modern literature which I once attended. The lecturer explained that to understand modernism you must understand its history, its conditions of growth, what preceded it, etc.; to understand Z you must understand Y. In the seventh row some of us were laying bets as to how far back the lecturer would go. I think I staked five pence on the Middle Ages. In fact he got as far as the Ancient Etruscans. Such procedures of explanation are locally persuasive but globally doomed. At the practical level one will necessarily come to a place in a chain of cultural causes, say, where information simply gives out. How is one really to understand the Etruscans? They came, says Herodotus, from Lydia. We sense that the chain is disappearing from view. But a chain suspended from a vacuity offers small security. To take the chronological method to its conclusion is precisely to discover that no conclusion, no terminus, is to be had. Similarly, to press hard on the synchronic sense of meaning as context-dependent is to be thrown upon increasing circles, ever larger context, until one loses control of one's material. You cannot understand X unless you understand the context which alone confers identity and significance on X. But you cannot understand the context of X unless you understand its context, and so on. Therefore you cannot understand anything unless you understand everything.

Thus, in Sterne, an initial disorientation is created by starting the counter-flow of explanation before the flow of narrative is properly begun; the *inherently* problematic character of explanation is then permitted to loom in the background. There is some truth in the old-fashioned notion that *Tristram Shandy* is a kind of hybrid, a cross between *Don Quixote* and Locke's *Essay Concerning Human Understanding*. It is noteworthy that of these two primal sources it is not the comic work but the serious which exhibits most clearly the Shandean absurdity. Cervantes seems to have no trouble in beginning his work. The opening words are easy, comfortably sequential: 'At a certain village in La Mancha, of which I cannot remember the name, there lived not long ago one of those old-fashioned gentlemen . . .'.[6] Now hear poor John Locke in the Epistle to the Reader prefixed to the *Essay*:

. . . I should tell thee that five or six Friends meeting at my Chamber, and discoursing on a Subject very remote from this, found themselves quickly at a stand, by the Difficulties that rose on every side. After we had a while puzzled our selves, without coming any nearer a Resolution of those Doubts which perplexed us, it came into my thoughts, that we took a wrong course; and that, before we set our selves upon Enquiries of that Nature, it was necessary to examine our own Abilities, and see, what Objects our Understandings were, or were not fitted to deal with. This I proposed to the Company, who all readily assented . . . When I first put Pen to Paper I thought all I should have to say on this matter, would have been contained in one sheet of Paper; but the farther I went, the larger Prospect I had.[7]

Notice the general air of sweet reasonableness, with an underlying note of panic. The idea is that by moving back to a prior level, the sources of difficulty can be dealt with and a more rapid progress will then be possible. The phrases 'to make plain' and 'to make clear' are used over and over again in the remaining pages of the Epistle, together with the Cartesian catch-phrase, 'clear and distinct ideas'. But we all know what happened. Alps rose on Alps and the preliminary difficulty of clearing the way proved to be a task beyond anyone's powers. Instead of one, lucid page we have the vast, ramshackle *Essay Concerning Human Understanding*. John Locke is not like Sterne, because Sterne perceived and rejoiced in the latent absurdity. But he is very like Tristram. The *Essay* is in no sense a Sternean

---

[6] *The History of the Ingenious Gentleman, Don Quixote of La Mancha*, trans. P. A. Motteux, 4 vols. (Edinburgh: John Grant, 1902), i. 17.

[7] John Locke, *An Essay Concerning Human Understanding*, ed. Peter Nidditch (Oxford: Clarendon Press, 1975, see corr. repr. of 1984), 7–8.

work, but those few who have read it through know that it *is* Shandean.

The thought, once started, continues to dog the more reflective novelist. More than a hundred years after Sterne, Henry James wrote in the preface to *Roderick Hudson*, 'Really, universally, relations stop nowhere, and the exquisite problem of the artist is eternally but to draw, by a geometry of his own, the circle within which they shall happily *appear* to do so.'[8]

Locke remains the fundamental analogue. But it is important to remember that there is an overspill of anxiety elsewhere in the century, arising from this (originally philosophical) ideal of exhaustiveness. We can catch it in Samuel Johnson's preface to his Dictionary:

When I first engaged in this work, I resolved to leave neither words nor things unexamined, and pleased myself with a prospect of the hours which I should revel away in feasts of literature, with the obscure recesses of northern learning, which I should enter and ransack, the treasures with which I expected every search into those neglected mines to reward my labour, and the triumph with which I should display my acquisitions to mankind. When I had thus enquired into the original of words, I resolved to show likewise my attention to things; to pierce deep into every science, to enquire the nature of every substance of which I inserted the name, to limit every idea by a definition strictly logical, and exhibit every production of art or nature in an accurate description, that my book might be in place of all other dictionaries whether apellative or technical. But these were the dreams of a poet doomed at last to wake a lexicographer . . . I saw that one enquiry only gave occasion to another, that book referred to book . . . and that thus to persue perfection was, like the first inhabitants of Arcadia, to chace the sun, which, when they had reached the hill where he had seemed to rest, was still beheld at the same distance from them.[9]

Johnson's reference to 'technical' as distinct from 'appellative' dictionaries reminds us that we are in the century of the encyclopedia. It is likely that the recurrent use in *Tristram Shandy* of the term *Tristrapaedia* is not only an allusion to Xenophon's *Cyropaedia* (a treatise on the upbringing of a prince)

---

[8] *Roderick Hudson* (London: Macmillan, 1921), p. x.
[9] *A Dictionary of the English Language* (London: printed by W. Strahan for J. and P. Knapton, T. and T. Longman, C. Hitch and L. Hawes, A. Millar and R. and J. Dodsley, 1755), not paginated. Available in facsimile (London: Times Books, 1979).

but is intended to awaken thoughts of Ephraim Chambers's *Cyclopaedia* (1728), a work which influenced Johnson's Dictionary. A little further back lies Pierre Bayle's *Dictionnarie historique et critique* (1697). Diderot began his twenty-year editorship of the *Encyclopédie* in 1747. It is thus likely that with his coinage, *Tristrapaedia*, Sterne brilliantly contrived a simultaneous reference to the incompatible ideals of biography (Xenophon) and comprehensive information.

The notion of a world constituted by relations cannot but suggest structuralism to a sophisticated reader in the 1990s. The further intuition that this world of relations is essentially intractable, because no stable terminus of signification is available, then, inevitably suggests the Deconstruction of Derrida. But of course this idea is by no means confined to Deconstructionists. Sir Thomas Elyot in *The Boke Named the Governour* (1531) argued metaphysically that individuality is not opposed in principle to relation, but is rather a product of relation: without relation we have, not individuals, but mere unmeaning chaos.[10] In the fourth century BC, Pyrrho (the original Pyrrhonist) argued from relativism to a form of nihilism. If all our understanding of the world is expressed by relations, and no description is ever intrinsic to the thing described, we know nothing. 'No single thing is in itself . . . any more this than that. And so there is nothing really existent, but custom and convention govern human action.'[11] These thoughts are, in a manner, perennial. I propose to turn to T. S. Eliot, rather than to Derrida at this point.

Eliot expresses the fundamental theorem very clearly: to understand one thing you must understand the system in which it occurs, and in Eliot this notion is evidently grounded in a coherence theory of truth (as opposed to a correspondence theory) derived from F. H. Bradley. His observation in his essay on John Ford (1932),[12] that in order to understand any part of Shakespeare one must understand it all, may seem a harmless local observation. In fact the notion is wider. Indeed, it is of the

---

[10] In the edn. by H. H. S. Croft, 2 vols. (London: Kegan, Paul, Trench, 1883), i. 3.

[11] See Diogenes Laertius, *Lives of the Eminent Philosophers*, ix. 61; in the Loeb edn. with an English translation by R. D. Hicks, 2 vols. (London: Heinemann, 1925), ii. 274.

[12] 'John Ford', *Selected Essays* (London: Faber and Faber, 1951), 193.

essence of this idea that it spreads in broadening circles. In 'Tradition and the Individual Talent' (1919) Eliot had written that works of literature formed an ideal order, such that the addition of a new work always produces a modification of the whole system.[13]

Bradley's friend Harold Joachim argued in a somewhat similar manner that the mathematical mind was not left unaltered by the addition of the differential calculus, but rather that its 'entire character' was changed.[14] Some years later Bernard Bosanquet carried the idea further: 'The end or purpose can be nothing but the nature of the whole . . .'. Should contradictions arise in the course of this pursuit of the whole, he explains:

Within the world which constitutes the individual's being, the contradiction has in some way shifted its place, and this fact cannot possibly mean . . . an additional idea, tacked on, so to speak, without affecting the organized system. . . . There must have been, in principle, a dislocation of the whole system. . . . His world has been dislocated and reshaped itself.[15]

Neither Joachim nor Bosanquet is speaking of literature, but the structural affinity with Eliot's language is inescapable.

If we turn to the youthful dissertation on Bradley, we can find in Eliot himself the full, metaphysical generality. He begins with a (far from exact) quotation from Bradley: 'We cannot attend to several disconnected objects at once. We organize them into a single object.'[16] He then goes on, 'This I believe to be true, but what does it mean? That the world, so far as it is a world at all, tends to organize itself into an articulate whole. The real is the organized.'[17]

It follows that only the whole truth will do. Remember here

---

[13] *Selected Essays*, 15.

[14] *The Nature of Truth* (Oxford: Clarendon Press, 1906). 94.

[15] *The Principle of Individuality and its Value* (London: Macmillan, 1912), 118–19.

[16] T. S. Eliot, *Knowledge and Experience in the Philosophy of F. H. Bradley* (London: Faber and Faber, 1964), 82. Eliot cites Bradley's 'On Active Attention', *Mind*, 11 (1902), 1–30. This essay is reprinted in Bradley's *Collected Essays*, 2 vols. (Oxford: Clarendon Press, 1946), ii. 408–43. Bradley's actual words are, 'Apart from oscillation, and again apart from abnormal states, to attend to a plurality is always to attend to it as one object, and it is not possible to have really several objects of attention at once'. *Mind*, 11 (1902), p. 21; *Collected Essays*, ii. 431.

[17] *Knowledge and Experience*, 82.

Tristram's emphasis on *completeness*. Other things—local, particular things—are not separately real at all. As Richard Wollheim says,

[Bradley] rejected the Empiricists' view of reality and their view of knowledge. For them . . . Reality was the sum of particular events or objects, Knowledge the totality of true particular judgements. For him Reality was an unanalysable whole: and anything that fell short of this was a mutilation of knowledge, not either an instance or a component of it.[18]

Bradley loved to stand Locke's terminology on its head, and affirm that it is the discrete event of the empiricists which is truly an abstraction. Wollheim adds that the artistic analogy, which surely fertilized the literary criticism of Eliot, was strong for Bradley too: the whole world for him, he says, is not like a jigsaw puzzle but more like a work of art, to be seen as a whole.[19]

It will be apparent that Bradley, like Parmenides long before him, is a Monist. But Bradley's Monism arises from a reaction against empirical pluralism. Bradley employed against pluralism, first, a critique of the notion of a successful uniqueness in designation or reference[20] and, secondly, an argument from the interdependence of facts.[21] By the first argument Bradley suggests that uniqueness of reference can never be secured within a singular judgement and so the singular judgement can never so much as refer to a particular fact. This includes as one of its implications something highly congenial to both structuralists and post-structuralists: namely, that the idea of a specific thing or event, given in a form untainted by human mentality, uninterpreted by theory, is chimerical. This leads us in turn to the second argument, that from the interdependence of facts. Bradley's sense of the indefinite deferral of a satisfying terminus seems to me to have a strong affinity with the thought of

---

[18] *F. H. Bradley* (Harmondsworth: Penguin, first pub. 1959, 1969), 45.

[19] Ibid. 46.

[20] *The Principles of Logic*, 'Second Edition, Revised, with Commentary and Terminal Essays', 2 vols. (London: Oxford University Press), 1922, i. 41–113. See also the 'Terminal Essay', 'Uniqueness', ibid. ii. 647–58, and, for a brisk recapitulation, Bradley's *Essays on Truth and Reality* (Oxford: Clarendon Press, 1914), 234–6, 261–5.

[21] *The Principles of Logic*, i. 100.

Derrida. In *Essays on Truth and Reality* he writes, 'Uniqueness in a word means difference, and difference in a word means a quality',[22] and in *The Principles of Logic* he writes,

We are fastened to a chain, and we wish to know if we are really secure . . . The practical man would first of all ask, 'Where can I find the last link of my chain? When I know that is fast, it is time enough to inspect the connection.' But the chain is such that every link begets, as soon as we come to it, a new one; and, ascending in our search, at each remove we are still no nearer the last link of all, on which everything depends.[23]

Bradley is clear that we must know everything to know anything. As Wollheim says, for him there could not be facts such that we could know one fact and not know another . . . 'All facts are one fact.'[24]

COMEDY AS BODILY CRITIQUE

We are in the interlocked universe of an extreme coherence theory of truth. According to coherence theory, to say that a statement is true is to say only that it coheres within a system of other statements. According to the correspondence theory of truth, on the other hand, a statement is true if it corresponds to the real: 'The cow is in the meadow' is true if the cow is in the meadow. The interlocking universe of coherence theory is in a manner impregnable (Sterne, by the way, were he here, would bring out the sexual metaphor in *impregnable*). If truth were thus, no one could ever learn, knowledge could not advance. *One could never enter the system.*

The literary problem echoes the philosophical—no accident, since one is rooted in the other. Tristram cannot really get on with his ostentatiously naturalist beginning, because even that is fatally impeded by a potentially infinite train of prior conditions.

But this brings me to the turning-point of this chapter. For Sterne, quite simply, sees all this as lunacy. He perceives, so clearly as strikingly to anticipate, pragmatically, the observations of a Bradley or a Derrida, the indefinite and intractable field of presuppositions. But he never for a moment advances

---

[22] *Essays*, 263.   [23] *Principles*, i. 100.   [24] *F. H. Bradley*, 90.

this grand analysis as serious philosophy. The infinite regress which so fatally encumbers poor Tristram (not Sterne) has proved fatally congenial to twentieth-century readers, in some cases almost to the point at which comedy vanishes. Similar things happened with the Existentialists. If you are an *absurdiste* you tend to lose your nose for ordinary absurdity.

For Sterne subjects this lunacy of spirit to a bodily critique. It might be thought strange, given the provenance of *Tristram Shandy*, that it should contain no Pantagruel, no overspilling Bakhtinian carnival body. But this anxiety is misplaced. In Sterne it is the intractable, immensely physical world itself which figures as Pantagruel. The spectacle of Tristram's endeavouring to enter upon his autobiography is immediately exposed to a gross parallel—quite invisible to Tristram, but brilliantly managed by Sterne and therefore visible to the reader. Mr Shandy also experiences a problem of entry, after which poor baby Tristram makes his own uncertain and bedraggled entrance into the world. Matter is made to parody and belie form. A purely formalist criticism will discover, with a relentless inevitability, the formalist elements in a given work. In the case of *Tristram Shandy* this is both initially fruitful and finally mistaken; fruitful, because formalist tropes are developed in this book with an energy and intelligence elsewhere unmatched in eighteenth-century fiction; mistaken, because the comedy of *Tristram Shandy* is produced over and over again, by an unlooked-for collision with the material world. Walter Shandy, at a stand in his discourse, bites a pin-cushion.[25] Whatever you do, you must not deconstruct that pin-cushion, or the comic dialectic will simply evaporate.

We must allow, of course, that the picture is intermittently qualified (for, in Sterne, everything is qualified). This grossly material world is shot through with images of death and sexual incapacity. Moreover, one senses that Sterne loves the erotic incompetence of Uncle Toby, as a mode of innocence. When Trim sketches (with his stick) the delights of celibate freedom available to Toby if he does *not* marry the Widow Wadman,[26] we may begin to feel that in some quite fundamental way

---

[25] *Tristram Shandy*, III. xli; New, i. 283.
[26] Ibid. IX. iv; New, ii. 743.

Sterne's moral allegiance has shifted, from materiality to the play of wit, from earth to air. But such moments are not typical of the book.

Esse est obstare, 'To be is to block, to get in the way' is the old, succinct expression of an unrepentant materialism. Dr Johnson notoriously stubbed his toe to refute the idealist, Berkeley.[27] Sterne's way is to have his idealists bump their noses (or analogous, more disquieting parts of their anatomy). The indefinite frustration of intellection in *Tristram Shandy* is continually both echoed and opposed by physical blockage, of the most definite kind. The unmanageable ambiguity of the word 'Where?' is thrown into comic relief because the Widow Wadman is made to utter it in what is for her an urgently physical, real context: 'And whereabouts, dear Sir, quoth Mrs. Wadman, a little categorically, did you receive this sad blow?'[28] Her concern, you will recall, is that Toby's wound may have unfitted him for matrimony. Toby, delighted by the question, sends for a map, so that Mrs Wadman may lay her finger 'on the very place'.[29] Wollheim says that Bradley never considers that judgements are made in a real physical context.[30] Sterne, conversely, never forgets this fact. It may be that the word *obstetric* pleased Sterne because of its etymological hint of blockage in the very process of inducing passage. Certainly we as readers must never forget the physical character of procreation and birth. Socrates, with his celebrated maieutic technique, assisted the passage of others' ideas. Dr Slop is a man-midwife of another, more ordinary kind.

Some people have a taste for Bradleian metaphysics; others prefer Stephen Leacock. Leacock's memorial of his friend Juggins—'The Retroactive Existence of Mr. Juggins'—should be read by all serious students of *Tristram Shandy*. Leacock explains how he first met Juggins; someone was trying to nail a board to a tree and Juggins told him that he needed to saw off the end of the board before he did anything else; Juggins then found that the saw needed to be sharpened and, after that, that the sharpening file needed a new handle. The reader will by now

---

[27] Boswell's *Life of Johnson*, 6 Aug. 1763, in the edition of G. Birkbeck Hill, 6 vols. (Oxford: Clarendon Press, 1934–64), i. 471.
[28] *Tristram Shandy*, IX. xxvi; New, ii. 793.
[29] Ibid. IX. xx; New, ii. 773.   [30] *F. H. Bradley*, 66–7.

have got the idea: the process extends itself indefinitely. Juggins's retroactive malaise was not confined to practical activities; it spilled over into his intellectual life. He wished to study French but found that he needed first to master Old French and Provençal, and before *that* Latin, and before *that* Sanskrit, and before *that* Ancient Iranian. Ancient Iranian, however, is a lost language. Leacock tells how Juggins in old age began to look more and more like a small boy. At the end he writes,

So then I realised where Juggins' retroactive existence is carrying him to. He has passed back through childhood into infancy, and presently, just as his annuity runs to a point and vanishes, he will back up clear through the Curtain of Existence and die,—or be born, I don't know which to call it.[31]

The fable, terminating as it does in a baffled confusion of death with birth, is apposite.

I have argued that Sterne's comedy presupposes, again and again, a common-sense access to the physical world. This view of Sterne would appear to place him squarely as an ally of the new science and of Lockean empiricism, and as hostile to aprioristic schemes (always associated in the English mind with the continent of Europe), the enemy of Spinoza and Leibniz. It is true that Sterne follows his master Rabelais in attacking Scholasticism and the bizarre precisionism of the Roman Catholic Church, which fits our scheme well enough. But the overall picture remains puzzling. If Sterne is an empiricist why does he (on occasion) make fun of Locke?

The answer, I think, is that he comically exposes those elements in Locke which are *not* a matter of piecemeal acquaintance with material bodies, but rather essay some systematic universal understanding of the limits of knowledge. To do this *is*, implicitly, to expose a contradiction in empiricism, to show that empiricism really is (that which it affects to despise) a metaphysic. Sterne is, in fact, a Realist. This implied critique of empiricism can easily be mistaken, especially in the current climate of thought, for an espousal of some sort of

---

[31] *Laugh with Leacock: An Anthology of the Best Work of Stephen Leacock* (New York: Dodd, Mead, the 1981 repr. of 1913 edn.), 251. My attention was drawn to this by Lorraine York.

formalist coherency theory, but it is nothing of the kind. For Bradley the given, the particular, is an abstraction; for Sterne it is never so, but on the contrary remains his best weapon against the idiocy of theory. I am saying, note, that Sterne is anti-theory, which should come as no surprise to those acquainted with the tradition of learned wit. It is nevertheless remarkable, in one who is manifestly so good at theory that he can easily outstrip our best modern practitioners, before cocking his own materialist (or sentimentalist) snook at them. He never attacks Locke for being empirical; he attacks him for being an empiricist. Meanwhile he knows that in a very important way he and Locke are on the same side. There is no reason to suppose that Sterne's frequently expressed admiration of the *Essay* is not fundamentally sincere. Here perhaps Sterne has set a certain wheel spinning, the motion of which he cannot arrest. For if Locke's very hostility to metaphysics is itself a metaphysic, by like reasoning Sterne, in so far as he recommends the piecemeal application of common sense *as a general principle*, is himself a theorist. But this is one irony we are not invited to perceive.

As with Locke, so with the scientists. In the famous opening, say, or in the episode of Phutatorius and the chestnut, Sterne picks on the doctrine of animal spirits. He homes in, not on the new, general emphasis on common sense (which he consistently respects) but on a point of real, metaphysical difficulty in Cartesian philosophy, the point at which thinkers were driven to desperate hypotheses to account for the unthinkable yet ubiquitous interaction of mind and body.

For Sterne body is prior to spirit, matter to form. That is why *Tristram Shandy* is part of the history of the English novel, as *Rasselas*, say, or *Gulliver's Travels,* is not. When I say that *Tristram Shandy* is part of the history of the English novel, my meaning is almost the reverse of Shklovsky's notorious epigram. Shklovsky, as a good formalist, held that *Tristram Shandy* was *the* typical novel because it exposes all those formal dodges which comprise the essence of all other novels, the shadow of reference now frankly discarded.[32] I mean, on the contrary, that

[32] 'Sterne's *Tristram Shandy*: Stylistic Commentary', first pub. Petrograd, 1921; in *Russian Formalist Criticism*, trans. with introduction by Lee T. Lemon and Marion J. Reis (Lincoln and London: University of Nebraska Press, 1965), 25–57.

Tristram Shandy is a major novel because, though we never meet Tristram, we do meet Trim, the Widow Wadman, 'my father', 'my mother', 'my Uncle Toby'. They are, in John Bayley's phrase, characters of love. Sterne, as we saw earlier, nourished the genius of Dickens, but not for Shklovsky's reasons. There is an oddly revealing—almost a neurotic—sentence in Bradley's *Principles of Logic*, in which the Comprehender of the Whole confesses his almost desperate exclusion from ordinary reality: 'We may never see [reality], so to speak, but through a hole.'[33] I once wrote that in Sterne the richly substantial forms of human beings gradually loom through the flying spume of theory, as the corner of a sofa, say, looms through the oceanic spray of light in one of Turner's 'late interiors' (at Petworth or East Cowes).[34] It may be thought that, if in Sterne we are restricted to glimpses and surmises, his case is like Bradley's; but it is not. Bradley's sentence gives us only the subject of perception, straining to see out from his metaphysical prison. What he sees, we are not told. In Sterne the characters triumphantly reach us through—in spite of—Tristram's pathological narrative stammer. Indeed he could never be content to write a work of, so to speak, inert empiricism, in a wholly plain style. Sterne the empiricist works, for comic effect, through a converse persona, Tristram the intellectualist. The comic mechanism is itself materialist. The moral surely holds as much for us modern theorists as it did for Tristram: 'Human beings are harried not by things, but by opinions about things.'[35]

[33] *Principles*, i. 70.
[34] *A Common Sky* (London: University of Sussex Press, 1974), 64–5.
[35] From Epictetus, cited on the title page of *Tristram Shandy*.

6

David and Pip

The Magus Zoroaster, my dead child
Met his own image, walking in the garden
(Shelley, *Prometheus Unbound*, 192–3)

THE DISCARDED FACE

David Copperfield, like *Tristram Shandy*, begins with the beginning of a life.

Chapter I
I Am Born

WHETHER I shall turn out to be the hero of my own life, or whether that station will be held by anybody else, these pages must show. To begin my life with the beginning of my life, I record that I was born (as I have been informed and believe) on a Friday, at twelve o'clock at night. It was remarked that the clock began to strike, and I began to cry, simultaneously.

We do not think of *David Copperfield* as a 'problematized' text. Nevertheless this opening is laced with reflexive ironies. The very words 'I Am Born' are a faint joke. It may be said that these words lie outside the book, but a moment's thought will show that they are quite unlike the (merely editorial) 'Book I' which precedes, say, Virgil's *Arma virumque cano*. Dickens's wit is already at work. It relishes the mismatch of a bland present tense (of the kind used in chapter headings—'In which our Hero is Suddenly Rescued'—and the like) with the queer, defeated intimacy of a first-person reference to the one thing none of us can remember.

Wittgenstein once wrote that death is not an event in life (*Tractatus Logico-Philosophicus*, vi. 4311). Birth, as Sterne

All quotations are from *David Copperfield*, ed. Nina Burgis (Oxford: Clarendon Press, 1981).

strenuously explained, certainly is an event in life, since it
is preceded by embryonic existence. But, for all that, birth lies
beyond the illuminated area of memory. It is notable that when
Wittgenstein made his curious observation about death, he was
thinking of the peculiar character of the visual field as it is
presented to us. We are aware of what we see, and yet, try as we
might, we cannot inspect the *limit* of what we see. There is no
more immediate datum of experience than the visual field, yet
none of us can say with confidence what shape is the picture
constantly presented to us. We may decide that it is certainly not
square, that it is round, say, or a horizontal oval, but this
account is arrived at obliquely, by inference, not from direct
inspection. Dickens seems anxious to offer a temporal equivalent of this mystery in the opening words of the second chapter,
called 'I Observe':

The first objects that assume a distinct presence before me, as I look far
back, into the blank of my infancy, are my mother with her pretty hair
and youthful shape, and Peggotty with no shape at all (I. i. 11)

The play on shape and shapelessness may carry a sexual charge.
John Carey observes[1] that 'shape' is a Victorian euphemism for
'figure' or 'breasts'. David's mother has what Peggotty has not.
But there is, beyond this, a further allusion to the unimaginable
idea of formlessness, to that which precedes all distinct creation.
Poor waistless Peggotty here signifies—with the help of the
word 'blank' a little before—primal Chaos. Meanwhile, here at
the true beginning of the novel, the three words, 'I Am Born',
have a nuance of absurdity and miracle simultaneously. The
following conceptual zeugma, 'To begin my life with the
beginning of my life', is wonderfully light, yet complete in its
perception of the difference between life and writing-about-life.
The chiming cadence, the apparent tautology, seem for a
moment to heal the wound of arbitrariness; in nature lives must
begin with birth, but writers, we all know, can begin anywhere.
     Thus Dickens, like Sterne, having given his opening a
biological basis and authority, for an instant at least subjects this
majestic naturalism to the critique of wit. It may even be that
Dickens had Sterne in mind when he wrote this (John Carey has

[1] In a letter to the author.

shown how Dickens could, on occasion, be taken over stylistically by Sterne).[2] Notice that there is a clock in *David Copperfield* as there is a clock in *Tristram Shandy*. Here, however, the paths diverge. Sterne's clock is, like everything else in the book, the occasion of a digression. In Dickens the clock *frees* the narrative; it strikes as the child's first cry is heard. There is something almost Elizabethan in *this* sonorous simultaneity ('When we are born we cry that we are come | To this great stage of fools . . .'[3]). The majestic progression of the novel has begun and will not falter.

There is a story that a professor of English telephoned a fellow professor and told him, 'I've just written the first sentence of my study of Dickens. It says, "Dickens was the last great English novelist who was also a popular entertainer".' His friend answered, 'Well, now, that's very odd, because I've just written the first sentence of *my* book on Dickens, and it says, "Dickens was the first great English novelist who was also a popular entertainer".' Can it be that Dickens was the *only* great English novelist to achieve genuine mass popularity? G. H. Ford goes along with Edgar Johnson's guess (based on the wholly reasonable assumption that a single copy was passed from hand to hand, read aloud, etc.) that one person in every ten read him.[4] Fielding reached many readers, but not as many as were reached by Dickens. *Pickwick Papers* easily beat Scott's *Waverley*.[5] Kipling came close to winning a Dickensian range of readers but still could not match him. The crowd which poured down to the quayside in New York to meet the ship which bore (perhaps) the instalment containing the death of Little Nell[6]— this crowd is a kind of Witness, as a Puritan might say, which is not offered to any other writer in this most literate of genres (for the novel, far more than epic or lyric, is designed primarily for solitary reading). The confinement, indeed, was too narrow for Dickens, who 'broke back' into reading aloud, to performance. He was therefore popular as Shakespeare was popular (as

[2] In his *The Violent Effigy* (London: Faber and Faber, 1979), 166.
[3] *King Lear*, IV. vi. 186–7.
[4] *Dickens and his Readers* (New York: Norton, 1965), 76.
[5] Ibid. 6.
[6] See Malcolm Andrew's introduction to Charles Dickens, *The Old Curiosity Shop* (Harmondsworth: Penguin, 1972), 27.

Homer was popular). Virgil, Milton, Wordsworth, Sterne, are coterie writers, by comparison.

If we fully understand the nature of this extraordinary feat, we shall acknowledge, against the trend of much academic criticism which favours the later, more labyrinthine Dickens, that *David Copperfield* is the great novel of the century—in Silvère Monod's words, 'le sommet de l'œuvre'.[7] This most moving of love stories (the love is that of David for Steerforth, who is beautiful and a corrupt bearer of death) is in a certain sense primitive. Moreover the primitive quality is directly linked to its enormous moral and imaginative impact, and to its sheer, statistical success. Its naturalism, its beginning from the beginning, is an unconscious rejection of Greek poetic art, a richly Victorian Philistinism which proves, against all the odds, to have *imaginative* power.

The *in medias res* opening is, after all, thoroughly integrated in the novel by this date. It is true that the formula, 'Two persons might have been observed, making their way up the white road which leads to . . .', was not yet securely established, and further true that Sterne's fireworks were largely forgotten ('Nothing odd will do long'[8]). In *Barnaby Rudge*, however, Dickens himself had already written a skilful *in medias res* opening which already 'feels central': the landlord of the Maypole Inn, after a brief, mildly insane, entirely wonderful exchange with a customer about the moon, allows his eyes to wander to a mysterious young stranger. The reader is made aware that the two *have met before* (we may think here of the opening of Scott's *Kenilworth*, with the stranger arriving at the inn at Cumnor). In *The Old Curiosity Shop* Dickens had actually essayed a quasi-Chaucerian *in medias sententias* opening: 'Night is generally my time for walking . . .'. And of course the eighteenth-century epistolary novel had made a species of *in medias res* opening entirely familiar.

'I Am Born' therefore represents an artistic decision, a special assertion. Aristotle, we remember, despised the poet who

---

[7] In his *Dickens Romancier* (Paris: Hachette, 1953), 247.

[8] Dr Johnson's (in the short run, cogent, in the long run, ill-fated) observation on *Tristram Shandy*. See James Boswell, *Life of Johnson*, 21 Mar. 1776, in the edn. by R. W. Chapman, corr. J. D. Fleeman (London: Oxford University Press, 1970), 696.

narrated 'everything that happened to Theseus' (*Poetics*, 1451^a). Dickens, we surmise, intends to do just that: to tell 'everything that happened to David'. This is apparent from the trial titles, jotted down by Dickens and later rejected: 'COPPERFIELD'S ENTIRE', 'COPPERFIELD<'S ENTIRE > COMPLETE / BEING THE WHOLE PERSONAL HISTORY . . .[9] Dickens, after all, is not Sterne. This time we find that the great exhaustive project of an embodied life is not perceived as a philosophical absurdity, to be foisted upon a deluded persona. There is a sense in which Sterne despised poor Tristram. Dickens loves David as himself. Dickens shares with Shakespeare an ability to register sophisticated nuance without impairing the elemental force of his design (in this way keeping clever readers happy). Thus instead of following Smollett's bald dictum: 'I was born in the northern part of this united kingdom, in the house of my grandfather',[10] we have instead the self-referential wit of the chapter heading. But the drive towards a profoundly naturalist opening is, as it were, stronger than the wit.

One effect is that a bridge is built between Sterne's almost suicidal, conscious 'crossing' of birth with intervention and Wordsworth's imperfectly articulate pressing backward to his own real origin for the springs of his poem. I do not mean Dickens needs to be thinking of either of these as he writes (it is clear that he is not thinking of Wordsworth at all and of nothing except perhaps the clock in *Tristram Shandy*). The author of *David Copperfield* is within an ace of autobiography. David is the young Charles. Modern editions of the novel rarely print its full title as it appeared on the first published monthly part: *The Personal History, Adventures, Experience & Observation of David Copperfield the Younger of Blunderstone Rookery*. Within the story the word 'younger' means merely that the principal character has the same name as his (entirely fictitious) father. But— because we become aware quite soon that 'David' is Charles— we intuit the meaning, 'my younger self': 'There was a boy . . .'. This impression grows stronger if one reads through the full sequence of trial titles. The word 'younger' occurs no less than eleven times; the equivalent, 'junior', twice.[11] In one

[9] See *David Copperfield*, 755.
[10] The first words of *Roderick Random* (1748).
[11] *David Copperfield*, 754–5.

entry we have '<Mr. David> Charles Copperfield <the Younger> Junior'.[12] D.C. is of course the reversal of C.D.

The effect in Wordsworth of a certain fusion of the poem with the real life of the poet was that the Muse or inspiring agent of the work was shifted from outside to inside the work; Wordsworth *narrated* the poem's inspiration and inception and this narration is then echoed in the story he tells of his childhood memory. This indeed releases the poem, but not in the clear, extrinsic manner of a Homeric Muse. The Virgilian or pseudo-Virgilian *ille ego*, 'that man I' began the strange movement of epic towards autobiography. The *distance* of *ille* ('that man'), combined with the *presence* of *ego* ('I'), which reverberates through *The Prelude*, also informs the opening of *David Copperfield*; 'that infant I'. The child is father to the man: by a kind of fond symmetry Dickens always felt, meanwhile, that he was father to the novel: 'Of all my books I like this the best . . . I have in my heart of hearts a favourite child. And his name is DAVID COPPERFIELD.'[13] The shifting of the spirits of origin to the interior of the work is likewise repeated in the opening of *David Copperfield*. Instead of Muses we have Powers (woman, witches, angels) Attendant upon Birth.

Neither David nor Dickens himself is haunted by solipsistic fear as Wordsworth was. D.C./C.D. is not tangentially related to his own body nor does he pass through the world enclosed in a bubble of mediating sensibility. Yet the curious Wordsworthian idea of the work killing the earlier self perhaps half shows itself in a strangely energetic joke. Dickens wrote in a letter to the editor of an American paper 'I may one of these days be induced to lay violent hands on myself—in other words to attempt my own life'.[14] Or, in yet other words, to father his favourite child by writing *David Copperfield*.

The Attendant Powers appear in the second paragraph, as the sound of the chiming clock is dying away. We may note that the function of these beings is to *declare* a birth:

In consideration of the day and hour of my birth, it was *declared by the nurse, and by some sage women in the neighbourhood* who had taken a lively interest in me several months before there was any possibility of our

[12] Ibid. 754.
[13] Preface to the Charles Dickens Edition, 1867. In Burgis, p. 752.
[14] Ibid. p. xvii.

becoming personally acquainted, first, that I was destined to be unlucky in life; and secondly, that I was privileged to see ghosts and spirits; both these gifts inevitably attaching, as they believed, to all unlucky infants of either gender, born towards the small hours on a Friday night. (I. i. 1, my italics)

The word 'nurse' perhaps carries, for those born after Florence Nightingale's reforms, associations inappropriate to this passage. It is likely that Dickens is referring here to a wet-nurse. Moreover, even if we allow the wider meaning to enter our minds, the nurse of the earlier nineteenth century belongs to an ancient underworld. Nurses were associated with loose morals and drunkenness (think of Sarah Gamp). It is no great step from this to the village 'cunning woman' or witch; Dickens, very precisely, makes this step for us with the words, 'some sage women in the neighbourhood'. He is writing of course, in a light manner, so that the entire passage could be thought parallel in its humour to Sterne's account of Tristram's ill-starred birth, launching him upon a life which would prove indeed to be a chapter of accidents. But, once more, the mythic force of the language is somehow stronger, or more subtly persistent, than the minimizing wit of the civilized narrator. The new-born child is elected to see marvels, the election being linked to his worldly misfortunes. In George Romney's famous painting for Boydell's Shakespeare Gallery, 'the Infant Shakespeare' (a noble babe with an already impressive cranial development) 'nursed by Tragedy and Comedy', is shown surrounded by variously weird women. Dickens, perhaps, is telling us, as Milton told us, that he is a Chosen Poet.

These sage women are replaced, as the story begins to unfold, by a stronger emissary, Miss Betsey Trotwood. Miss Trotwood, like the bad witch in the fairy tale, turns up at the baby's appearance in the world. Like Miss Havisham in *Great Expectations* she has been betrayed by a man. After the separation from her husband Miss Trotwood resumed her maiden name and adopted a life of inflexible celibacy. When she looks down at the childlike but heavily pregnant Mrs Copperfield, she muses, 'She must be well brought up, and well guarded from reposing any foolish confidences where they are not deserved. I must make that *my* care' (I. i. 6–7). Even such was Miss Havisham's aim in life. Miss Trotwood will admit to her house, we learn later, an adult male, but one desexualized by mild lunacy. Like Miss Havisham, Miss Trotwood is to take over a child born fatherless, to become the source of nourishment (though this is later curiously cancelled in the narrative of *Great Expectations*) while never being, biologically, the parent. Miss Trotwood, though always treated comically, is in some ways superhuman. Seemingly contemptuous of all softness and yielding, she is herself both feminist and feminine. Despite the constant barrage of 'male' signals, we never forget that she is a woman. Unlike the bad fairy, unlike Miss Havisham, she is entirely good.

She comes on a bright day in March to the house where David is about to be born and gives signs of her identity, as a good ghost should:

When she reached the house, she gave another proof of her identity. My father had often hinted that she seldom conducted herself like any ordinary Christian; and now, instead of ringing the bell, she came and looked in at that identical window, pressing the end of her nose against the glass to that extent, that my poor dear mother used to say it became perfectly flat and white in a moment. (I. i. 4)

The face at the window is inherently alarming (as Henry James knew when he wrote *The Turn of the Screw*). We may think of the women who shriek when they see 'a face at the pane' in Yeats's poem, 'High Talk'. Dickens himself had already caught this terror in the famous moment when Fagin appears (with Monks) in a window in *Oliver Twist* (a moment seized on, with good reason, by the illustrator, George Cruikshank).[15] Ordinary human beings (Dickens's use of the word 'Christian' hints a daemonic character in Miss Trotwood) ring the bell or knock at the door. She suddenly and inexplicably moves laterally and surprises her niece by appearing like a bird at the window. 'My poor dear mother used to say', with its frequentative verb, is a marvellously economic way of giving the moment a special status. This was something which was told and retold afterwards.

The effect of this appearance of an improbable Gabriel to a still more implausible (though oddly virginal) Mary is nothing less than to precipitate the birth:

[15] See edn. by Kathleen Tillotson (Oxford: Clarendon Press, 1966), facing p. 228.

She gave my mother such a turn, that I have always been convinced I am indebted to Miss Betsey for having been born on a Friday. (I. i. 4)

Tristram's birth was almost dissipated by distracting thoughts acting upon the animal spirits; David's birth, on the contrary, is convulsively induced by this maieutic spirit.

We sense that, somewhere in the upper reaches of Miss Trotwood, a tile or two may be loose, but also that this does not matter. We trust her. From the beginning to the end of the story she remains a bizarre but competent grown-up. David is born of a woman who is almost infantile in character ('a wax doll', 'a very baby' to Miss Trotwood, pp. 3 and 4). Later David himself, having failed properly to grow up, will marry a child-bride. Mr Dick, Miss Trotwood's friend, is capable of occasional practical advice (more by luck than judgement) but, alas, he sucks his thumb. Steerforth is always the glorious sixth-former, Traddles an inky schoolboy. Mr Micawber and Mr Wickham are both children in the world of grown-up finance. Mr Peggotty and Ham are natural inhabitants of a strangely salty Arcadia. Little Emily is, precisely, little Emily. Even Uriah Heep seems somehow like an evil boy, the school sneak. At the very least it seems that in this novel the children outnumber the adults. Even if we concede adult status to Mr and Miss Murdstone, Creakle, Rosa Dartle, and Agnes, they are not saving, organizing grown-ups, as Miss Trotwood is. Indeed, Miss Trotwood is the more grown-up for being seen from below, through the eyes of a child who is moving from initial fear to a grateful sense that she is a loving person and can be trusted. Her very contempt for the softness of Mrs Copperfield is, crucially, laced with affection: David's mother had a fancy 'that she felt Miss Betsey touch her hair, and that with no ungentle hand' (I. i. 5). She is, gloriously, more than a match for Mr Murdstone.

Meanwhile the most amazing image of all in the opening chapter is still unmentioned. David was born with a caul, that is a portion of the amnium, or skin-bag from the womb, still adhering to his face and head. Taking the cue from 'sage women', Dickens describes how this unpleasing object was hawked around, as a thing having some supernatural potency, a good luck charm:

I was born with a caul, which was advertised for sale, in the newspapers, at the low price of fifteen guineas. Whether sea-going people were short of money about that time, or were short of faith and preferred cork-jackets, I don't know (I. i. 1–2).

In Lucretius's *De Rerum Natura* (iv. 29–44), dreams and visions are caused by fully material *membranae*, 'skins' or 'films', flying in the night, cast off by real, physical bodies. A caul becomes shapeless almost at once, but at first it is moulded to an infantile physiognomy. In Jonson's *The Alchemist* it is, appropriately enough, Face, the ingenious servant who gulls Dapper by telling him that he was born lucky with a caul and is near kin to the Queen of the Fairies (Dickens, incidentally, rehearsed in the role of Sir Epicure Mammon in *The Alchemist* in Miss Frances Kelly's house in December 1847, after he had begun work on *David Copperfield*[16]). In Jonson as in Dickens the light comic manner cannot altogether defuse the power of the primitive material. Here, in grotesque form, is the prenatal face of David, sent before him as a fetish to prevent drowning by sea. The narrator David tells us that the old lady who eventually bought it did indeed die in her bed but that she never went near the sea anyway. We smile, but we know—or will know before long—that this is a story which will indeed lead in the end to a drowning by sea, and that David himself will be spared. The entire paragraph is funny but it is also eerie, not least when David describes how ten years after his birth, he was present at the raffling of his caul and felt quite uncomfortable (p. 2).

The dead face is sold in the market-place. Here perhaps, behind the wit (which I would not wish away) is the strangest transformation of the Muse—a grotesque terminus to its long declension: goddess, angel, fairy, midwife, dead self, caul. In Michelangelo's *Day of Judgement* the artist's own features are recognizable in the fearful skin held up for us to see. Greek myths have a way of living on in later writers who may be wholly unconscious of them. Dickens is Marsyas, the flayed poet, Apollo's prey. He has indeed attempted his own life.

Oliver Twist and *Nicholas Nickleby* are both earlier then *David Copperfield* and both begin with births. But these are not

---

[16] See Edgar Johnson, *Charles Dickens: His Tragedy and Triumph*, 2 vols. (London: Victor Gollancz, 1953), ii. 623.

intensely conjured: they offer pseudo-biographical information in an eighteenth-century mode; they do not essay the imagining of the unimaginable dawn of consciousness. But in *David Copperfield* all this is suddenly performed. This is a birth *ex nihilo*, where the nothingness is emphasized, mythically, by having a dead father (so different from Sterne's baffled but evidently living Walter Shandy) and a symbolic white gravestone (p. 2). Moreover, after a proemial first chapter, filled, as we have seen, with strange emissaries and attendant spirits, the second chapter directly addresses the glimmering upon infant consciousness of the first objects of perception. The Shakespeare play most closely concerned with such liminal consciousness is *The Tempest*: 'The fringed curtain of thine eye advance, | And say what thou seest yond'; 'What seest thou else, in the dark backward and abysm of time?' (I. ii. 409–10, I. ii. 50). The second chapter of *David Copperfield* has something of the same quality. Miranda, in response to Prospero's prompting, remembered the shadowy forms of the four or five women that attended her (I. ii. 47). In Dickens, as he turns distance into presence (*Ille . . . ego*) we have, wonderfully, whiteness before we have darkness: 'The first objects that assume a distinct presence before me, as I look far back, into the blank of my infancy are . . .' (I. ii. 11). Only afterwards are we given the 'dark abysm' in the remembered corridor: 'Here is a long passage—what an enormous perspective I made of it!—leading from Peggotty's kitchen to the front door. A dark store-room opens out of it . . .' (p. 12). The writing has the density and energy of lyric poetry. The 'long perspective' is offered first, within the fiction, as the natural result of the small child's eye level: that is what little David saw. But then, with the present tense of 'I make of it' we sense some reference to the adult art of constructive memory—even to the act of literary composition, for at this point the novelist casts a long perspective in his time-scheme.

Dombey and Son also opens with a birth, and this time there is a focusing on the physical detail, if not of the birth itself, at least of the immediately post-natal scene. But *Dombey and Son*, as the title announces, is about familial continuity, not origin. Indeed, when we compare the opening sentences, with their confident employment of the third-person form, with the opening of

David Copperfield, we may well feel that the move to the first person has an extraordinary effect. In *Dombey* the 'family firm' title is instantly incorporated in the first paragraph:

Dombey sat in the corner of the darkened room in the great armchair by the bedside, and Son lay tucked up warm in a basket bedstead, carefully disposed on a low settee immediately in front of the fire and close to it, as if his constitution were analogous to that of a muffin, and it was essential to toast him brown while he was very new.[17]

No gates of horn or ivory here. The opening is comfortably pivotal between past and present, father and son. Mr Dombey is neither a ghost nor a gravestone, but very much himself.

MODES OF SELF-REFERENCE

The time was to come when Dickens would write *David Copperfield* all over again, and call it *Great Expectations*. Evelyn Waugh once complained that novelists, unlike painters with their repeated Nativities and the like, are not allowed to have second shots at a target.[18] Of course, *Great Expectations* differs from *David Copperfield* in many ways, not least in having, instead of a primitivist plot-structure ('A life is a life is a life'), a plot of brilliant intricacy: the hero paralogically misreads his own life, mistakes his parentage and, for much of the novel, conducts the reader down a long blind alley of misconstruction. But it is like *David Copperfield* in its personal intensity. It, too, has a *potent* opening in which the 'I' is a child of death:

My father's family name being Pirrip, and my christian name Philip, my infant tongue could make of both names nothing longer or more explicit than Pip. So I called myself Pip, and came to be called Pip.

I gave Pirrip as my father's family name, on the authority of his tombstone and my sister—Mrs. Joe Gargery, who married the blacksmith. As I never saw my father or my mother, and never saw any likeness of either of them (for their days were long before the days of photographs), my first fancies regarding what they were like, were unreasonably derived from their tombstones. The shape of the letters on my father's, gave me an odd idea that he was a square, stout, dark man, with curly black hair. From the character and turn of the

---

[17] Ed. Alan Horsman (Oxford: Clarendon Press, 1974), 1.
[18] *The Ordeal of Gilbert Pinfold* (Harmondsworth: Penguin, 1962), 10.

inscription, '*Also Georgiana Wife of the Above*,' I drew the childish conclusion that my mother was freckled and sickly. To five little stone lozenges, each about a foot and a half long, which were arranged in a neat row beside their grave, and were sacred to the memory of five little brothers of mine—who gave up trying to get a living exceedingly early in that universal struggle—I am indebted for a belief I religiously entertained that they had all been born on their backs with their hands in their trouser-pockets, and had never taken them out in this state of existence.

Ours was the marsh country, down by the river, within, as the river wound, twenty miles of the sea.[19]

This manages in some degree to dazzle the intelligence even while it engages those simpler, more magical energies of the imagination which are involved, so to speak, with memories we never had. The first-person narrator enters the book by naming himself; his childish incoherence crystallizes in a name and, although we are simultaneously made aware of an adult world in which the hero is called, of all things, Philip Pirrip, it is the childish nomenclature that is to stick, through the whole of the huge novel which follows. Pip in his infancy names himself as Adam named the beasts in the infancy of the world. As the book begins out of nothing, so Pip comes out of nothing. Especially brilliant is the swiftly defeated connection with the half-life of faded daguerreotypes: 'Long before the days of photographs'. This presentiment of coming out of nothing is at once enhanced by Pip's orphaned state. Like David Copperfield, he is born, not from the living, but from the dead. His parents and even his brothers are stones in a churchyard. The stones, to be sure, are inscribed, so that the family is allowed to assume a spurious bodily existence derived from, of all things, the form of *the letters recording their disappearance from the world*. The Cartesian *cogito* was certainly far from Dickens's mind, yet its sequence is loosely followed: Pip first secures his own identity and then gives body to his fellow creatures. But the body so given is derived from written characters.

This flurry of knowing reference to written discourse is very different from the near-translucency of the natural beginning of *David Copperfield*. Wit frequently betrays some form of anxiety.

[19] All quotations are from *Great Expectations* (London: Oxford University Press, 1953).

Here one senses that some impediment is slowly rising, an unwanted degree of consciousness tending to block the birth of the novel. Release comes, as it came at the beginning of *The Prelude*, with the memory of a river: 'Ours was the marsh country, down by the river, within, as the river wound, twenty miles of the sea . . .'. Here, however, conscious figuration is probably more vigorously at work than it is at the analogous moment in Wordsworth. It is part of the point of this book about openings that we should, even when reading novels, be willing to think mythically, to understand that mythology is a kind of language. In that language we may say that Wordsworth's Derwent is Milton's Alpheus; it is the River of Poetry. Pip's river is the River of Life. The direction of the figurative reference is forward, into the ensuing narrative: the sea towards which the river flows is the Great World into which Pip will find his way. It is *intra poema,* within the fiction.

In Dante the notion of an *in medias res* intervention was transferred from the poet to his maker—a maker who sends certain beasts and then Virgil as guides. Dante the pilgrim was surprised in the middle of the dark journey of his life by strange emissaries. In *Great Expectations* we have a surprisingly similar structure. The opening appears at first to fall unequivocally on the 'natural' side of our 'natural/interventionist' divide. It is an 'I Am Born' opening, not an 'Under a lowering February sky a travel-worn figure might have been observed' opening. But *athwart* this comes, as in Dante, an explosive intervention from outside. It is done with deliberate abruptness.

At first, indeed, the pace is notably unhurried. Dickens gives us a childish solitary in a darkening landscape, peopled only by images of termination: a churchyard overgrown with nettles, a great space beyond, an almost Dutch landscape of flats, dykes, and feeding cattle with, at its utmost rim, the sea sending its wind across the marshes to blow upon Pip, who has been left alone, stranded in the encroaching dark. It is in a way like a mixture of Wordsworth and Gray ('leaves the world to darkness and to me[20]') but Dickens is not in the business of registering such echoes. Pip does not, however, meet with an answering self, a double who yet mysteriously merges with the landscape,

---

[20] *Elegy in a Country Churchyard,* 4.

nor do his thoughts have leisure (as it turns out) to muse on a dead, rustic *alter ego* who in former time inhabited this place:

'Hold your noise!' cried a terrible voice, as a man started up from among the graves at the side of the church porch. 'Keep still, you little devil, or I'll cut your throat!'

A fearful man, all in coarse grey, with a great iron on his leg. A man with no hat, and with broken shoes, and with an old rag tied round his head. A man who had been soaked in water, and smothered in mud, and lamed by stones, and cut by flints, and stung by nettles, and torn by briars; who limped and shivered, and glared and growled; and whose teeth chattered in his head as he seized me by the chin.

'O! Don't cut my throat, sir,' I pleaded in terror. 'Pray don't do it, sir.'

'Tell us your name!' said the man. 'Quick!'

'Pip, sir.'

'Once more,' said the man, staring at me. 'Give it mouth!'

'Pip. Pip, sir.'

'Show us where you live,' said the man. 'Pint out the place!'

I pointed to where our village lay, on the flat in-shore among the alder-trees and pollards, a mile or more from the church.

The man, after looking at me for a moment, turned me upside down, and emptied my pockets. There was nothing in them but a piece of bread. When the church came to itself—for he was so sudden and strong that he made it go head over heels before me, and I saw the steeple under my feet—when the church came to itself, I say, I was seated on a high tombstone, trembling, while he ate the bread ravenously. (i. 1–2)

The fearful man with the great iron on his leg is Magwitch the convict, who proves, before the end of the novel, to be the source of Pip's enormous wealth. Before we begin to understand—to 'interpret'—the convict it is important that we recognize his initial, terrifying unintelligibility. He pops up like the Demon King in a pantomime—or, perhaps, more accurately, like some ogre in a fairy-tale. 'What fat cheeks you ha' got', he says to Pip, licking his lips (p. 2); 'What big teeth you've got', said Little Red Riding Hood, conversely, to the wolf-grandmama (Robert Samber translated Perrault's fairy-tales as *Mother Goose Tales* in 1720). Quilp, the wife-biting dwarf-giant in *The Old Curiosity Shop*, who is a sort of nightmare Mr Punch pursuing a frightened child, little Nell, refers continuously to her rosy cheeks and, on introducing himself, generously explains, 'I don't eat babies' (ch. xxi).

Peter Brooks is right to say that *Great Expectations* presents at its outset the search for an origin; Pip consults the tombstones as an *authority* in the matter of identity, struggles to make the graphic symbol directly mimetic ('freckled and sickly'): 'Magwitch, the father-to-be, the fearful figure of future authorship . . . will demand of Pip, "Give us your name".'[21]

I have so far linked Miss Trotwood, by resemblance and opposition to Miss Havisham (both are 'man-haters', one a pseudo-nourisher and therefore bad, the other genuinely protective and therefore good). Structurally (improbable as it may seem) Miss Trotwood corresponds, quite clearly, to the convict. Both are irruptive emissaries from the future, blown in with the wind at the beginning of the book. True, the convict in *Great Expectations* does not appear alarmingly at the window, but we sense that he could easily have done so. Fagin, we have already seen, does appear at a window and Quilp, who has affinities with both Fagin and (through his potential cannibalism) with the convict, also shows his face at the window (this time the powerful illustration marking the moment in chapter lx is by C. Gray). The reader may be troubled by the wild oscillation of these characters between evil and good (for the convict will prove, like Miss Trotwood, to be good). But this ethical lurching, this violent latitude of possibilities is entirely appropriate to the child's world of mingled fear and dependence. A sense of the potentially daemonic character of goodness—that not only geniality but even charity may appear momentarily monstrous—is something which usually gets lost in 'mature' fiction. In the underworld of Victorian children's books it is strong—and strongest of all in Dickens.

There are resonances in the encounter with the convict which can grow in the mind only after the novel as a whole has been understood. Just as Miss Trotwood moves into the place vacated by David Copperfield Senior, so the convict in *Great Expectations* abruptly usurps the place of Mr Pirrip Senior and becomes a second father to Pip. We begin to see that *evoked*

---

[21] *Reading for the Plot: Design and Intention in Narrative* (New York: Alfred A. Knopf, 1984), 115–16.

persons in Dickens are not other selves but rather alternative parents. David is threatened early on in the story by a bad foster-father in Mr Murdstone. Pip, more obscurely, is threatened by a *second* convict, a shadowy double of the first but as evil as Magwitch is good. Magwitch, to frighten Pip, says, 'That young man has a secret way pecooliar to himself, of getting at a boy, and at his heart, and at his liver' (i. 3–4). With inadvertent prophetic truth he also says, 'There's a young man hid with me, in comparison with which young man I am an Angel' (i. 3).

All this forward reference is unavailable to the first-time reader whose consciousness is dominated by the apparent danger presented by Magwitch, by his desperate need and, in due course, by the fact that he is protected and fed by the shivering child, Pip. But a sense of these things can grow retrospectively for, as is the way with good novels, the opening continues to figure in one's mind as one reads further, and can itself be deepened and transformed.

Thus, when the convict turns Pip upside-down the whole novel (as John Batchelor pointed out to me) is foreshadowed. The moment is brilliantly rendered through a sudden assertion of subjective perspective: the church jumps over its own steeple. By a kind of Copernican revolution of the private imagination, the world is made to turn when really it is Pip who is upside-down. This is an exact mythical translation of the inversion of worlds, from blacksmith's boy to gentleman, experienced by Pip in the story which follows. M. Bernard Brugière has further suggested (orally, at a conference) that, in another fashion, we have a birth scene: the inversion of Pip is like the traditional turning upside down of the new-born baby, to ensure that it breathes and lives. The effect of this would be to link Magwitch, tenuously enough, with the maieutic references of the first chapter of *David Copperfield*, the nurses and sage women, Miss Trotwood inducing birth through shock and terror. Magwitch as a goblin midwife is not too wild an idea for the licentious imagination of Dickens but this one I cannot quite believe. I wish that I could.

I have suggested a connection between Dickens and Sterne and also between Dickens and Wordsworth. The first of these is intuitively acceptable: we know that Dickens read and enjoyed

the work of Sterne. With Wordsworth the case is very different.
There is little temperamental affinity and no sign of direct
influence as that word is usually understood in literary history.[22]
Yet the basis of the comparison is very simple. *The Prelude*,
David Copperfield, and *Great Expectations* are all large,
nineteenth-century books about their own authors, stories of
the evolving self. All treat childhood with a special intensity. All
convey a sense of a falling away in visionary or perceptual
power as maturity comes on. *David Copperfield* is even about
'the growth of a poet's/novelist's mind' (for David like Dickens
is a writer), but as soon as one avails oneself of this apparently
corroborative feature one becomes uneasily aware that the
argument is, at this point, weaker than it appears to be. For
David's writing is not at the heart of his story as Wordsworth's
poetry is at the heart of *The Prelude*. *David Copperfield* is
conceivable with David making his living as, say, a country
doctor. *The Prelude* is inconceivable without a poet at its centre.

It may be said, in the spirit of the New Critics, that reference
to the real, historically existent author is in any case an
extra-literary affair, which cannot properly figure in criticism.
Yet Wordsworth is so far a figural poet[23] as to make a point of
the reality of his poem's reference, in contradistinction to the
fantastic, artificial productions of others (he has little interest in
real*ism*, which is quite another matter).

The New Critics sought to draw a firm distinction between
the genesis of a poem (in the mind and immediate circumstances
of the writer) and its import. The former is 'extra-literary', the
latter is alone the proper province of the critic. Subsequent
Structuralist and post-Structuralist criticism had pushed this
thesis still further with its 'abolition' of the author. It may be
that the death of the author is one which, in the language of
'whodunnits', occurred in suspicious circumstances. Was the
author perhaps murdered, and, if so, who murdered him or her?

As the New Critical doctrine took root in people's minds it
was taken to imply that the kind of reading which looks for the
real author as somehow continuously latent in the work was
now outlawed, especially when this interest took the form of an

[22] For what it is worth (not much) Dickens admired Wordsworth's 'We Are
Seven'. See Carey, *The Violent Effigy*, 136.
[23] See above, pp. 34-5.

enjoyable detection of analogies between fiction and life. The most challenging of these was always the grand Miltonic analogy, inescapable for all except the most determinedly doctrinaire, between the blindness of the shattered champion Samson and the blindness of the poet, 'Dark, dark, dark, amid the blaze of noon' (*Samson Agonistes*, 80). For most readers, and perhaps for all readers uninstructed in critical police-regulations, there was an easy transition from such moments of poignantly intuited analogy to, say, the sonnet 'On his Blindness', in which the poet makes his own, real condition the manifest subject of his poem. The analogy with Samson can, at a pinch, be ignored, but by the sonnet the naïve New Critic is brought up short. Certain works of literature themselves break the *cordon sanitaire* of fictionality: they bend back upon themselves and *refer* (term of scandal) to the writer. One way for the New Critic to deal with such occasions is to affirm that, say, Pope's presentation of himself in *The Second Epistle of the Second Book of Horace, Imitated* should be treated exactly like any other fiction. The Pope presented in the poem is a *character*, utterly distinct from the Pope who sits there writing the lines, and to interpret the one by the other is a critical solecism, identical in kind with the antiquarian sentimentalism of books which 'interpret' Wordsworth with photographs of Dove Cottage. We sense in all this a certain straining for false clarity. When Pope writes about Addison it is wholly natural that (*a*) biographers of Addison should be interested in Pope's lines and (*b*) that readers of Pope's poetry should want to find out about Mr Addison himself.[24] So with the poet. Take the lines in which Pope contrasts himself with his father:

> He stuck to Poverty, with Peace of Mind,
> And me, the Muses helped to undergo it;
> Convict a Papist He, and I a Poet.   . (65–7)

The art here is emphatic. Life, as we all know, is never as neatly antithetical as this. But (and now the 'illicit' biographical interest begins to make itself felt) it is very striking that Pope tells us that Roman Catholicism is not for him the ruling principle it was for his (mildly persecuted) father and that he

---

[24] See Laurence Lerner, 'The Famous Mr. Joseph Addison', in his *The Frontiers of Literature* (Oxford: Basil Blackwell, 1988), 29–46.

should say that poetry became for him the most important thing of all—which would amount, from the father's point of view, to a confession of idolatry. By what right are such reflections forbidden to us? Our New Critic has tried in effect to get rid of the problem of the text which refers to the author by denying the fact of *reference*. Instead, we are told, what we supposed to be reference to a specific reality is simply another fiction, which is made—for fun?—to bear the same name as the writer. This thesis is, to say the least, implausible.

Often it is tacitly allowed that a general reference, as opposed to reference to individuals, is permitted. A poem can be about love, love being something which happens in the non-literary world, but a poem cannot be about Beachy Head, in a critically important sense. The distinction is inwardly weak. Beachy Head itself will turn out, if we adjust our focus appropriately, to be a complex aggregate, blurred at the edges, changing in time, just as the famous Mr Joseph Addison turns out not to be an atomic primary datum but a complex, fluid whole. It is entirely reasonable that we should move easily between these far from ultimate extremes. If a poem can be about love, it can be about Beachy Head, in the same sense of 'about'. Even Arnold's 'Dover Beach' is partly (though not importantly) about, of all things, Dover Beach. If 'general reference' is allowed, as distinct from some ideal, terminal, *pure* fictionality (never, so far, found) then reference to individuals—Addison, Pope himself—follows.

Meanwhile the Newer Critics who would brazen it out and deny reference even to the most general material make one exception. They will allow—indeed they will rejoice in—the reference of literature to literature. It is curious that few take the line that, where literature appears to refer to literature, what is really happening is that the reader is bemused by an eidolon: the invented, free-floating fiction masquerading as the (real) invention: literature itself. By parity of reasoning with the treatment given to 'authorial reference' one might expect a severe distinction to be drawn between extra-fictional analogies, transformations, influences of one work upon another (this being the matter of literary *history*) and the fictionally presented eidolon of a literary reference—now, of course, a pseudo-reference. The odd thing is that this really could be done since there is obviously fictional transformation in literary reference just as there is in authorial (in neither case, normally, is the reality simply mirrored). Earlier I granted that Pope transformed himself, only denying that in doing so he severed *all* links with preliterary reality. But by and large the Newer Critics have not followed this path. Real reference in the full-blooded sense is allowed, so long as it is to 'text', not 'world'.

One suspects that this anomalous concession is sustained by an elementary metaphysical confusion. It is thought that reference to literature is 'all right' because literature is not real; there is therefore no danger of the 'scandal of reality'; we are safely ensconced in the purely formal realm. But in fact literature in the sense required is firmly and unequivocally a part of ordinary reality. Poems and novels exist. The matter can be clarified if we consider dreams. Dreams are unreal in the sense that their contents do not actually occur. But the dreams themselves certainly do occur and, in that perfectly ordinary sense, dreams are real. Baron Munchausen never had a horse which was cut in two and then sewn together again. But Rudolph Eric Raspe's *Baron Munchausen: Narrative of his Marvellous Travels* (1785) is a perfectly real book which has now been turned into a perfectly real film. Therefore the critic who allows literature to refer to literature may find that he has let in the Trojan Horse: reference to reality. Textual reference can, of course, take the extreme form (and this, especially, receives applause) of reference-to-itself-as-text.

There are, then, two kinds of self-reference, textual and authorial. The first is allowed, the second not. Yet we live in a period of burgeoning literary biography. The trouble is that the burgeoning has happened, as it were, by mere displacement of pressure—as if the long-continued embargo has simply forced our natural interest in authors to issue, like steam, in another place. There has been little in the way of an argued reintegration of authorial self-reference.

Certainly the difference between the two can be striking. *Tristram Shandy* is strong on textual self-reference and therefore fashionable among theoretically minded critics, but *The Prelude*, contrariwise, is a source of obscure embarrassment because here the self-reference is to Wordsworth himself.

I will make no attempt to build on the link between Tristram and Sterne, though Sterne himself had fun with the connection. *The Life and Opinions of Tristram Shandy* is, quite simply, *not* the life and opinions of Laurence Sterne. Sterne signed letters 'Tristram' and 'Yorick' but we should not mistake the direction of the stream, on such occasions. This is fiction invading reality, not vice versa as in *The Prelude*. All the famous writer-to-reader intimacies in *Tristram Shandy*, when the voice seems breathily close to one's very ear—'Look, here's a blank page—*draw* the Widow Wadman if you like'—are *pseudo*-intimacies. A reader who actually drew on the blank page would be literal-minded to the point of near idiocy, would be missing the joke, which turns on the fact that this oh-so-intimate author is completely hidden from our view. Some pages back I asked, rhetorically, whether when a writer gives his own name to the protagonist, this is done 'for fun' (implying, of course, that it is *not* done for fun). But with Sterne the converse enterprise, the substitution of Tristram for Laurence, is exactly that. It is done for fun.

Meanwhile, however, there may be works which effectually and successfully refer the reader to the author without ever mentioning him by name. One such is Cowper's 'The Castaway' which described a drowning man in language which is somehow the more frightening for its very eighteenth-century blandness. Self-reference of the barest kind is afforded in line 3,

> When such a destined wretch as I . . .

Thereafter the poem is all about a shipwreck until the last two stanzas:

> I therefore purpose not, or dream,
>   Descanting on his fate,
> To give the melancholy theme
>   A more enduring date:
> But misery still delights to trace.
> Its 'semblance in another's case.
>
> No voice divine the storm allay'd,
>   No light propitious shone;
> Where, snatch'd from all effectual aid,
>   We perish'd, each alone:

> But I beneath a rougher sea,
> And whelm'd in deeper gulphs than he.[25]

The 'he' of the poem, though receiving the weight of narrative and imagery, is quite clearly a projection of the 'I', and the 'I' is none other than Cowper himself. There is no tricksy masquerade here. At first the reader may not understand how 'destined' bears all the terror of Calvin's doctrine of predestination to eternal damnation. To know this is to draw information from biographical materials. But that is exactly what the word means, in the poem. This is a poem about a death excluded from the love of God, about horror. To treat it as the presentation of a persona is, in every sense, an impertinence.

But the 'I' of *David Copperfield* and of *Great Expectations* is, in each case, technically fictitious. Such technicalities must be respected, since it is they that plant from the first the appropriate 'mental set' in the reader. Dickens makes it perfectly clear that neither work is an autobiography. In the bluntest sense of the word, we know that we are reading a *novel* when we read *David Copperfield*. But the 'I' of these works is not a locus of delighted differentiation, where the whole point is to stress the manifest distance from the author. Sterne's use of the inept, endlessly defeated Tristram is light years away from Dickens' use of David; it is indeed hard to remain unaware of a contrary pressure: 'This, reader, is really myself: no one but I.' Dickens writes not from an assumption of prurient, intrusive personal interest in the curious reader (though even that is not unambiguously outlawed) but from a humane sympathy with the anguish of personal memory. The artistic play of *David Copperfield* is not a play of *différance* but something much more dangerous for the writer: a play of similarity, of mere likeness.

With *Great Expectations* the matter is a little more complex. I have contrasted David in *David Copperfield* with the much more strongly differentiated Tristram. I might have extended the comparison to Conrad, whose 'teacher of languages', in *Under Western Eyes*, is strongly differentiated from the more knowing author (Marlow, Conrad's more habitual persona is much more weakly differentiated, though an interestingly variable factor of

---

[25] William Cowper, *Poetical Works*, ed. H. S. Milford, 4th edn. with corrections by Norma Russell (London: Oxford University Press, 1934), 432.

difference is present there also[26]). Associated with a degree of incomprehension in the narrating voice is a device admirably termed 'delayed decoding' by Ian Watt.[27] This device is employed over and over again by Conrad. What Marlow sees as 'sticks, little sticks' in *Heart of Darkness*, ch. 2, will afterwards be explained as arrows. In *Under Western Eyes* it is suggested that the entire story is unintelligible to the person telling it. The 'I' of *Great Expectations* is only weakly differentiated: we sense that Pip is Dickens himself. But *Great Expectations* is a spectacular example of delayed decoding. Pip is telling a story which, while it happened, was unintelligible to him. Indeed the plot of *Great Expectations* is fascinatingly double. There is the real story, in which a grateful ex-convict masterminds from afar the social elevation of the small boy who befriended him, and there is the pseudo-story of the rough boy raised to dignity by Miss Havisham. The story in which we are involved as readers for many hundreds of pages is wrong. The voice which gives us all our information misinterprets that information and we share in this misinterpretation. The 'deep' story, to which we come in due course, perhaps exposes a vein of gynophobia—for the men prove good and the women bad. Miss Havisham, grandly extending a macabre bounty, proves malevolent (though with a partly legitimate project of revenge upon the male sex). Biddy, to be sure, is good but she is not a strong presence. Estella really belongs to Miss Havisham and her fell designs, for the 'hopeful ending' is notoriously incredible. It is as if the wolf in *Little Red Riding Hood* turned out to be a friend and Grandmama an enemy.

But if Pip fails to understand the story does not this, necessarily, differentiate him fundamentally from the real author, who must, as artist, have a complete overview of the whole, a complete understanding, from the beginning, of the 'deep story'? A narrative which is misread to the reader by its own, uncomprehending first-person narrator looks closer to the 'tricksy' world of *Tristram Shandy* than to the clumsy-serious, infinitely moving self-exploration of *The Prelude*.

[26] See John Batchelor, *Lord Jim* (London: Unwin Hyman, 1988), esp. 46, 49, 84.
[27] *Conrad in the Nineteenth Century* (London: Chatto and Windus, 1980), esp. 175–8.

It ought to be so and yet it is not. There can be no stronger witness to the strength of the self-reference in *Great Expectations* than its power to survive the brilliantly duplicated plot. Throughout, the sense of a barely withheld personal identification is importunately present. And before the end Pip, unlike Conrad's teacher of languages, really does understand. It is not so very difficult to make sense of this, after all. Such a person may say, especially if he is writing about a previous self, 'I did not understand this, but now I do.'

It may be, then, that the idea of 'delayed decoding' needs to be reformulated. We need to know who does the decoding. The 'little sticks' in *Heart of Darkness* are in fact decoded for the reader by the narrator, Marlow. In *Under Western Eyes*, as we have seen, the narrator *never* understands his narration and *we*, the readers, perform the operation of decoding (covertly assisted, of course, by Joseph Conrad). If a further term in the series is desired, we may think of Golding's *The Inheritors*, in which an entire species, through whose consciousness everything is filtered, fails to comprehend what we readers understand. It may be said that the more firmly the process of decoding is located *within* the text the more the narrator is allowed personally to decode what *he* had previously misinterpreted—the closer the persona will be to the real author. And indeed Marlow, though demonstrably at times a 'limited narrator', is shrewd, sad, much travelled, as was Conrad. *Pollōn d' anthrōpōn iden astea, kai noon egnō*, 'He saw the cities of many men, and learned their mind' (*Odyssey*, i. 3).

There is in Dickens another kind of opening which we may call 'the scene-setting' opening. This can be of almost modernist audacity. Long before Hardy wrote his famous 'Egdon Heath' first chapter of *The Return of the Native* (1878), Dickens wrote the amazing first chapter of *Bleak House*. It is an opening which simultaneously sets the scene (in Lincoln's Inn, London) and erases it, in fog.

LONDON. Michaelmas Term lately over; and the Lord Chancellor sitting in Lincoln's Inn Hall. Implacable November weather. As much mud in the streets, as if the waters had but newly retired from the face of the earth, and it would not be wonderful to meet a Megalosaurus, forty feet long or so, waddling like an elephantine lizard up Holborn

Hill. Smoke lowering down from chimney-pots, making a soft black drizzle; with flakes of soot in it as big as full-grown snowflakes—gone into mourning, one might imagine, for the death of the sun. Dogs, undistinguishable in mire. Horses, scarcely better; splashed to their very blinkers. Foot passengers, jostling one another's umbrellas, in a general infection of ill-temper, and losing their foot-hold at street-corners, where tens of thousands of other foot passengers have been slipping and sliding since the day broke (if this day ever broke), adding new deposits to the crust upon crust of mud, sticking at those points tenaciously to the pavement, and accumulating at compound interest.

Fog everywhere. Fog up the river, where it flows among green aits and meadows; fog down the river, where it rolls defiled among the tiers of shipping, and the waterside pollutions of a great (and dirty) city. Fog on the Essex Marshes, fog on the Kentish heights. Fog creeping into the cabooses of collier-brigs; fog lying out on the yards, and hovering in the rigging of great ships; fog drooping on the gunwales of barges and small boats. Fog in the eyes and throats of ancient Greenwich pensioners, wheezing by the firesides of their wards; fog in the stem and bowl of the afternoon pipe of the wrathful skipper, down in his close cabin; fog cruelly pinching the toes and fingers of his shivering little 'prentice boy on deck. Chance people on the bridges peeping over the parapets into a nether sky of fog, with fog all round them, as if they were up in a balloon, and hanging in the misty clouds.

Gas looming through the fog in diverse places in the streets, much as the sun may, from the spongey fields, be seen to loom by husbandman and ploughboy. Most of the shops lighted two hours before their time—as the gas seems to know, for it has a haggard and unwilling look.

The raw afternoon is rawest, and the dense fog is densest, and the muddy streets are muddiest, near that leaden-headed old corporation: Temple Bar. And hard by Temple Bar, in Lincoln's Inn Hall, at the very heart of the fog, sit the Lord High Chancellor in his High Court of Chancery.

Never can there come fog too thick, never can there come mud and mire too deep, to assort with the groping and floundering condition which this High Court of Chancery, most pestilent of hoary sinners, holds, this day, in the sight of heaven and earth.

On such an afternoon, if ever, the Lord High Chancellor ought to be sitting here—as here he is —with a foggy glory round his head, softly fenced in with crimson cloth and curtains.[28]

---

[28] (London: Oxford University Press, 1948), 1.

Dickens does not plunge us immediately in the fog. He wants us to know first that we are in London. There must be *something* there (nothing less, indeed, than the largest city in the world) to be swiftly effaced by the amazing, obliterating consequence. So the first sentence of the novel is a verbless disyllable: 'London'.

The second paragraph gives us the fog—again, verblessly. We are somehow relegated to a primal world of mere nouns. All syntactically deployed complex signification is abruptly curtailed—still-born. I have called this almost modernist because it is strikingly similar to certain features of the French *nouveau roman* which are commonly considered especially audacious, quintessentially twentieth century. Take, for example, the opening of Robert Pinget's *Passacaille*: 'Le calme, le gris, De remous aucun' ('Stillness, greyness. Not an eddy').[29] Raymond Jean writes,

L'*incipit* de ce très beau récit qu'est *Passacaille* n'est rien d'autre qu'une suite de courtes phrases nominales. *Le calme, le gris*, ces touches sont exactement l'équivalent *aplats* de couleurs neutres (de non-couleurs, plutôt) posés sur la toile de la manière la plus délibérément non figurative. Cela ne *figure* rien, en effet.[30]

The *incipit* of this admirable story, *Passacaille*, is nothing but a succession of short noun-phrases. *Calmness, greyness*, these strokes are the exact equivalent of flat washes of neutral colour (or rather, of non-colour) laid on the canvas in a manner which is, expressly, non-figurative. Indeed, nothing is here *figured*.

In *Passacaille* the greyness (unlike the fog in *Bleak House*) is immediate and total. But, for all that, Jean's observation about the noun-phrases is applicable at once to the opening of *Bleak House*. The effect of the differentiating factor, the initial, specifying 'London', is to impart a vertiginous, backward-dynamism to the following swift transition to unbeing.

It may be thought that the 'scene-setting opening' is remote from the long dialogue between genesis and intervention which forms the central, vertebral subject of this book. But Dickens, through his eerie sense of reduction to *primordial* slime (soup?)—that is to the formless, original, unmeaning Chaos—succeeds in

---

[29] (Paris: les Éditions de Minuit, 1969.)
[30] 'Ouvertures, phrases-seuils', *Pratique de la littérature, roman poésie* (Paris: Éditions du Seuil, 1978), 21.

instituting that dialogue once more, in a highly original manner. If he was anticipated it was by someone who was certainly not in his mind when he wrote this chapter—by Alexander Pope, in the 'reversed' Genesis conclusion of *The Dunciad*, itself a great poem about London as an *Inferno*. There is a curious, highly instructive, traditional rectitude in Dickens's sequence of images. From the figure of Justice we proceed to mud (in various myths of origin human beings are formed from mud or clay), and then to our Saurian ancestors, before we reach the utter formlessness of the fog itself.

The Megalosaurus is, technically, an *adynaton*; that is, he belongs to the ancient trope sometimes known as the 'fishes in the trees' topos, whereby things are transposed, with surrealist violence, from their usual context. I have written elsewhere on the history of this topos.[31] The important point is that this history is double. The *adynata* can be used either to express some laughable absurdity or else to refer to cosmic marvels, at the beginning or end of time. John Conington observed long ago that the style and cadence of those passages in Virgil in which the shepherd imagines a world turned crazy are oddly akin to certain other passages in which the Golden Age is evoked (*Eclogues*, i. 59, viii. 53, as against iii. 89, iv. 30).[32] Ovid, more pertinently still, employs this topos in his myth of creation from chaos:

> modo quae graciles gramen carpsere capellae
> nunc ibi deformes ponunt sua corpora phocae
> (*Metamorphoses*, i. 299–300)

Where, but a moment before, the slender goats had cropped the grass, now shapeless sea-calves spread their weight.

Ovid's sea-calf is a not-so-distant relation of Dickens's Great Lizard. The word 'megalosaurus' is itself, at the date of the novel, obscurely monstrous. Darwin's *Origin of Species* was still seven years off, in the future. Francis Buckland, the fearless eccentric who claimed to have eaten or drunk everything in the animal kingdom, coined the word in 1824. Gideon Mantell

---

[31] 'Fishes in the Trees', *Essays in Criticism*, 24 (1974), 20–38. Repr. in my *The Stoic in Love* (Brighton: Harvester, 1989), 68–81.

[32] *P. Vergili Maronis Opera*, ed. with a commentary by John Conington, 4th edn., 3 vols. (London: Whittaker, 1881), i. 93.

found his petrified iguanodon in the sandstone of Tilgate forest
in the following year. But most of Dickens's readers would not
have known the word; hence the helpful gloss, 'elephantine
lizard' in the following clause.

Perhaps the most brilliant intimation of regression comes
with the curious, parenthetical retrospective cancellation of
daybreak, 'Since the day broke (if this day ever broke)'. By this
point we have already been informed of the death of the sun.
There are other, fainter *adynata*, for example, the unwonted
mingling of blackness with snow. This too is strangely like
Pope in his London-apocalyptic vein:

> Thro' Lud's famed gates, along the well-known Fleet
> Rolls the black troop, and overshades the street,
> Till show'rs of Sermons, Characters, Essays,
> In circling fleeces whiten all the ways:
> So clouds replenish'd from some bog below,
> Mount in dark volume, and descend in snow.

> (*Dunciad* (1742), ii. 359–64)

The notion of a suffocating tide of paper is absent from
Dickens's opening but not, we may remark, from the novel
which follows. The fog of the first chapter becomes indeed a
paper fog, in which all lose their way. J. Hillis Miller writes,
'*Bleak House* is a document about the interpretation of
documents.'[33]

There is no Miltonic matching of the work's beginning with
the world's. Instead with comic heroism Dickens, like a genial
ogre, steps bravely into a nightmare of accelerating non-
existence. Unlike Kafka's K he is 'man enough' (as people used
to say) for even this Augean confusion. The *Zeitgeist*, even as I
write, is pressing me to say that *Bleak House* will demonstrate
negatively the impossibility of all interpretation by dismantling
itself, enacting the defeat of Structure by Deconstruction,
incorporating the misreading Pip brought to his own career in
the very fabric of the book, which is now nothing but a tissue of
misconstructions. But I believe none of that. Dickens, with the
clew of art, is Jason in the labyrinth; he is Hercules. The *adynata*
at the beginning of *Bleak House* are finally more comedic than

---

[33] Introduction to the Norman Page edn. (Harmondsworth: Penguin, 1971), 11.

apocalyptic. Here be monsters, and dragons are for slaying. This is a nightmare from which we can be led to light and that is why Dickens, unlike the genuinely apocalyptic Pope, places his reversed Genesis at the opening, not at the end. He is confident that the reversal can itself be reversed. *Bleak House* is therefore not irradiated with the idea of origin as *David Copperfield* was. Rather it has fun with a false ghost—and then tells its story.

7

The Sense of a Beginning

THE IDEA OF A NATURAL BEGINNING

In Frank Kermode's sense of an ending is my sense of a
beginning: his Mary Flexner Lectures delivered at Bryn Mawr
in 1965 set a wholly new standard. Thereafter we had all either
to think or else, in a manner, to declare ourselves enemies of
thought. *The Sense of an Ending* (the title given to the lectures in
their published form) exposes the problematic ontology of
literary form. It caused my mind to race, even at first reading,
between the seemingly antithetical poles of a natural end and a
formal ending. At the same time I was obscurely uneasy lest, by
some trick of an unperceived conceptual hyposhere, the polarity
itself might be resolved into an identity. What if all supposedly
natural beginnings and ends are really cultural fictions, read into
the world but never, in truth, read off from it? In *La Nausée*
Annie says to Roquentin, 'Il n'y a pas d'aventures.'[1] There is
something heady—even delicious—in the glissando of this
thought. For a while it feels a little like flying. Nevertheless,
even then, I resisted. Every death is a natural termination.
Births really are natural beginnings. And so, I thought, are
many other things. The foundation of a new university is, very
clearly, an ideological act which is translated into natural fact. In
1936 there was no University of Sussex. In 1966 there was one.
The precise moment of its inception between those dates may be
indistinct, confused, and muffled by pre-echoes and corroborative ceremonies, but we are forced to say, nevertheless, that it
had begun to exist. We often speak as if the world of discourse
were absolutely separate from the natural world, but in fact this
separateness is a partial, relative affair. It will be said that we can
contrast words with things because words are used to refer to
things, while things are not so used. But this is just a serviceable
shorthand, a simplification. The truth is that words *are* things

[1] Jean-Paul Sartre, *La Nausée* (Paris: Gallimard, 1938), 206.

(for anything—any thing—is a thing) but they are of course very curious things, having the power to symbolize and refer to other entities. As words are things, so particular utterances are real events. The comfortably absolute division which we make between the beginning of a poem and a beginning in the real world is inwardly weak. For poems, likewise, really exist in no other world than this one. We may hear the words, 'There are no beginnings in nature, we make all the beginnings', but if an artist has constructed an opening paragraph and given it to the world, then that beginning, at least, is there for all to see. It is true that 'beginning actually to compose *Paradise Lost*' is distinct from 'the beginning of *Paradise Lost*', and both are distinct from 'the beginning of human history' which *Paradise Lost* recounts. Of course, a piece of discourse may offer as fact a beginning which is wholly feigned, but we can no longer feel confident that the question is settled in advance by a prior knowledge that there are no beginnings in nature. If poem can begin, why not, say, a period of political office, or a biological species (I am deliberately moving gradually from artificial to inartificial sequences)?

I was willing to grant that religion might be wholly fictitious and that we shape history in accordance with our desires, but in assessing such spectacular feats of cultural fiction I felt myself to be reviewing a tensely contested field, rather than the flat, unbroken surface of a foregone conclusion. Whig History, it seemed to me, while manifestly enforcing a certain fiction, contained a higher quotient of natural fact, of ordinary true propositions than, say, Mormonism. Most crucially, I thought that every demonstration of the ways in which we actively shape the world was a demonstration of distortion, and the notion of distortion presupposes a natural Is, a fact or set of facts which is fictively transformed. Indeed, to say that *everything* is fiction and nothing is fact is like saying that everything is left and nothing right (I plagiarize G. K. Chesterton here). 'Is it a fact, then', one is tempted to add, 'that there are no facts?'

It is sometimes said that all beginnings are social constructions. 'Construction' is a slippery word. If it is used with a conscious implication that the appropriate verbal form is 'construe' ('interpret', 'dispose', 'shape') rather than 'construct', I can have no quarrel with the user. In this sense even our simplest conceptions—individual material bodies, say—are constructions of our environment. Where Jane sees a table an ant would see something else. Births and deaths are, *a fortiori*, social constructions in this sense of the word. Such construing, clearly, is not an unconstrained activity (a sentence will 'bear' this construction, but not that). Jane is 'set', biologically, socially, and culturally, to construe 'table', and the ant in this same room is 'set' to construe (say) 'dust-boulder'. Neither party is feigning the object; the table and the dust-boulder are both real. But sometimes the separate existence of that-which-is-construed is denied. This happens when people notice every time they try to *specify* in language that which exists before the construing takes place, lo!—they have construed it. They infer from this that everything is construction, that nothing precedes construction. The reasoning is indeed frail. It is as if one were to notice that every time one tried to specify the objects in one's back garden one became aware that one had used a *word*, and were to infer from this that there were no objects in the back garden, but only words ('I thought I had a lawn-mower but now I see that I have only the word "lawn-mower"'). Construction is now indistinguishable from 'making things up'. It may be said that the constraint of cohering with the other constructions persists, but this constraint will swiftly lose its urgency as its real character (that is, being nice to the other fictions) is reflected upon.

As the habit of rebellion grew, I found myself doubting where before I had easily acquiesced. It seemed harder and harder to find the truly unconstrained, pure fiction, uncontaminated by nature. I suddenly wished to answer Sartre's Annie, 'Yes, there are, in addition to the adventures we retrospectively construct, certain real adventures.' In 1871 Stanley really did find the emaciated Livingstone in Ujiji. The note of converse excitement, the rebellion of earth against air, bearing the standard of nature some distance into territory conventionally held by fiction, can be sensed in George Orwell's sudden and astonishing concession: 'Revolutionaries keep their mouths shut in the torture chamber, battleships go down with their guns still firing when their decks are awash.'[2]

---

[2] From 'The Art of Donald McGill', in *The Collected Essays, Letters and Journalism of George Orwell*, 4 vols. (Harmondsworth: Penguin, 1970), ii. 193.

Usually, I grant, such things are either constituted or improved in the telling. But not always.

It is, then, too easy to consider all human discourse as a field of variable fictions. Rather one's thought must be dialectical: no form without matter, no art without nature. Even within the field of manifestly fictive, artful poetry, the dialectic is sustained. The most arbitrary conclusion is in some remote sense the mimesis of a death. Literary beginnings, meanwhile, group themselves with surprising clarity, either as devoutly natural (David Copperfield's 'I Am Born') or as proudly artificial. The Bible (which may or may not be seen as literature) provides most people's example of *the* natural beginning, the Genesis of the world. But Homer in the *Iliad* begins in the middle of the Trojan War and presents a narrative unity which presumably did not pre-exist the poem, the unity of Achilles' wrath. Though Hesiod wrote a *Theogony*, with a 'deep' natural beginning, it remains in general a striking characteristic of Hellenic culture that it should, so to speak, make a point of the non-natural character of its own greatest literary openings. Aristotle, as we saw, praised Homer for his interventionist opening and scorned the low writer who imagines that unity is to be attained by recounting 'all the things that happened to Theseus' (*Poetics*, 145^{1a}16–22). Horace was never so Greek-minded as when he gave the world the approving phrase, *in medias res*, 'into the midst of things' and disparaged the practice of beginning *ab ovo*, 'from the (natural) egg' (*Ars Poetica*, 146–9). Although the 'framing' of a story by placing it within another (necessarily incomplete) sequence is quite distinct from the epic interventionist opening, it remains mildly surprising to find it in places where there can be no question of Greek influence. In the ancient Egyptian 'Tale of the Shipwrecked Sailor' a certain official, having reached port, is anxious about an impending interview; one of his attendants then attempts to encourage him by telling the *main* story, about a shipwreck followed by a safe home-coming.[3]

It is now time to draw together, in rough summary, the

---

[3] The story survives in a single papyrus, known as P Leningrad 1115 (now in Moscow). A literal translation is given in Miriam Lichtheim, *Ancient Egyptian Literature: A Book of Readings*, 3 vols. (Berkeley, Los Angeles, London: University of California Press, 1975), i. 211–15.

different strands of this book, beginning with Virgil. The *Aeneid* defers to the powerful Greek assertion of *les lois du texte* against the laws of nature. It begins *in medias res*. Yet there is another side of Virgil (traditionally regarded as in some sense Hebraic) which betrays a nostalgia for the other, natural beginning. The poet inside the poem (the Carthaginian bard Iopas at the end of Book i) sang, as Caedmon sang in the first English verses to come down to us, of the origins of men and beasts, a creation song (*Aeneid*, i. 740 f.). Aeneas himself, caught in the artful literary toils of analepsis and prolepsis, strains with a sort of famished desire for something better than this mess of shadows, spectral cities, Greek images—for a Roman home which is also an origin. Again, older critics were less afraid than we are to say, 'Here Aeneas is Virgil, who was turned out of the farm he loved, deracinated from his proper earth.'

After Virgil we found, especially among texts regarded as canonical, beginnings which are dialectically stretched between natural origins and artful intervention. The word *mezzo* in the first line of Dante's *Commedia*:

> Nel mezzo del cammin di nostra vita

owes something to the *medias* of Horace's *in medias res*.[4] The *Commedia* is commonly regarded as the paradigmatic medieval poem, merging the world and the book in an eschatologically structured unity: nature is now the work of a divine author, and the poem's author, Dante, is a pilgrim within his own poem—which is itself the universe. Yet, as we saw, Benvenuto da Imola in the fourteenth century discovered the lineaments of a classical proem behind the *visio* opening of the *Commedia*. The supposed grand fusion of world and book is in fact excitingly incomplete. I have suggested that Dante's *mezzo* echoes Horace's *medias*, but that where the Horatian term connotes authorial intervention Dante's word directs us to the point at which God intervened in his mere fiction of a life, reappropriating it to the Major Poem, the divine creation (and here we remember Auerbach's argument in his essay 'Figura' that in Dante's universe it is we who are the fictions, the shadows). This huge feat of theological imagination, this turning inside-

---

[4] See above, p. 37.

out of the relation of poetry—God's poetry or making—to a now *posterior* nature, has, in addition to its power to move us, an almost mathematical elegance. Yet it cannot quite work, and Dante knows this. A gritty, pragmatic knowledge that it is Dante, the Florentine poet, who orchestrates his own erasure cannot be destroyed. Some three hundred years later, in another country, we shall meet the same problem in an altered form. In poem after poem of George Herbert's *The Temple*, the mere creature, Herbert himself, is illuminated and transcended by words which only the Creator can utter. Yet Herbert the poet writes the lines for the creature, Herbert, and for the creator, God. The divine concluding corrections, represented within the fiction as *essentially* trans-human, are palpably Herbertian in style and cadence. With all the sharpened sense of individual identity which Protestantism could confer, George Herbert remains, irremediably the poetic master of his own, repeated, elegant-devout self-effacements. God for Dante is indeed the volume in which the scattered leaves of the universe are gathered:

> legato con amore in un volume,
> cio' che per l'universo si squaderna   (*Paradiso*, xxxiii. 85–7)

I have stressed, however, that it would be wrong to forget, in the exaltation of this vision of unity, the force of the words *si squaderna*, 'are scattered' or 'scatter themselves'. The leaves of the world are for us—that is, in ordinary experience—scattered before the mellowing of time. Through this dispersal room is made for human poetic art—for Dante's art. C. S. Singleton is not wrong when he says the *Commedia* means to mirror God's world,[5] but the glass is flawed, by time, humanity, and fallen nature. This transforms the various relations—between the author of the poem and the author of the world, between the poet and the pilgrim, between arrogant fiction and devout transcription—into continuously dynamic, unresolved engagements.

We saw in the openings of the *Aeneid*, the *Commedia*, and *Paradise Lost*, an ever-shifting process of imaginative negotiation between natural and formal inception. Virgil plunges *in medias res*,

---

[5] *Journey to Beatrice* (Cambridge, Mass.: Harvard University Press, 1967), 95.

in Greek fashion, by beginning with Aeneas sailing before the wind, with his dispossessed followers. But in the preliminary invocation he obtrudes—in un-Homeric contrast with one another—his own personality and the declaration that the subject of his poem is the *real* beginning of the Latin race, the lords of Alba, the walls of towering Rome. If we accept from Donatus the restoration of four *preceding* lines, we have a syntactically odd 'opening-before-the-opening'; Virgil presents himself as emerging from a forest, leaving behind the flute (of pastoral *Eclogues*) to subdue the farmlands (*Georgics*), thereafter turning, at last, to arms and the man. The effect of this is greatly to strengthen the intuition of the personal significance of Virgil's placing '*cano*', 'I sing', before the Homeric 'Tell, O Muse'. The sentence thus restored is indeed strangely extended, producing a reduplicative effect through the tacking-on of relative clauses, first to the poet and then to the hero, who has likewise *emerged*, embarked upon a journey. Thus in Virgil the beginning of the *poem's* story is matched (and deliberately mismatched) with something Homer could never admit (or even, perhaps, conceive), with the beginning of a real, organized History, the true story of those then and there listening to the poem. Yet even as this deep engagement with the natural is proudly declared, the poet's sense of his own separate individuality is not healed but exacerbated, and the grand progression of Roman History is eerily pre-echoed by a sequence which is personal and literary.

Dante's poem is of course thoroughly medieval, unequivocally Christian, but even here the negotiation with the other, 'counter-natural' opening is sustained. The poem begins *in medias res*, in the middle of the journey of Dante's own life. Yet, as we have seen, Dante is here in one way the object, the matter of the poetry; we are asked to believe that the intervention is not the poet's but God's. *He* enters *in medias res* and in beginning the poem starts a transformation of Dante himself in which the poet grows into accord with the real shape of the universe. The ordinary march of events is broken in upon, not by something confessedly less real, an artful fiction, but by something more real, by that which is itself the beginning and end of all things, Alpha and Omega. We are as far as literature will permit, it would seem, from Valéry's formula for the weakly arbitrary novel-opening: 'La marquise sortit à cinq heures.'[6] As with Virgil, so with Dante, we come to see that the circle is not closed. We are made aware, not only of the real story of the world, but of the real poet: as Virgil speaks of himself as *egressus silvis*, 'emerged from the woods', so Dante finds himself in 'una selva oscura', 'a dark wood'. *Mezzo* is moreover implicitly structured not only with reference to the real but also with reference to the structure of the poem. The word is indeed stiffened by a sense of symmetry which is fundamentally medieval (think of triptychs) and is wholly absent from the Horatian formula.

The narrative of *Paradise Lost* begins with Satan, now cast out from Heaven, staring wildly on the surrounding desolation. It begins *in medias res*. But, as with Virgil but still more radically, the preceding invocation joins the beginning of the poem to the beginning of the Story of Us All, as we are fallen creatures. As Johnson wrote more than a hundred years later, 'All mankind will, through all ages, bear the same relation to Adam and Eve, and must partake of that good and evil which extend to themselves.'[7] The first line, 'Of man's first disobedience, and the fruit', tells of the first, constitutive act of humanity as we know it in ourselves. It is not, indeed, a Creation-of-the-World opening, but we are moving closer to that Hebraic extreme.

I am suggesting that an exclusively formalist account—an account which admits no concept of beginning other than that created by a fictive reading-*in*—will never be adequate for these canonical openings, for all their manifestly literary character. Even when we wish to register an appropriation of nature by art, we must notice the temporarily separate identity of that which is ineluctably appropriated. This feature of binary negotiation is continued, into the classic period of the novel. For all the elegant, self-referential wit of the opening chapter-heading, 'I Am Born', the beginning of *David Copperfield*, is, with Victorian gusto, triumphantly fused with the natural beginnings of birth. Dickens is, to be sure, too intelligent to

---

[6] André Breton says that Valéry told him he could never write in this manner. See A. Breton, *Premier manifeste du Surréalisme* (1926), in *Œuvres Complètes*, ed. M. Bonnet *et al* (Paris: Gallimard, 1988–), i. 314.

[7] *Life of Milton*, in Johnson's *Lives of the English Poets*, ed. G. Birkbeck Hill, 3 vols. (Oxford: Clarendon Press, 1905), i. 174–5.

proceed without negotiation. It will be said by the Formalist that the wit here confesses what the narrative mode mendaciously denies, that all is art. This however will not quite do; where birth is once named, real beginning cannot be quite forgotten.

The wittiest of all openings is surely that of *Tristram Shandy*. Here the Horatian opposition between a despised beginning-from-the-egg and an admired plunge *in medias res* is joyously exploded. Tristram, the supposed teller of the story, begins indeed from his own insemination, invoking as he does so, with crack-brained inverse scholarship, the authority of Horace. But Sterne simultaneously bewilders the first-time reader, who is pitched *in medias res*, into the middle of an ill-conducted marital engagement, which is simply unintelligible until we know the *previous* history of those concerned.

Here the comedy works not simply by the incongruous juxtaposition of the formal and the natural, but by a sudden wilful movement (having, I think, real philosophical force) into the territory of the natural, which can be made to appear *inherently* opposed to the notion of a beginning. The ploy is to show, first, that there is something which appears to be a far more radical beginning than birth, namely conception, and *then* to show, in the same breath, that if you *look* at a conception you will find that you are not looking at a beginning but merely at a nodal point in a larger process. Frank Kermode (who was not, as far as I know, thinking of Sterne at the time) had the same thought: 'We die', he says, '*in mediis rebus* and are born *in medias res*.'[8] To show the conception of Tristram is to show two mid-life persons in a relation which is, necessarily, only partly intelligible. They, not he, will fill the screen, if only because they are so much bigger! Sterne, as if in response to this very thought, switches his attention to the microscopic operations of spermatozoa, but here too we encounter not a clear inception but rather a baffled and baffling multiplicity of *process*.

At this point my resistance suddenly becomes radical. For the logical tendency of this insight is to abolish all beginnings from the order of nature, to relegate them firmly to the Indian Reservation of Discourse—with one (empty) concession: the

---

[8] *The Sense of an Ending* (London: Oxford University Press, 1967), 7.

mystic, inherently uninspectable Genesis of the Universe may stand as the sole permissible natural beginning. The wholly erroneous idea that only that which has nothing before it is truly a beginning has a long history. Cicero gives his support to it at *Tusculan Disputations* (I. xxiii. 54), knowing as he does so that he has the backing of Plato (*Phaedrus*, 254). If a beginning is that which is unconnected with any previous event, then only the origin of the world will serve. Even the beginning of the Bible, seemingly the most absolute of all written openings, does not satisfy the criteria, for this creation was preceded by a Creator. The matter is further complicated by a strange tremor in the Hebrew: *bereshit* perhaps properly invites, as the most literal translation possible, not 'In the beginning God created . . .' (Authorized Version) but 'In a beginning when God created . . .' (though this in its turn is attended by problems which propel the mind back in the direction of the Authorized Version).[9] The ghost of that extra 'when' can ever so faintly reinforce our sense of a history before History began, of creation as intervention rather than radical beginning.

To put the matter at its lowest and simplest, a concept which has only one application, and that to something which is intrinsically unavailable, is surely unlikely to figure prominently in language as one of our commoner words. Cosmic origin makes other paradigms of latency, such as the Freudian Unconscious or the *Dieu caché* of the Protestants, look like vividly familiar, friendly faces by contrast. It is possible indeed that the concept is in fact never employed at all (for I set aside biblical Genesis). Even those physicists who speak of creation allow, I understand, the notion of prior conditions. The truth is that the word is common because the thing is common. The world is full of natural beginnings. If Shakespeare did not exist in 1563 and did exist in 1565, then between 1563 and 1565 Shakespeare began, or, as we say, was born. This is not a social construct in the sense that class, say, is a social construct. It is true that Shakespeare's birth was preceded by a complex biological process, that he did not arise from nothing and it is further true that we are in a manner 'set' as organisms to read off

⁹ See Gabriel Josipovici, *The Book of God: A Response to the Bible* (New Haven and London: Yale University Press, 1988), 53–74.

the point at which Shakespeare, so to speak, crystallizes, as having especial importance. Again, an insect watching the whole affair would notice something else. The perspectival schemata operated by different organisms or different cultures may on occasion be interrogative rather than constitutive, as I have argued elsewhere. If you are 'set' to read off bicycles, say, from the given field, this need not mean that you are feigning 'bicycles' within a featureless and therefore infinitely indulgent environment; rather, you may be *asking*, 'Bicycle?' and receiving a perfectly clear 'Yes' or 'No' from the world. Once this converse thought is allowed and nature, so often driven off with a pitch-fork, has come running back, it becomes clear that even indistinct natural beginnings can be allowed—the beginning of manned flight, say, or even the beginning of the Reformation.

We are accustomed in the late twentieth century to seeing the apparently natural suddenly appropriated by form: propositions like 'Zolaesque naturalism is really pure convention' are the rule. But the ball *can* roll back. I began by contrasting the opening of the *Iliad*, as fundamentally formalist and fictive, with the natural beginning of the Bible. But if the Trojan War was real history, as the first listeners to Homer may have assumed, it is conceivable that the wrath of Achilles is a real though doubtless indistinct beginning. Alternatively, if the *Iliad* was taken as fiction, it was certainly taken as more or less plausible fiction, in which case the beginning of Achilles' wrath is founded, as plausible hypothesis must be, on real risings-up of anger in real, dangerous persons. In fact I do not suppose that the first listeners to Homer were so foolish as to believe, with the hard credulity of a modern, in the details presented to them. Preliterate or quasi-preliterate cultures tend, as it were, not to hope for—not to expect—exactitude, but are instead content with an exciting Limbo of possibles. A kind of wisely passive sophistication may have been destroyed by the Sophists, when they appeared on the scene with harshly binary questions, 'True or false? Yes or no?' Either way, fact or fiction, there turns out to be a more or less firm link with the natural. Thus my strong contrast between a confessedly fictional, interventionist opening (Homer) and a natural beginning (Genesis) begins to blur, to transform itself perhaps into a weaker antithesis: between culturally prominent, publicly baptized beginnings, and more fugitive, *shyer* beginnings, which the individual artist chooses to make prominent.

Kermode's *Sense of an Ending*, indeed, sometimes follows the other, stony track. By this path, all beginnings are merely suppositions or impositions. 'What can be thought must certainly be a fiction.' This shrill apophthegm from Nietzsche stands as an uncontested epigraph, and the infinitely subtle, discriminating Kermodian prose which follows seems, with its use of 'make sense of the world' as a recurring catch-phrase, to be gently urging what is at last the same desolating view. The famous paradigm of sense-making is our ability to 'hear' a merely serial 'tick-tick-tick-tick' as the symmetrically organized 'tick-tock, tick-tock'. Even as we think we are hearing, we are in fact composing. Some people in response to this passage pointed out (what is true) that older clocks make two distinct sounds in repeated sequence—that is, they actually do go 'tick-tock, tick-tock'. Meanwhile, however, it is equally true that people can do the thing of which Kermode speaks, they can hear 'tick-tick-tick-tick' as 'tick-tock, tick-tock'. The basic counter-argument was always, therefore, to point out that Kermode's demonstration, where it succeeded, depended on a prior ability to determine what sound the clock was really making (otherwise this remarkable self-deceiving dexterity of mind could never have been exposed to view). And that means that there is such a thing as an unconditioned apprehension of reality.

But *The Sense of an Ending* does not acquiesce in this false simplicity. The dialectic is sustained. It may be that Professor Kermode thinks, fairly modestly, that historical 'periods', at least, are purely imposed shapes, read *into* the past. I imagine that for most historians 'periods' are excitingly indistinct natural beginnings, rich material for dispute precisely because their credentials are in doubt. If it were easily admitted on all hands that there are no natural credentials at all—that there is no cognitive sense in saying, for example, that classical civilization was succeeded by a different order—then of course the argument tails off into silence. Kermode suggests near the beginning of *The Sense of an Ending* that the notion of an epoch is 'something entirely in our own hands' (p. 7), but later observes, with all the energy and engagement of one who still

believes in such things, that we live in a technological age
(p. 101). Here he uses—without the apologetic inverted
commas which have become *de rigueur*, the phrase 'in fact'.
Within a few pages he is commending W. B. Yeats's 'regard
for the reality which will not be reduced' (p. 106) and
suggesting that the contempt for reality (including ethical
reality) which we find in the early Modernists is a 'treason of
the clerks' (p. 109). Indeed in this lecture, 'the Modern Apoc-
alypse', he ascribes to Eliot—by no means derisively—a critical
position which is almost the opposite of the one from which he
began. Instead of saying, 'That which is preceded by anything at
all is no true beginning,' he forces us to attend to a more
complex proposition: 'Anything which is importantly new—as
distinct from the trivial posturing of the *avant-garde*—must
emerge from a context: Nothing on its own can be new'
(p. 121). It is a mistake, then, blankly to oppose genesis and
metamorphosis. Here below the level of the moon, every
genesis involves a transformation, but there are real beginnings
because in this way things which did not exist before came into
being.

If what I have suggested is true, we are left with an enigma.
Homer is the grand puzzle. Why did he, at the start of European
poetry, enter obliquely with the seemingly non-natural opening? Everyone else followed the advice of the King of Hearts:
'Begin at the beginning'—that is, the known public beginning.
We have creation myths, the lives and exploits of heroes, battles
and wars serially expounded, chronicles. 'Carles li reis, nostre
empereur magne | Set anz tres plein ad ested in Espagne',[10] and
away we go.

In other narrative poems of the Middle Ages a brief prologue
offering a résumé of the whole is followed by a 'real' beginning.
Greek dramatists, notoriously, begin their plays 'near the end'.
Sophocles' *Oedipus Rex* begins after Oedipus has solved the
riddle of the Sphinx and married Jocasta, but the anonymous,
medieval *Roman de Thèbes* begins, as the 'deep story' begins,
with Oedipus's father, Laius: 'De Thebes fu et reis et dus . . .'.[11]

---

[10] *La Chanson de Roland*, ed. Cesare Segre (Milan, Naples: Riccardo Ricciardi,
1971), 3.
[11] Line 38, ed. Leopold Constans, Société des anciens textes français, 2 vols.
(Paris: Firman Didet, 1890), i. 3.

Even Benoit de Sainte-Maure's *Roman de Troie*, after its huge, proleptic prologue extending to line 714, begins firmly at the beginning of the story: 'Peleus fu uns riches reis'.[12] Sometimes there is a drive to locate the ultimate historical origin (as with Wace's *Roman de Brut*), at other times the poet is able to work without any extra-literary impulse towards an Origin, to follow the simple inner logic of the story *qua* story. Thus *Guy of Warwick* begins like an eighteenth-century novel: 'There was a very powerful earl who had a daughter and there was a certain young man, the son of the Steward, who was cup-bearer to the Earl; one Whitsuntide the Earl instructed this young man to wait upon his [the Earl's] daughter . . .'.[13] One may feel that it is those texts which push the story back to an Origin which exhibit the more primitive, less developed instinct. We saw how Coleridge observed,[14] apropos of Mistress Quickly in Shakespeare's *Henry IV, Part Two*, that uneducated persons, lacking any firm sense of 'point', are obliged to recount an event laboriously from some point of acknowledged origin far removed from the immediate needs of the listener. The curious 'Trojan' induction of *Sir Gawain and the Green Knight* can indeed look like an almost barbarous prefix to an otherwise masterly narrative fiction. There are, further, problematic 'historical' openings like that of *Beowulf*, in which the strange, brief account of the Danish king Scyld (who came from nowhere, rose to do great things for his people, and then departed) provides not so much the historical cause of the main story as a haunting analogy to it. But in all this material it is hard to find a truly Greek *in medias res* opening. It seems absurd to suggest that something as universal as rationalist philosophy should have a single, identifiable cultural source, yet Greek culture seems to be exactly that. The Greeks invented rationalism. But long before the rise of the pre-Socratics, the original discovery of the point of 'point' appears to have been repeated, within the sphere of an already organized ('pointful') story-telling. Homer, quite clear-

---

[12] Ed. Leopold Constans, Société des anciens textes français, 6 vols. (Paris: Firman Didet, 1894–1912), i. 38.

[13] *The Romance of Guy of Warwick* (the fifteenth-century English version, but using an older French source for p. 1, missing from the English), ed. Julius Zupitza, Early English Text Society (London: Trübner, 1875–6), 5.

[14] See above, p. 60.

ly, not only knows how to tell a story without extraneous
preliminaries, from its poetically proper beginning to its
poetically proper end; he further knows how to frustrate and
then satisfy, in a wholly deliberate manner, the auditor's
appetite for due sequence and relevant matter with artfully
delayed analepses. This represents a secondary level of abstraction which does not occur naturally in other cultures.

Perhaps we can advance our understanding if we narrow the
enquiry, for a moment, to a technical question of language.
There is a difficulty, long familiar to commentators, about the
meaning of *ex hou*, 'from when', in line 6 of the first book of the
Iliad:

> Sing, goddess, of the wrath of Peleus' son, Achilles, the accursed
> wrath which laid ten thousand woes upon the Achaeans and cast down
> many strong ghosts of heroes into the house of Hades and gave their
> bodies to be the spoil of dogs and all the birds, and the purpose of Zeus
> was accomplished, [*ex hou*] from when Atrides, King of men and
> godlike Achilles first fell out in strife.

The question is whether *ex hou* is to be taken with *aeide*, 'sing',
in line 1 or with *eteleieto*, 'was accomplished', in line 5. By the
first interpretation the general sense is, 'Begin your song, Muse,
at that point in the saga where . . .'. By the second interpretation, *ex hou* is firmly located within a story already begun:
'Sing, goddess, of the wrath which ruined all—and how Zeus's
purpose began to be accomplished [*ex hou*] when those heroes
first quarrelled . . .'.

I should say first that the second interpretation may well be
the right one. *Ex hou* is a very long way in the sentence from
aeide, 'Sing', and it can be argued strongly that the most natural
presumption is to take it with the nearest preceding verb, 'was
accomplished'. But we cannot be certain. It remains possible
that, instead, a reflexive reference to the *poet's* memorial feat
was marked and made conventionally clear by, say, a pause and
a loud stroke upon the lyre, when Homer sang. Auerbach
taught us that there is no latency in Homer, that, despite the
technique of flashback and anticipation, the surface presented is,
so to speak, at a uniform distance from the eye. Yet if *ex hou*
means 'from the point in the saga at which', there is a huge

latent poem, a poem behind the poem we possess. The bard's performance (memorial feat, inspiration) entails his temporary immersion in an immense, ever-flowing Iliad. The Middle Ages continue instinctively to understand this, for they have a name for the poem behind the poem. They speak of 'the Matter of Rome' or 'the Matter of Britain'; here we must say, 'the Matter of Troy'. At the equivalent moment in the opening of the *Odyssey*, there is, incidentally, no doubt. *Tōn hamothen, thea*, '[Beginning] from these things, goddess', are the first words of the sentence which concludes the invocation. Moreover, when the Phaeacian minstrel Demodocus begins his *Iliad*, he sings 'taking up the story [*enthen helōn*] from the point at which the Greeks threw fire among the huts' (*Odyssey*, viii. 500–1). For Homer the division is not between poetic invention and objective reality. Almost certainly he never saw the pre-existing poem of Troy in a book. Rather, it lived in the throats and memories of singers, and, to a lesser degree, in the memories and responses of their listeners. The poem and the history were therefore in a manner one thing. The poem lies outside the ego of the particular bard who is in some ways an executant rather than a maker. It follows that the divinity who is to inspire the process is a divinity of *song*, a Muse, and not one of the usual Olympians. One senses that Horace's *in medias res* might have been *in medium poema* ('into the midst of the poem') but for the fact that Augustan Romans, with their books in their hands, could see that the *poem* began with the first line on the page. Note that we are not dealing here with a poetic ambiguity. *Ex hou* means one or the other of the above, not both.

Look now at a sophisticated post-Virgilian, Ovid. The *Metamorphoses*, so many centuries after Homer, has a beginning of primitive, elemental naturalism; it narrates the genesis of form from chaos:

> In nova fert animus mutatas dicere formas
> Corpora; di coeptis (nam vos mutastis et illas)
> Adspirate meis primaque ab origine mundi
> Ad mea perptuum deducite tempora carmen!
> Ante mare et terras et quod tegit omnia caelum
> Unus erat toto naturae vultus in orbe
> Quem dixere chaos

My spirit moves me to tell of forms changed into new bodies; gods (for it was you who changed those forms) breathe kindly on the work I have begun and draw out the thread of my perpetual song from the origin of the world to my own times. Before sea, or lands, or sky covering all, nature in all her round had but one face, and this they have called Chaos.

For all its primordial weight, however, this is manifestly the work of a late-born poet, not primitive but primitivist. The poet betrays the initiating role of his own separate, individual psyche in the fourth word, *animus*. The poem is brought into being not by a poetry-god, a Muse, but by Ovid's own mind. When gods are addressed, they are the Olympians who act upon the world—upon that world towards whose origin the poet gestures with what might be called ontological nostalgia. We saw in Virgil an un-Homeric reduplicative effect, in the opening sentence (as given by Donatus), doubling the poet and the hero. In Ovid the deep, Mosaic note of 'In the beginning' is counterpointed from the first by a lighter, more capricious music, which translators cannot catch. *In nova fert animus*, the first four words, naturally suggest a wholly literary meaning: 'My spirit moves me to treat a new subject', but then, as the inflected sentence gradually unfolds, a different grammar is asserted, and we realize that we must take *in nova* with *mutatas* rather than with *fert*, that we must think, within the narrative, of forms changed into new bodies rather than, extra-poetically, of a spirit propelled into new subject-matter.

All this suggests that Homer is able to perform his feat of intervention partly because he is exempt from the anxiety of individual consciousness. He is not making up a poem, in antithesis to the known sequence of reality. He is entering a pre-existent saga, guided and inspired by a goddess who is herself saga. In Ovid, conversely, we may glimpse the beginning of consciously false cosmological thinking. There is a marvellous passage in *The Sense of an Ending* (p. 38) in which Kermode describes the Third Reich as having a cosmology which it always knew, in a manner, to be false: the most disquieting example extant of what philosophers call 'making it true'. Ovid's phrase, *carmen perpetuum*, 'perpetual song', similarly combines sophisticated doubleness with nostalgia. The phrase itself is knowingly literary—almost an arrogant joke, for it echoes the *aeisma diēnekes* of Callimachus.[15] Callimachus notoriously thought a great book was a great bore and coined the phrase, 'continued song' as a pejorative description. Within his grand opening, Ovid is therefore impudently contradicting his Hellenistic teacher. Although Troy and Rome enter Ovid's poem in Book xii, I do not agree with Brooks Otis's suggestion that the reader will feel in the *Metamorphoses* 'a definitely historical structure: a temporal movement from the Creation to the present reign of Augustus'.[16] The labyrinthine interwoven narrative of the *Metamorphoses* contrasts strongly with the teleological majesty of the *Aeneid*. Nevertheless we *may* hear, in Ovid's phrase, an allusion to the now distant, ever-flowing river of saga, whether this be the matter of Troy, or the vast body of god-stories. Remember the question Nisus asked:

> Dine hunc ardorem mentibus addunt,
> Euryale, an sua cuique deus fit dira cupido? (*Aeneid*, ix. 84–5)

Do the gods put this spirit in our hearts, Euryalus, or does each man's fierce desire become a god for him?

Here the suggestion is planted that these are not coexistent states of affairs but rather rival languages, with the implication that 'god-language' could be replaced by psychological language. In which case the Muse herself might die, replaced by the *animus* or spirit of the individual poet. In Virgil the *ego* is already growing strong but the Muse is still (though belatedly) invoked. In Ovid *animus* is the confessed origin of a poem which terminates, likewise, in the personality of the poet; *vivam*, 'I shall live', is the last word of the *Metamorphoses*.[17] The gods invoked are the gods of a nostalgically viewed cosmology, something other than the poet and the poem.

I have moved somewhat from my original antithesis. The difference between a natural and a formal beginning becomes, as we close with the mystery of the Homeric intervention, less important than the growing distance between the poet and the matter of this poem. The Muse is, by this process, slowly

---

[15] Fragment 1, in R. Pfeiffer (ed.), *Callimachus*, 2 vols. (Oxford: Clarendon Press, 1949–53), i. 1.

[16] *Ovid as an Epic Poet* (Cambridge: Cambridge University Press, 1970), 47.

[17] See G. Karl Galinsky, *Ovid's Metamorphoses: An Introduction to the Basic Aspects* (Oxford: Basil Blackwell, 1975), 44.

starved. In the centuries which followed we may watch the
Muse becoming in her turn, as *mythos* was for Ovid, the matter
of nostalgia, or else the object of a systematically defeated quest.
In Milton the separate individuality of the author reaches a
crisis, out of which the poet *strains towards* the divine guarantor
of the first blind poet. There is a sense of terrible need:
'Something other than I must sing this song.' The first fourteen
lines of *Lycidas* tell of a voyage made in a strange darkness, in
which seasons are confused, Spring with Autumn, unripeness
with brown myrtle and frail, scattering leaves. Virgil's already
sharply personal *cano*, 'I sing', is transposed into an elaborately
deployed future: 'I—come—to—sing—again—soon—yet—
before—due—time.' The poem must find its own voice before
the sisters of the sacred well can touch their lyres. Nor are they
the sources of the poem in any stronger sense than Milton is, or
Edward King, or Orpheus, or that eeriest of 'doubles', the
genius of the shore. We are in a world in which poets will seek
nourishment from ghost-muses, dead versions of the poets
themselves (as in Gray's *Elegy*, say), from prompting friends,
urging them to write, from unseen readers who are, again
with conscious falseness, depicted as *semblable* and *frère* to the
poet writing. Otherwise, as with Wordsworth's *The Prelude*,
the poem will begin at last to flow with the remembered
sound of water, not Arethuse but the stream behind his father's
house.

In *Paradise Lost*, the great work of Milton's blindness, this
process is indeed thrown into reverse; the Muse revives. But the
reform could not hold for other (sighted, literate) poets. In
Jonathan Swift's 'Occasioned by Sir William Temple's late
illness', the Muse is at last roundly pronounced a fraud, creation
not creator of the poet's breath:

> There thy enchantment broke, and from this hour
> I here renounce thy visionary power;
> And since thy essence on my breath depends,
> Thus with a puff the whole delusion ends.[18]

Here as the Muse dislimns in secondary images of herself, my
own thoughts *si squadernano* in questions: who or what was the

---

[18] Lines 151–4, in *Jonathan Swift: The Complete Poems*, ed. Pat Rogers
(Harmondsworth: Penguin, 1983), 79.

Muse? Are poems and novels now inertly free to begin *in any way at all*? 'One may as well begin with Helen's letters to her sister . . .'.[19] When Henry James wrote his famous sentence in the preface to *Roderick Hudson* on the novelist's need to draw a circle in order to enclose the matter of the novel at *some* point, he seems to have no idea of a conceivable foundation for what is otherwise a strangely arbitrary exercise in pure geometry. What would Shakespeare (himself no naïve lover of the Origin opening) have thought of these words? Could it have struck him that James, the supersophisticate, is here rather the inept rustic, standing gaping, halfway across the *pons asinorum* of his craft? Why did Homer, as his sole contribution to the *Iliad* (for everything after the first paragraph is from the Muse) *tell* the Muse where to begin, instead of being told by her? And, still overarching all the other questions, how did Homer ever come to do what he did?

FINDING THE MUSE

The first of my questions, 'Who or what was the Muse?' can perhaps be partly answered. The Muse is that, other than 'I', here and now, which makes the poem. Already, however, the phraseology is potentially misleading, since the twentieth-century reader could easily take this to be an impersonalist theory. Although the Muse is other than the poet's ego, the Muse is herself a person. We have traced a tolerably clear sequence. Homer begins, 'Sing, Muse', and all that follows is hers, not his. Virgil begins, 'I sing', and so asserts his own, literate sovereignty over what is now manifestly a text. Wordsworth wants an 'I who is yet not the present I' to be the source of his poem. The oral or quasi-oral poet seems to regard it as intuitively obvious that *he* is not making the richly organized poem which issues from his lips. He quite simply has no leisure for deliberate construction, once the performance is under way. It may be said that in ascribing the poem to a Muse, the bard simply christens (names) the problem, rather than explains it. The earlier twentieth century would have assumed with the utmost confidence that the *category* of explanation must be

[19] The first sentence of E. M. Forster's *Howard's End*.

psychological: whatever is not done by the conscious mind must be done by the unconscious.

It has now become evident that the explanatory promise offered by the shift into the psychological mode has scarcely been fulfilled. First there is an initial difficulty: how does one know that one has an Unconscious at all? One is after all never conscious of it (Bishop Berkeley would appreciate this argument). The usual answer to the primitive objection, 'if the Unconscious is unconscious, we cannot know that it is there', is to say that the Unconscious is a necessary hypothesis, if we are to account for manifestly interconnected chains of behaviour which do not flow from conscious intention. But as long as the hypothesized cause is not itself accessible to some form of independent inspection it will, so to speak, simply mirror the original difficulty; it will answer only as Echo answered Narcissus.

The situation might be caricatured thus: 'Coherent behaviour usually issues from mind; we explain it by referring to the mind which produces it; *this* coherent behaviour does not, obviously, proceed from mind; we therefore explain it by deriving it from an *un*-obvious mind, mind no. 2, which (for some reason) we cannot perceive.' There is a connection here with the real writings of Freud, for example with those parts of the essay, 'The Unconscious', in which he finds himself forced to explain that, since the Unconscious is goal-directed and to that degree intelligent, it is rather an infra-consciousness ('under-consciousness') than a non-consciousness. Even the simplest emotions, in so far as they differ from mere physical actions, turn out to pose the same problem. Freud himself concedes that it is of the essence of an emotion that it is felt—and yet we speak of 'unconscious love, hate, anger'.[20] At the end of the essay the tension between some sort of seething 'anti-mind' and an alternative intelligence with its own consciousness remains unresolved. Note that, by the second conception, the word 'unconscious' is applicable only in a curious, inverse manner: Mind 1, the mind from which we ordinarily speak and write is indeed unconscious of Mind 2; but Mind 2, paradoxically,

---

[20] 'The Unconscious', in *The Complete Psychological Works of Sigmund Freud*, trans. James Strachey (London: Hogarth Press, 1957), 159–215, esp. 177.

appears to have access to the flimsy illusions of Mind 1. In such circumstances it is perhaps odd that the privative epithet is applied to Mind 2.

But of course Freud did in fact believe that other modes of access to the Unconscious were available to him, though all are in some degree oblique. Dreams and the free associations of patients were richly informative. From this vantage point he was able to give character and colour to what might otherwise have been a fatally translucent hypothetical infrastructure. The character which emerged was libidinal, appetitive, suggesting a hirsute beast—hardly, at first sight, a likely source of complex art although, as we have seen, tainted from the first by intentionality. The picture carried conviction for a bad reason; it reminded people of things *within* the field of consciousness, such as the conflict between reason and passion. Milton's *Comus* looks splendidly Freudian not because Milton anticipated psychoanalysis but because Freud shamelessly pillaged traditional Stoic materials.

What is more worrying, however, is the fact that the increase of 'character' or 'colour' seems actually to impede rather than assist the original project of explanation. Before Freud there were, roughly speaking, three notions of the unconscious mind: first the repository of memory, noticed by empirical philosophers (we know things without being continuously conscious of them; the light is not always on in the attic of the mind but, on the contrary, the conscious mind thriftily switches it on only for its brief visits to retrieve material). Second comes much Romantic talk of dark winds blowing from the Africa of the mind,[21] appetitive drives working before and below the appetitions of which we are conscious. Third is the version for which the evidence is perhaps strongest of all: 'Poincaré's unconscious'. Notoriously, Poincaré would on occasion become stuck in a mathematical problem, would stop trying to solve it, and go for a walk, whereupon something offering itself as a solution would pop up in his mind, like a number from a cash register.[22] He then had laboriously to link the 'solution' to

[21] See Lancelot Law Whyte, *The Unconscious before Freud* (London and New York: Julian Friedmann, 1978), 133.
[22] H. Poincaré, *Science et méthode* (Paris: Ernest Flammarion, 1927), 52.

the problem. Often enough the 'answer' proved to be, indeed, the answer. The hypothesis that someone, somewhere, must be doing real mathematics is here very difficult to resist. Yet Freud was more interested in the second model than in the third. This meant, in effect, that a hypothesis framed to account for otherwise inexplicable coherencies was internally characterized as primarily incoherent, irrational. 'Poincaré's unconscious' was obviously no hairy beast but more like some glittering, MIT intellectual.

Poetry, to be sure, is not mathematics. But poets speak of the Muse because of the presence of rich organization in what is uttered, an organization which they know they have not managed consciously. Good poetry is always full of live, tender intelligence. *Something* is thinking and feeling. Indeed, since in general we say 'someone' rather than 'something' when we think of a subject capable of thought and feeling, we should say here, 'Someone is doing this.' In a society in which poetry is still felt as communal rather than as the idiosyncratic product of a single ego, this 'someone' will, naturally and properly, on the basis of the evidence, be construed as operating on many different individual performers. In those circumstances it grows harder and harder to say that the old account in terms of a Muse is irrational, while the newer account in terms of the Unconscious is rational. That the two categories of explanation are in any case more nearly equivalent than is commonly recognized was noticed many years ago by Edmund Husserl, who remarked that 'by a change in the shading' we could transform 'a pure psychology of the inner life into a self-styled transcendental phenomenology'.[23] 'The Muse breathes genius in the poet'; 'Repressed libido articulates what the conscious cannot of itself express.' Which makes greater sense?

When Socrates was told by the Delphic Oracle that he was the wisest of all men, he strove like a good Popperian to falsify the proposition, calling on all those who seemed wise in order to prove, if he could, that their wisdom was greater than his. He tried first the philosophers, then politicians, and then, last of all, the literary artists:

---

[23] *Ideas: General Introduction to Pure Phenomenology*, trans. W. R. Boyce Gibson (London: G. Allen and Unwin, 1931), author's preface to the English edition, p. 16.

I went to the poets; tragic, dithyrambic and all sorts. And there, I said to myself, you will be instantly detected; now you find out that you are more ignorant than they are. Accordingly I took them some of the most elaborate passages in their own writings, and asked what was the meaning of them—thinking that they would teach me something. Will you believe me? I am almost ashamed to confess the truth, but I must say that there is hardly a person present who would not have talked better about their poetry than they did themselves. Then I knew without going further that not by wisdom do poets write poetry, but by a sort of genius and inspiration. (*Apology*, 22a–c)[24]

I have quoted from Jowett's scholarly and careful Victorian translation. Oddly enough, however, Jowett may have biased his version a little too much towards inspiration, away from the psychological, since the word which he translates 'genius' is *phusei*, of which the more usual translation would be 'by nature'. Plato is, with great prudence, hedging his bets. But he plainly includes inspiration and indeed gives that category greater prominence in the sentence which immediately follows. The reasoning is perhaps not absolutely 'tight', but is quite as rigorous as many of the inferences in modern scientific publications.

That the notion of the Muse or inspiration continues to possess, for working poets, an obvious plausibility is clear from T. S. Eliot's dexterous observations on Virgil's fourth Eclogue. The fourth Eclogue is the poem which (because, some years before the birth of Christ, it speaks of a virgin, of a new-born child sent down from Heaven, of the death of the serpent, and of taking away the sins of the world) has seemed to many readers, especially in the Middle Ages, to be obviously prophetic. Eliot was anxious to assure his twentieth-century readers that he certainly did not suppose that Virgil with his conscious mind had anything in view but some recent developments in politics and perhaps the birth of a child to an important Roman family, But this, he felt, did not, so to speak, dispose of the matter:

Whether we consider the prediction of the Incarnation merely a coincidence will depend on what we mean by coincidence; whether we

---

[24] *The Dialogues of Plato*, trans. Benjamin Jowett, 5 vols. (Oxford: Clarendon Press, 1875), i. 354.

consider Virgil a Christian prophet will depend on our interpretation of the word 'prophecy'. That Virgil himself was consciously concerned only with domestic affairs or with Roman politics I feel sure: I think that he would have been very much astonished by the career which his fourth Eclogue was to have. If a prophet were by definition a man who understood the full meaning of what he was saying, this would be for me the end of the matter. But if the word 'inspiration' is to have any meaning, it must mean just this, that the speaker or writer is uttering something which he does not wholly understand—or which he may even misinterpret when the 'inspiration' has departed from him. This is certainly true of poetic inspiration: and there is a more obvious reason for admiring Isaiah as a poet than for claiming Virgil as a prophet. A poet may believe that he is expressing only his private experience; his lines may be for him only a means of talking about himself without giving himself away; . . . a prophet need not understand the meaning of his prophetic utterance.[25]

It seems clear that for the Christian Eliot as for Milton there is a pressure to say that the agent of inspiration is God (for under Christianity polytheism is not allowed). But, equally clearly, he does not suppose himself to be aprioristically assuming a divine origin for poetry; rather the notion of inspiration is forced upon the mind by some very peculiar facts.

Eliot's thought propels us back to models of divine causation, but also forward, away from the *Grand Guignol* of psychoanalysis to the cooler world of Structuralism. That Eliot was some sort of proto-structuralist is clear from his observations, already noticed, that to understand Shakespeare one must understand it all,[26] and that works of literature form an ideal order such that the addition of a new work always produces a modification of the whole system.[27] It is hard to decide whether Structuralism represents a fresh explanation of non-ego-directed literary achievement or rather an elegantly deployed refusal to explain. The New Critical down-grading of authorial intention was epigrammatically exaggerated by Roland Barthes as 'the death of the author'. There was some show of doing for literature what Noam Chomsky was thought to have done for language. The ultimate codes and oppositions which 'generate' particular

[25] *On Poetry and Poets* (London: Faber and Faber, 1957), 122–3.
[26] 'John Ford', in *Selected Essays* (London: Faber and Faber, 1951), 193.
[27] 'Tradition and the Individual Talent', ibid. 15.

literary works (as sentences are 'generated' in Chomskian linguistics) were, it was supposed, identifiable. But 'generate' in this usage is quasi-figurative. It connotes a logical rather than a practical genetic relationship. It was soon clear (long before Deconstruction dissolved the primary codes) that the detailed character of particular works could not be securely predicted on the basis of the available codes alone. The feeling nevertheless persisted that it was somehow barbarous—or sentimental—to ascribe an elaborate literary production to any sort of mind. Even the notion that an intelligently expectant readership produced the work was not welcome. The consequent *aporia* found expression in a new sort of self-reflexive epigram, confessing, in a sophisticated yet helpless manner, its own vacuity: 'Poems are the authors of poems'; 'Literature writes itself.' It is as if one were presented with a sudden vista of a vast phylogenetic development in which no single causative or propulsive agent could be identified. The austere refusal to countenance any extra-formal explanation—the once proud *Non fingo hypotheses*[28] ('I make no hypotheses')—began to sound merely hollow.

It would seem that we have made little progress. If the transcendental flavour of the old Greek terminology offends our modern sensibilities (though few deities have been more immanent, less transcendent, than the Greek Muse) we may speculate (a little desperately?) on the frequency in nature of elaborate behaviour leading coherently to the achievement of a goal, a frequency which in no way worries the hardest Darwinian. Then link this frequency to the clear priority, in many human instances, of 'knowing how' to 'knowing that' (we know how to walk long before we know fully what we are doing when we walk; we know how to speak English long before we can explain a single rule of English grammar). It is now perhaps, half intelligible that human beings should be equipped with such stupendous powers of coherent, gratuitous fiction, as a kind of wild by-product.

The story I have told, beginning with 'Sing, Muse', passing

---

[28] Originally Isaac Newton's. See the General Scholium to Book 3 of the *Principia*, in Florian Cajori's revision of Motte's translation, 2 vols. (Berkeley: University of California Press, 1962), ii. 547.

on first to 'I sing' and then to 'An "I" which is not I sings this song', may be thought nevertheless to confirm the essential claim of Structuralism, which is that literature is a supra-personal product. By this reasoning, the Virgilian project of personal sovereignty over the poem, though initially encouraged by the opportunities afforded to ego-control by developed literacy, would be forced in the end to confess its own incompleteness.

The figure of Wordsworth does not sit entirely comfortably within this scheme. I have argued that late-born Wordsworth felt impelled to found his poetry on a prior self-as-source. I have gone far—many will feel much too far—in naïve agreement with this proposal, to the point where I have affirmed that the *childish* self, now dead, really did in some sense generate the poetry (the child is father to the man, but the man is murderer of the child). This looks like a 'solution' which, as it were, proclaims its own cultural distance from the experiential Muse of the archaic oral poet. One cannot imagine that Homer ever thought that the Muse who caused the poem to surge in his lungs and throat could somehow be the same person as himself—as a child! The thought simply makes no sense. Yet it would be unwise to infer too confidently that Wordsworth's idea can have nothing to do with the real process of making a poem. *The Prelude* began to flow when he remembered the river Derwent. Wordsworth, being Wordsworth, did not simply remember the river; he also remembered the subjective correlative, the tender interior of a consciousness (his), now very far off in time. Even the Greeks thought the Muses were the daughters of memory, though they were thinking of the poet's memory of the lay rather than of autobiographical recollection. In *The Prelude*, however, the early life *is* the lay. The child Wordsworth is in one sense an anti-Muse, since he is artless, unskilled in the technical craft of poetry, but we have seen that not only in Romanticism but in pastoral long before there is a nostalgia for an art which is nature, an art which is artless (the untutored shepherd, the Aeolian harp played by the wind, the languageless nightingale). The obstacles are smaller than they at first appear.

What obstinately remains to offend the Structuralist is 'the scandal of substance'. Wordsworth is certainly guilty of the barbarity of seeking a real *fons et origo*, a source outside the formal structures of poetry itself. This in its most primitive form produces the strange-factual 'pedantry' which, predictably, upset Geoffrey Hartman.[29]

Twentieth-century literature is full of variously elaborated authorial personae and in general a formalist criticism can be happy that this is so. But whenever we hear the beating of the Muse's wings, we shall be aware of the scandal of substance. In Joyce's *Ulysses* we are alerted by the suggestion (with Homeric overtones) of father-and-son relationship. Stephen Dedalus is Telemachus to Bloom's Odysseus. Bloom is a *fictional* parent-self, complicated and ironized by art. Because of the high quotient of distancing, objectifying elaboration he is more persona than Muse (outside not inside the poet's head). But even Bloom is touched by the mystery of subjective, generative power. With Stephen we are certainly nearer to the 'I which is not I, but is nevertheless the source of the book'. He is by several degrees more firmly objectified, more 'wrought', than the Stephen of *Portrait of the Artist* (or, still more, of *Stephen Hero*), but a figure formed from autobiographical recollection, exalted by a name which means 'craftsman', must be, in however vestigial a manner, some sort of Muse and not just a coldly controlled fictional persona. Similar things might be said about the shifting, variable figure of Marlow in Conrad's novels.

In the work of Joyce and Conrad there can of course be no question of the authorial double having the uncontested authority enjoyed by the Homeric Muse. That complete, joyously fruitful deference to the supervening voice was never recovered. Literary biographers often overplay the element of historical reference in poetry, but the New Critics and succeeding formalists, conversely, are mysteriously prevented, by the rules of the game they have chosen to play, from noticing that there is a necessary intersection with reality at this point of literary genesis. They are interested in the life of the book but cannot feel its inspiring breath, even when it is warm upon the reader's cheek.

The line I have traced in this book is heavily canonical: a sadly phallogocentric business, some would say, of fathers and sons (with some interference, however, from deviants like Sterne). It may be thought that the line is lost in the twentieth century, but that is not so. Joyce writes 'out of' Homer and Eliot 'out of' Virgil and Dante. In Eliot indeed we find an acute sense of an inherited poetic task; this American must reverse the pilgrimage of the Plymouth Fathers and, in a quest which seems to belong simultaneously to the worlds of Virgil and Henry James, must make his way through the chattering collage of the Jazz Age to the ancient source of literary strength. *Vergilium tantum vidi*, 'I once caught sight of Virgil', wrote Ovid in his *Tristia* (IV. x. 51). Pope told Wycherley how at the age of eleven he sat in a coffee house and watched the great Dryden.[30] For Eliot there was no such glimpse, no unbroken sequence of the laying-on of hands. In some ways he was more like Milton (whom he at first instinctively disliked), straining in his proper darkness to hear the voices of a remote past. Like Milton he meditated his *Arthuriad* (*The Waste Land*). Everyone knows that in Eliot 'tradition' is a word of power.

The Waste Land begins with the vernal word 'April' and at once subjects it to an almost hysterical destruction. It is the cruellest month, breaking up the comfortable oblivion of winter. Then, as the voice of the poet becomes the voices of the poem, overheard fragments of asthenic complaint, after all, reconfirm our original intuition of life in 'April'. The warm forgetfulness under the snow is death and the cruelty of April is the hurt of life. The person who reads much of the night and goes south in winter is a person who, despite the memories of a sharper reality in the different winters of childhood ('hold on tight . . . there you feel free') is now 'screening out' reality.

Chaucer's *Canterbury Tales* begins on the same note:

> Whan that Aprill with his shoures soote
> The droghte of March hath perced to the roote
>
> .   .   .   .
>
> Thanne longen folk to goon on pilgrimages

---

[30] See *The Correspondence of Alexander Pope*, ed. George Sherburn, 5 vols. (Oxford: Clarendon Press, 1956), i. 1–2. See also Joseph Spence, *Observations, Anecdotes, and Characters of Books and Men*, ed. James M. Osborn, 2 vols. (Oxford: Clarendon Press, 1966), i. 25.

Here the reference to Spring is immediately and unproblematically linked to the notion of a holy pilgrimage to Canterbury. In Eliot the sense that the life implied at the opening may have religious character is simultaneously powerful and wholly indistinct. For those who relish improbable truths I would say that Chaucer's genuine pilgrimage is in some ways like a works' outing, while Eliot's disintegrative excursion is a real pilgrimage (Nevill Coghill would wish me to add, however, that in the long run the authentic character of Chaucer's pilgrimage is harmoniously clear). In *The Waste Land* as in the *Commedia* and *Paradise Lost* there is a negotiation between the disorientation and arbitrariness of art on the one hand and some sort of supernaturally authorized beginning on the other. But of course all this is in *The Waste Land* designedly disputable. In 'East Coker', printed as the second of the 1943 *Four Quartets*, we have at last an explicit meditation on *archē* and *telos*, origin and end.

> In my beginning is my end. In succession
> Houses rise and fall, crumble, are extended,
> Are removed, destroyed, restored, or in their place
> Is an open field, or a factory or a by-pass.
> Old stone to new building, old timber to new fires,
> Old fire to ashes, and ashes to the earth
> Which is already flesh, fur and faeces,
> Bone of man and beast, cornstalk and leaf.
>
> (1–8)

The title 'East Coker' is the name of the village in Somerset from which Andrew Eliot set sail for the New World in the seventeenth century. The first six words are an inversion of the legend on Mary Stuart's chair of state. The dalliance with familiar actuality in 'by-pass' (think of Betjeman, or even Larkin) is expertly managed; the vividness is fugitive, because relegated to a secondary status by a major order which we do not yet understand. 'In an open field, or a factory' is similarly tender towards ordinary usage yet somehow remote from it.

Ordinary people who think history and progress are real can sometimes be heard saying, 'It was all fields here, when we first came.' In Eliot the idea of linear progress is replaced by meaningless cycle or mere flux. It is already evident that we are far from the Virgilian notion of a progressively shaped history, expressing a divine order. We saw the Virgilian historical scheme break up in Dante, whose notion of *imperium* is beginning to betray its weakly retrospective character, leaving an absolute disjunction between the benighted world and the order of eternity. For Eliot, nourished (if that is the word) by the Bradleian Absolute, history can become wise only by confessing its futility. The voyage out becomes a circumnavigation, rotation becomes stillness. The road up and the road down are one and the same. When Eliot writes,

> I am here
> Or there, or elsewhere. (49–50)

the line division produced a Dantean effect. What for Eliot is *mediae res*, a certain intermediate position, is by some imminent larger perspective no such thing. The thought becomes explicit in a clear echo of the *Commedia* at lines 173–4:

> So here I am, in the middle way, having had twenty years—
> Twenty years largely wasted, the years of *l'entre deux guerres*—

Nel mezzo del cammin di nostra vita . . . For Eliot, however, there can be no serious pretence that what for him is 'middle' is really the point of God's intervention, and therefore a deep beginning; nevertheless, it is just that which is powerfully desiderated. *The Four Quartets* are a conjuring pre-proemium to a *Commedia* which god fails visibly to compose. The fire and the rose at the end of 'Little Gidding' figure as a still-removed future, lying beyond the confines of the poem. The work as a whole therefore has the character of a prayer, not a narrative. There is a sense in which '*l'entre deux guerres*' returns us to the Virgilian order of history, since it exactly describes Aeneas's situation, between the Trojan and the Latin wars: the *errores*, 'wanderings', of *Aeneid*, iii. *Entre*, 'between', is another word of power in Eliot, this time working within the poetry itself.

> Between the idea
> And the reality
> Between the motion
> And the act
> Falls the Shadow
> > 'For Thine is the Kingdom'
> > (*The Hollow Men*, v.)

Who walked between the violet and the violet
Wavering between the profit and the loss
In this brief transit where the dreams cross
The dreamcrossed twilight between birth and dying

. . . .

Between blue rocks

(*Ash Wednesday*, iv, vi)

One can see why Eliot responded strongly to St John of the Cross with his belief that God is nearest when he is least expected. In the 'shadow' of intermediacy we find—or else desire—the primacy of the Kingdom. All Eliot's 'betweens' are breathless with hope, though threatened with despair. Throughout, the false starts, the gleams and vanishings, the shored-up fragments of a Modernist *œuvre* are plotted with reference to an absolute stability, which is theological. The common twentieth-century technique of 'stiffening' contemporary randomness by allusion to the canon can mimic this Eliotic relation, though in the end it is only a weak, sublunary echo.

Epilogue

I have deliberately abstained in this book from any substantial reference to dramatic openings, but now I will loosen that restriction. Shakespeare is the most canonical of English writers and perhaps the one who cared least for the idea of a canon. It is noteworthy that his one foray into 'the Matter of Troy' is that of a freebooter rather than an heir. *Troilus and Cressida* is disintegrative almost to the point of nihilism. Meanwhile the best known of Shakespeare's plays, famous beyond the shores of his own country, does not have a classical hero but is instead about a Danish prince.

Hamlet begins, not with the ghost of Hamlet's father, but with the ghost of a joke.

BARNARDO. Who's there?
FRANCISCO. Nay, answer me. Stand and unfold yourself.

A change in this shading—or the lighting—could transform this, swift as it is, into a familiar comic routine. The sentry, issuing his sonorous challenge, is answered not by a stranger but by a fellow sentry whom he has arrived to relieve. If the comic structure were more emphatic, we could say that Barnardo is first made a fool of and then, with marvellous rapidity, the same treatment is extended to Francisco (for *he*, absurdly, challenges Barnardo). One might infer that, since Barnardo has not yet formally taken over from Francisco, he is not yet on duty and that his first words are therefore not a sentry's challenge but a civilian's (alarmed) enquiry. Even if this is the case, the words fall into the pattern of the sentry's challenge (Francisco in reply immediately points out that Barnardo has, so to speak, stolen his line); the point is rendered finer still by the fact that Barnardo *is* a sentry, coming to take up his post.

By the time the play is over we know that the question, 'Who's there?' was in a manner prophetic, for standing behind Francisco, in the darkness, is a dead King, a most potent negation, having the power to undo the social fabric of Elsinore, to involve others in his own unbeing. Perhaps, since we know from Lodge's *Wit's Misery* (1596) that the old play of Hamlet contained a ghost,[1] Shakespeare could count on thoughts turning in that direction at the very first words of the play. Before he uttered the first words of the drama did Barnardo glimpse something or someone *other* than Francisco? Yet, in any case, the answers supplied by the ensuing action are non-answers, for the essence of the ghost is that he has no essence. We therefore never really move from the interrogative mood of Barnardo's first speech to an indicative resolution. His question remains truer than other peoples' answers.

Thus, even as the actors enter the public arena of the theatre, emerging with creaking of boards and rustling of costumes in broad daylight before a crowd of onlookers, a sense is created that we are somehow able to watch the passing of these same figures from the familiar world into the unintelligible world of death. It is often alleged (though with decreasing confidence) that the Elizabethans had no doubts about life after death. In fact Shakespeare relies absolutely in this play on our not knowing what death means. On this radical uncertainty the entire shadow-fabric of the drama is raised. Lear says, 'When we are born, we cry that we are come | To this great stage of fools (iv. vi. 182–3). The stage on which the actors arrive at the beginning of *Hamlet* is the dark obverse of that to which Lear alludes. The audience itself, in a good production, experiences a disembodying fear. The laughter is still-born.

The Greek example, in epic, of the interventionist opening is in some degree echoed by the development of Greek drama, but with a difference. The difference is neatly illustrated by Satan's speech on Niphates' top (*Paradise Lost*, iv. 33–41). Milton's friend Edward Phillips says that he saw these lines 'several years before the Poem was begun' and adds that they were designed for the beginning not of an epic but of a tragedy.[2] The fact that in these lines Satan addresses the sun makes it virtually certain that in the projected tragedy, as in the published epic, the speech came after Satan had reached our terrestrial globe. In the dramatic plot, then, the point of intervention is much later in the story, nearer to the point of crisis. But there appears to be no element of deliberate disorientation in the dramatic practice. No

[1] *The Works of Thomas Lodge* (a reissue of the Hunterian Club edition, Glasgow, 1883), 4 vols. (New York: Russell and Russell, 1963), i. 62.

[2] *The Early Lives of Milton*, ed. Helen Darbishire (London: Constable, 1932), 71.

one in antiquity records any sense of surprise at the customary Sophoclean playing-off of plot against myth. Individual plays, of course, could have disorienting openings. Aeschylus's *Agamemnon* begins, notoriously, with an apparently empty stage—but then the watchman, lying dog-wise on the roof, is suddenly noticed.[3] But this is a special theatrical effect. The surprise does not flow simply from the fact that the play begins at a late point in the Trojan story. The most majestically developed English drama of the Middle Ages, the great cycles of mystery plays, exhibit a powerful impulse to begin from the 'deep' beginning of all things. Such a beginning must be from that which has no prior beginning. The York Cycle opens with the soliloquy of God, a soliloquy which is also an announcement of self-hood. The playwright has no thought of plunging *in medias res*. Instead he finds that he must stress not so much the immortality of God as his 'birthlessness':

> I am gracyus and grete, God withoutyn begynnyng,
> I am maker unmade, al mighte es in me[4]

We are here as far as one can well be from the artfully interventionist opening of, say, *Othello*. The York dramatist gives us a far purer 'origin opening' than Dante does in the *Commedia*.

Ask an ordinary, educated person (not a student of English literature) how *King Lear* begins and you will receive the answer, 'The play begins with an old king dividing his kingdom.' In fact it begins, not with the ceremonial entrance of the King, but with a low-key, gossiping exchange between Kent and Gloucester. One needs to be fairly alert to take in the drift of the first words of the play: 'I thought the King had more affected the Duke of Albany than Cornwall.' The actor is given very little in the way of a formal send-off by the dramatist—not even the stiffening tempo of verse. It may be said that the first thirty lines or so of *King Lear* are mere 'filler', designed to occupy the time in which an unruly audience is settling down (corresponding, perhaps, to an orchestral tuning-up). But the lines contain important information, concerning both the

---

[3] See Aeschylus, *Agamemnon*, ed. J. D. Denniston and D. Page (Oxford: Clarendon Press, 1957), p. xxxi.

[4] *The York Plays*, ed. Richard Beadle (London: Edward Arnold, 1981), 49.

political world of the play and the question of Edmund's parentage. *The Winter's Tale* begins, in a somewhat similar fashion, with gossiping courtiers. All this suggests perhaps a surprisingly docile audience, which will fall silent at the first appearance of the actors—even when those actors (in this contrasting strongly with most late medieval drama) appear strangely negligent of their real-life auditors, to be wholly preoccupied with their own concerns. It may be, of course, that the audience was brought to order very simply, by a trumpet-call or the striking of a staff upon the stage. In which case the remarkable thing is Shakespeare's studious exclusion of the event from the inner texture of his frame. As far as I know, the surviving evidence (for example, Dekker's *The Gull's Hornbook*) points to an association of trumpets with formal prologue openings but tells us nothing about 'low-key' openings.[5]

Such a style of opening is the reverse of rhetorical, though Shakespeare, the master rhetorician, knows very well that people can be made to listen with a different sort of attentiveness to words which they conceive to be addressed not to them but to someone else. The queer false privacy of 'proscenium arch' theatre is already well developed, on the projecting stage of Shakespeare's Globe. In like manner, it is surely a mistake to think that the *scripted* 'improvisations' of the figures labelled A and B in the text of *Fulgens and Lucrece*, or the irruption of Ralph from the audience in *The Knight of the Burning Pestle*, are a simple contribution of the sort of improvisation achieved by the young Thomas More.[6] Such scripted pseudo-improvisation presupposes a high degree of docility in both actors and audience. But such audiences (as we know today) can still laugh in the wrong places.

It will be evident that *Hamlet* does not conform exactly to what we have described as the *in medias sententias* mode. Instead of an overheard continuity we have a pivotal movement (one sentinel replacing another), crisis replacing stasis at the very inception of the drama. Nevertheless, we enter the world of the

[5] See E. K. Chambers, *The Elizabethan Stage*, 4 vols. (Oxford: Clarendon Press, 1923), iv. 367, ii. 542.

[6] See William Roper. *The Lyfe of Sir Thomas More, Knyghte*, ed. Elsie Vaughan Hitchcock, Early English Text Society, no. 197 (London: Oxford University Press, 1935), 5. This work was written about 1556 and first printed in 1626.

play *after* the first two appearances of the ghost, though before its crucial encounter with the Prince. The further development whereby ordinary disorientation is suddenly extended into absolute mystery (life appropriated by death) might be supposed something essentially tragic. Yet there is a curious equivalent in comedy.

Twelfth Night opens, indeed, with a major chord, struck by the fantastical Duke in melancholic soliloquy, but at I. ii the play has what might be called a secondary opening:

VIOLA.	What country, friends is this?
CAPTAIN.	This is Illyria, lady.
VIOLA.	And what should I do in Illyria?
	My brother, he is in Elysium.

Barbara Everett has said of this exactly what needs to be said: 'Illyria is a name of a place that from the first maintains its own mocking half-echo of Elysium, a place of death as well as of immortality.'[7] 'Illyria' may draw on other echoes—'Idyll', 'delirium' (both words extant in English in Shakespeare's time, neither used by him) but Elysium is the word he planted in our minds. Viola, as she makes her first entrance on the stage, is half bewildered by a strange thought: that she ought to be—perhaps is—dead. Barnardo in *his* opening, nerve-stretching speech, was instantly wrong-footed on a point of personal identity. Viola is similarly wrong-footed but this time even more fleetingly, on a question of context, which in its turn throws into question her own identity as distinct from her brother's. In *Hamlet* we have a lurking emissary from beyond the grave; Viola conversely wonders why she has not followed her drowned brother, and then, with the echoic word 'Elysium', the dramatist plants the further, fainter thought that Viola may herself be a new arrival in a place of (strangely happy) death. In both plays our responses are quickened by a sense of death as an alternative world, eerily coinciding with the palpable unreality of dramatic performance (creaking boards, Illyrians). Yet the fictional 'lighting' of the scene is indeed quite different. *Hamlet* begins in an imagined darkness, *Twelfth Night*, I. ii. in strange brightness. It is remarkable that so complex a feat of emotional overlapping can be accomplished with such simple language, yet it is so.

---

[7] 'Or What You Will', *Essays in Criticism*, 35 (1985), 294–314, p. 295.

'Illyria', while it echoes 'Elysium', also figures as its living antithesis, so that the dominant character of the situation for her is its incongruity.

It is easy to 'hear' in 'What should I do in Illyria?' an echo of *Et in Arcadia ego*. Erwin Panofsky in his famous essay on the phrase did not succeed in tracing it back before Guercino's pastoral death's head, which may belong to 1623, the year of the Shakespeare First Folio. Panofsky argued that, by the rules of Latin syntax, the phrase properly means, not 'I too have lived in Arcadia', but 'Even in Arcadia, I (death) am'.[8] Anne Barton cited the Latin phrase, and the two great Poussin paintings in which it occurs, with reference to the momentarily disorienting intrusion of the idea of death towards the end of *As You Like It*.[9] Yet it is in the early, marvelling sequence in *Twelfth Night*, in which Viola finds herself new-lighted in Illyria, like the sea-stained Odysseus in Phaeacia, that Shakespeare comes closest to the cadence of the Latin phrase.

It may seem that my argument has doubled back and consumed itself, the attractive world of the dead now cancelled by a bright land of happy, living persons. But we must not allow the proper ambiguity of the scene to be lost. Elysium, like the Christian Heaven, is itself ambiguous: a place of dead people: a place where people find, to their joy, that they never died. Thus Viola's marvelling at the incongruous brightness of her surroundings does not automatically or unequivocally enforce the 'corrective' answer, 'She never died at all.' In a student production of *Twelfth Night*, directed by Edward Kemp in Oxford in 1985, Viola entered Illyria at the beginning of I. ii by appearing over a wall and descending a ladder into the world of the play. Although we can be reasonably certain that the original Elizabethan actor did no such thing, the device caught very exactly and economically the 'liminal' feeling of the scene. With her first words Viola crosses some magic threshold.

---

[8] Erwin Panofsky, '*Et in Arcadia Ego*: Poussin and the Elegiac Tradition', in his *Meaning and the Visual Arts* (New York: Doubleday, 1955), 295–320, p. 296. This is a revised version of '*Et in Arcadia Ego*: On the Conception of Transience in Poussin and Watteau', in *Essays Presented to Ernst Cassirer*, ed. Raymond Klibansky and H. J. Paton (Oxford: Clarendon Press, 1931), 223–54.

[9] '*As You Like It* and *Twelfth Night*: Shakespeare's Sense of an Ending', in *Shakespearean Comedy*, ed. Malcolm Bradbury and David Palmer, Stratford-upon-Avon Studies, no. 14 (London: Edward Arnold, 1972), 160–80, p. 164.

Shakespeare has found a way to turn the nervousness of the actors and the uncertainty of the audience to account. His method is to involve both parties in far larger uncertainties. Performances, *qua* performances, are real physical events, making clamorously importunate demands upon our senses yet at the same time the events displayed are not real events. This paradox of absence-in-presence is so familiar as to be normally almost unnoticeable. But Shakespeare reactivates the latent oddity by associating it with other antitheses: life/art, waking/ dreaming, being/unbeing, life/death. These in their turn can release further paradoxes: art may be more vivid than that quotidian existence, the undiscovered country may be lit by a brighter sun than shines on us. That is why, instead of employing some dramatic equivalent of the *in medias res* opening of classical epic, he finds his way, via various versions of what I have called the *in medias sententias* opening, to an entry not so much into the midst of (known) things as *between things*, or between whole orders of things. The ordinary indeterminacy of Elizabethan and Jacobean staging, with its rudimentary scenery and correlatively high demands upon the imagination of the audience, is made the vehicle of an ontological indeterminacy.

With *Twelfth Night* we allowed the notion of an opening to extend as far as I. ii. With *The Tempest* we must allow it to extend still further into the play. We begin *fortissimo*, with a crashing of chords. We are plunged in the centre of the storm which gives the play its name. The overriding voice is that of the tempest itself, not of the human agents. There is here no difficulty over the securing of audience attention since, according to the Folio stage direction, the first thing we hear is thunder. I suspect that the force of this particular audacious opening has been paradox- ically diminished by the rise of electronic wizardry in the twentieth century. In some present-day productions of *The Tempest* the sound effects are so overwhelming as to turn the actors into twittering, almost inaudible ghosts of themselves; the original *coup de théâtre* is intolerably coarsened.

The dialogue is as informal, as lacking in overt rhetorical address, as the low-key gossiping openings we have already noticed, but here the human agents, for all their shouting, are further reduced, to mere confused panic. At line 62 comes the cry, 'We split, we split, we split!' and the audience knows that the ship is wrecked. Can we say that at the beginning of the play we *see* the ship wrecked? The question is of some interest because it turns out later (v. ii. 224) that the ship is perfectly all right (either because magically reconstituted or because the wreck was some sort of illusion).[10] It is virtually certain that the King's men did not contrive to overturn the stage at this point. The trap was too small to have been of any use. Instead we may suppose that they relied on the auditory sense. In this they could be reasonably secure: in drama of the period the authority of the ear is higher than that of the eye. Irwin Smith writes that when a nocturnal scene was presented at the candle-lit Blackfriars theatre, all the artificial illumination was unchanged, though the character (night-shirted, carrying *his own* candle), would speak of darkness.[11] Audiences were educated to respond to verbal indications of action or situation (which is why the 'Dover Cliff' episode in *King Lear* is so disorienting—Edgar's vertiginous speech compels, as it were, an excess of assent). 'We split!' will therefore be believed. Moreover the words may well have been accompanied by some sound as of rending timber. The slightly odd Folio stage direction a couple of lines before, '*A confused noise within*', has usually been taken, since Capell's commentary, to refer to the quick-fire exclamatory speeches which immediately follow, but it is just possible that it points to some non-human sound effect—say, a creaking. At IV. i. 138, the masquing spirits vanish 'to a strange, hollow and confused noise'. There the noise is almost certainly inhuman. It must be weird and a little alarming—A piece of Jacobean avantgarde theatre. Further, the moment at which the spirits 'heavily vanish' may place some strain on our earlier confidence that the stage itself did not move. After all, we are dealing with a play which post-dates the leasing in 1608 of the Second Blackfriars Theatre (candle-lit performances, 'transformation scenes'). What if, both in I. i and IV. i, Shakespeare once more succeeded in exploiting a technical problem—this time the creaking of some ingenious mechanisms—either by deliberately throwing away the oil-can or by 'covering' with some louder noise, to induce yet another species of disorientation? In I. i, however, the

---

[10] See D. G. James, *The Dream of Prospero* (Oxford: Clarendon Press, 1967), 30.
[11] *Shakespeare's Blackfriars Playhouse: Its History and Design* (London: Peter Owen, 1964), 302–3.

sailors are all, manifestly, still in place *after* the confused noise has been heard. It may also be salutary to recall G. F. Reynolds on the scene in *The Two Noble Ladies* (1619–23) in which two soldiers crossing a river are drowned in full view of the audience;[12] we could easily have inferred from the text some minor miracle of illusionism but we happen to know how it was done: two Tritons entered and dragged the soldiers away.

With the beginning of I. ii we pass into the alternative shock of a strange tranquillity, from the wreck to the unhurried conversation of father and daughter. The contrast of 'volume' is so marked as to make us doubt momentarily the reality of what we just 'witnessed'. This intuition is reinforced as Miranda tells us, in her first speech, that the whole episode may have been an effect of (Prospero's) art. All this, to be sure, operates at the subordinate level only; the dominant impression is that Miranda has witnessed, as we have witnessed, a ship-wreck.

Yet a certain 'ecphrastic colouring' persists in the speech—a sense, that is, that we are listening to the description of a work of art rather than a reaction to a real disaster. 'O I have suffered with those that I saw suffer' (I. ii. 5–6) somehow suggests what we in the twentieth century have learned to call 'audience-empathy'. The disaster with 'no harm done' (I. ii. 14) succeeds in anticipating various psychological explanations of the pleasure of theatrical tragedy. The way Miranda gazed at 'the brave vessel, | (Who had no doubt, some noble creature in her)' (I. ii. 6–7), and the way she gasped at the fate of the 'poor souls' (9), seems not wholly unlike the way Leontes' soul is pierced by what he takes to be a statue of Hermione (*The Winter's Tale*, v. iii. 34). We may think also of the speech of the third servant on the painting of Daphne, in *The Taming of the Shrew*:

> Or Daphne roaming through a thorny wood,
> Scratching her legs that one shall swear she bleeds
> And at that sight shall sad Apollo weep
> So workmanly the blood and tears are drawn

> (*Induction*, ii. 56–60)

The special oxymoron of 'weep' and 'workmanly' is absent

---

[12] *The Staging of Elizabethan Plays at the Red Bull Theater, 1605–1625*, Modern Language Association of America, General Series, no. 9 (London: Oxford University Press, 1940), 43.

from Miranda's speech, but 'by your art' is only a few lines
away.

Meanwhile the sense we found in *Twelfth Night* of passing
through death by water to another world recurs here. The life of
the Island is not our life. When in II. i the castaways enter, as
Viola entered in I. ii, amazed to find their bodies and their
clothes intact, they see the Island differently: one sees lush
greenery while another sees a barren landscape (II. i. 54–6).
Once more, Shakespeare exploits the visual indeterminacy of
Jacobean scenery. Earlier in this book we saw how a certain line
in Virgil which is commonly assumed to describe the condition
of the dead,

> Clausae tenebris et carcere caeco
> Shut up in darkness and a blind prison   (*Aeneid*, vi. 640)

is in fact uttered by one of the inhabitants of Elysium to describe
the inhabitants of *our* world. When Prospero invites Miranda to
cast her mind back to 'the time before' (I. ii. 39), to the real,
living world of Milan, the image is not, as we might have
expected, of a far-off, brilliantly illuminated picture, watched
from the shadows by exiled spirits. Instead we have the line that
haunted Keats:

> What seest thou else
> In the dark backward and abysm of time?   (I. ii. 49–50)

The dream-island is brighter than the political reality.

In *The Tempest* the threshold between sleep and waking is
exploited to the same end, becoming indeed a place of transit
where we may feel the dream could cross. The wakings in the
play all lay stress on the equivocal character of perception at
such moments: Gonzalo and others at II. i. (the arrival in this
strangely transposed Elysium) and the sailors in v. i. Miranda
compares her dim memory image of the ladies who attended
her with a dream (I. ii. 45) and Prospero, in the play's most
famous speech, finally links the ideas of sleep and death ('our
little life | Is rounded with a sleep', IV. i. 157–8). The effect is
rather of a cycling movement than of a linear imaginative drive
to an unequivocal resurrection. Caliban, after all, having
woken, cried to dream again. At the end of the play the pastoral
pattern, whereby a golden world is entered and applauded but at

last eagerly exchanged for a return to court, is followed.

It is not necessary to discern any single 'law' or 'deep structure' in Shakespearean openings, though I have been concerned with a certain pattern of affinity, by which even plays as generically opposite to one another as *Hamlet* and *Twelfth Night* may be linked. Shakespeare, who endlessly recycles his imaginative intuitions, rarely if ever repeats himself. The drift of this chapter has been to find a strange equivalence between the world of the dead and various versions of Fairy Land. One may think of the medieval poem, *Sir Orfeo*, in which the classical story of Eurydice borne off to the world of the dead undergoes a Celtic transformation, so that she is carried away by a ghostly band of fairies. But none of it will, so to speak, keep still. If the eye is allowed to wander, it will notice that in *A Midsummer Night's Dream*, my notion of 'lighting', whereby an initially tragic conception is altered by a simple increase in illumination, is entirely overthrown, since in the *Dream* the silvan pastoral is made nocturnal. Shakespeare is not even thrifty enough to confine his openings to the beginnings of his plays. In *The Merchant of Venice* there is a secondary opening, at the end of the play, into the 'old money' lovers' Paradise of Belmont, once again nocturnal but now lifted high in the air, above the sordid traffic of Venice, a little nearer the ever-singing stars. Meanwhile—another 'meanwhile'—it all has its funny side:

SIR ANDREW.   Begin fool. It begins 'Hold thy peace.'
CLOWN.   I shall never begin if I hold my peace.
SIR ANDREW.   Good, i'faith. Come, begin.

(*Twelfth Night*, II. iii. 69–71)

Shakespeare, then, shares with the writers in the epic line an impulse to discover in the technical difficulty of opening a metaphysical or ontological resonance, but he differs profoundly from them in choosing to make ambiguity his end, rather than some presumed, structuring absolute. Where Virgil, Dante, Milton, and Eliot are hungry for an ultimate unitary truth, Shakespeare is—genuinely and deeply—happier with enriching questions than with conclusive answers.

By a familiar paradox, the more intense subversions of the 'origin' proem will be found within the strict classical tradition.

Shakespeare (who has after all a thousand other things in mind) can therefore never quite match the seismic effect of the conclusion of Pope's *Dunciad*. The reader may suspect that I have slipped unwittingly from openings to endings, but that is not so. This Popean ending belongs, quite clearly, in the category of proemia: it is just that everything happens to be running backwards.

> She comes! she comes! the sable Throne behold
> Of *Night* Primaeval, and of *Chaos* old!
> Before her, *Fancy's* gilded clouds decay,
> And all its varying Rain-bows die away,
> *Wit* shoots in vain its momentary fires,
> The meteor drops, and in a flash expires.
> As one by one, at dread Medea's strain,
> The sick'ning stars fade off th'ethereal plain;
> As Argus' eyes by Hermes' wand opprest,
> Clos'd one by one to everlasting rest;
> Thus at her felt approach, and secret might,
> *Art* after *Art* goes out, and all is Night.
> See skulking *Truth* to her old Cavern fled,
> Mountains of Casuistry heap's o'er her head!
> *Philosophy*, that lean'd on Heav'n before,
> Shrinks to her second cause, and is no more.
> *Physic* of *Metaphysic* begs defence,
> And *Metaphysic* calls for aid on *Sense*!
> See *Mystery* to *Mathematics* fly!
> In vain! they gaze, turn giddy, rave, and die,
> *Religion* blushing veils her sacred fires,
> And unawares *Morality* expires.
> Nor *public* Flame, nor *private*, dares to shine;
> Nor *human* Spark is left, nor Glimpse *divine*!
> Lo! thy dread Empire, CHAOS! is restor'd;
> Light dies before thy uncreating word:
> Thy hand, great Anarch! lets the curtain fall;
> And Universal Darkness buries All.

(Dunciad (1742), iv. 629–56)

This of course is mock-heroic and was intended to amuse. But it has become commonplace to observe that in these lines, against all the odds, a kind of dark sublimity asserts itself. The word 'sublime' connotes a dynamic aesthetic of the imperfectly apprehensible, while 'the beautiful' is that which is satisfyingly patterned and apprehensible (thus tending to the static). In English literature Milton is the master of the sublime. The central idea of chaos is both classical and counter-classical. In the creation myth at the beginning of Ovid's *Metamorphoses* the world of form and being rises out of a chaos which is as horrible as it is (because formless) unimaginable. Here at the end of the *Dunciad* that initial triumph of intelligible, bright reality is thrown into reverse. Pope is feeding on Milton. In the proem to *Paradise Lost* Milton allowed himself a cross-reference to Ovid in 'rose out of *Chaos*' (10) and at i. 543 'the reign of *Chaos* and old Night' is glimpsed as a kind of dumb evil, far older than Satan's brilliant transgression. Thereafter Chaos, as it were, grows rather than shrinks. The word re-echoes through the poem: 'Night | And *Chaos*, ancestors of Nature' (ii. 894–5), '*Chaos*, and ancient Night' (ii. 970), '*Chaos* and *Eternal Night*' (iii. 18), '*Chaos* and the inroad of Darkness old' (iii. 421), 'Far into *Chaos*, and the World unborn' (vii. 220), 'Wide Anarchice of *Chaos* damp and dark' (x. 283), 'Of unoriginal Night and *Chaos* wilde' (x. 477). I have here followed the emphatic typography of the 1674 edition, rather than the modernized Longman's edition. Pope, with his picture of a murky presiding figure, may well have had at the back of his mind Milton's 'He rules a moment; Chaos umpire sits' (ii. 907). Pope, notice, fuses the Miltonically distinct figures of Chaos and Satan. I have argued elsewhere[13] that Pope, who desired all his life to write an epic but could not proceed beyond mock-heroic or the polished pastiche of Augustan translation, nevertheless won through in *The Dunciad* to a kind of *nekuia*, a book of the dead which stands fittingly between the exalted tradition of Homer, Virgil, and Dante, and Eliot's twentieth-century urban *Inferno, The Waste Land.*

It is notable that this strange feat of epic sublimity is not by any means a straightforward victory for Enlightenment classicism but is rather a subversion of it. Pope at last finds his way (*tenuis qua semita ducit*) not to the sunlit, marmoreal ancient world celebrated by Winckelmann but to the dark and terrifying underworld explored later in Frazer's *The Golden Bough* (an

[13] In my *Pope's Essay on Man* (London: Allen and Unwin, 1984), 36–7.

important source for Eliot's *The Waste Land*). For the English the Enlightenment was summed up in the figure of Sir Isaac Newton and Pope expressed the national sentiment in a dexterous mixture of half-humorous piety and profound admiration when he wrote his epitaph for the great man:

> God said, *Let Newton be!* and All was *Light*

'Let there be light', the great traditional example of sublime utterance, is shifted by Pope from creation to cognition. He thus elegantly suggests that the spectacular expansion of knowledge produced by Newton's *Principia* is the intellectual equivalent of the primal *Fiat lux* (*The Beginning*). At the end of *The Dunciad* the same words from Genesis are evoked and joined to the Hellenizing opening of John's Gospel: 'In the beginning was the Word'. Pope, with more than Miltonic effrontery, is not content to reverse the creation myth of Ovid; he here reverses the biblical Creation.

> The sickening stars fade off th'ethereal plain

is a line of disquieting power, producing exactly the vertiginous disorientation needed before the thunderous, annihilating

> Light dies before thy uncreating word.

This has the accumulated strength which properly belongs to the most canonical, the most vertebral European poetry. But it is upside-down. Earlier in the book I suggested, with some hesitation, that the conclusion of *The Prelude* is still discernibly proemial. In Pope the queer imaginative feat of a proemial conclusion is a fully accomplished thing.

I had half hoped when I began this book to equip the reader with an interpretative 'kit', so that he or she could understand the inner workings of any literary opening, in terms of the opposition between a natural and a formal beginning. It is clear however, as I have already hinted in my Shakespearean digression, that the field of real openings is too rich for my scheme. The only honest course, then, is to end with an opening which simply does not fit:

Under certain circumstances there are few hours in life more agreeable than the hour dedicated to the ceremony known as afternoon tea. There are circumstances in which, whether you partake of the tea or

not—some people of course never do,—the situation is in itself
delightful. Those that I have in mind in beginning to unfold this simple
history offered an admirable setting to an innocent pastime. The
implements of the little feast had been disposed upon the lawn of an old
English country-house, in what I should call the perfect middle of a
splendid summer afternoon. Part of the afternoon had waned, but
much of it was left, and what was left was of the finest and rarest
quality. Real dusk would not arrive for many hours; but the flood of
summer light had begun to ebb, the air had grown mellow, the
shadows were long upon the smooth, dense turf. They lengthened
slowly, however, and the scene expressed that sense of leisure still to
come which is perhaps the chief source of one's enjoyment of such a
scene at such an hour. From five o'clock to eight is on certain occasions
a little eternity; but on such occasions as this the interval could only be
an eternity of pleasure. The persons concerned in it were taking their
pleasure quietly, and they were not of the sex which is supposed to
furnish the regular votaries of the ceremony I have mentioned. The
shadows on the perfect lawn were straight and angular; they were the
shadows of an old man sitting in a deep wicker-chair near the low table
on which the tea had been served, and of two younger men strolling to
and fro, in desultory talk, in front of him. The old man had his cup in
his hand; it was an unusually large cup, of a different pattern from the
rest of the set and painted in brilliant colours. He disposed of its
contents with much circumspection, holding it for a long time close to
his chin, with his face turned to the house. His companions had either
finished their tea or were indifferent to their privilege; they smoked
cigarettes as they continued to stroll.[14]

The beginning of Henry James's *The Portrait of a Lady* is indeed a
late-born, remote version of the *in medias res* opening. The word
'middle', Dante's *mezzo*, is important here as it was in 1300, but
James is not concerned to relate his work to any metaphysically
august order of origin and fulfilment. He is using the notion of
intermediacy in quite another way

the perfect middle of a splendid summer afternoon. Part of the
afternoon had waned, but much of it was left

James at the inception of his narrative majestically arrests the
flow of events in a tableau, a little like a photograph (we always
know that photographs are instantaneous, arrested sections of
something which really moved and changed). The intense visual

[14] Ed. Robert D. Bamberg (New York: W. W. Norton, 1975), 17.

effect is anticipated, lightly, in the opening, ponderously reflective 'ceremony known as afternoon tea'. To the knowing reader James is already signalling, 'I, the American, may see your customs as something exotic, like a Japanese ceremony, but at the same time I am very much at home, and know my ground.'

The house in the picture is beautiful, almost too beautiful as honey is too sweet. The figures who sit before it on the lawn are not integrated with it, socially or economically (this is part of the snap-shot effect). Contrast with James's picture this tableau from the fourth chapter of Tom Jones (and notice how the word 'middle' recurs):

It was now the Middle of *May*, and the Morning was remarkably serene, when Mr. *Allworthy* walked forth on the Terrace, where the Dawn opened every Minute that lovely prospect we have before described to his Eye. And now, having sent forth Streams of Light, which ascended the blue Firmament before him, as Harbingers preceding his Pomp, in the full Blaze of his Majesty, up rose the Sun; than which one Object alone in the Lower Creation could be more glorious, and that Mr. *Allworthy* himself presented; a human Being replete with Benevolence, meditating in what manner he might render himself most acceptable to his Creator, by doing most good to his Creatures. (I. iv)[15]

As befits a 'comic Epic-Poem in Prose'[16] this passage is a jubilant fanfare. Unlike the 'puny insect, shiv'ring at a breeze' outside his colossal house in Pope's *Epistle to Burlington* (108), Allworthy is big enough for the scene and is, with all his faults, loved by his creator. The active paternal benevolence which links him to his habitat is, we sense, unintelligent in a way which promises comedy, but for all that it is real benevolence. James's figures are conversely studies in non-relatedness. At the same time, however, the tranquil scene is instinct, to an extent which is almost sinister, with a sense of *potential* action and relationship. Technically it is superb. James has simultaneously

---

[15] Henry Fielding, *The History of Tom Jones, a Foundling*, introduction and commentary by Martin C. Battestin, ed. Fredson Bowers (the Wesleyan Edition of the Works of Henry Fielding), 2 vols. (Oxford: Clarendon Press, 1974), i. 43.

[16] The Preface to *Joseph Andrews*, in *The History of the Adventures of Joseph Andrews and An Apology for the Life of Mrs. Shamela Andrews*, ed. Douglas Brooks (London: Oxford University Press, 1970), 4.

given us a tableau of timeless social perfection and has contrived to suggest, not through anticipatory summary but by negation, the long narrative of pain which is to follow. He does this with the shadows on the grass. There is a story by Freeman Wills Crofts,[17] belonging to what Barbara Everett has called 'the classic English phase' of the detective novel,[18] in which the identity of the criminal is inferred from his shadow, as it appears in a photograph which he took himself. That kind of precision is not James's kind, but the shadows in the first chapter of *A Portrait of a Lady* are nevertheless of great significance. They are at first still, but then they grow:

The shadows were long upon the smooth, dense turf. They lengthened slowly, however, and the scene expressed that sense of leisure still to come

Even as a narrating voice assures us that even if the shadows do point to the future, it is a small-scale future holding nothing but ease and comfort, we know in a simpler, more poetic fashion that anything as dark as a shadow must point to future darkness. Each of the figures in the picture is attended by a taller, more obscure version of himself. *Quisque suos patimur manes*, 'Each of us suffers his own ghost' (*Aeneid*, vi. 743). Each will become that which the shadow promises.

There is here no sign of deference to a Muse, no hint of any need to found the fiction on some external supernatural authority. In this world the author is God. He holds these people in the hollow of his hand. In Virgil, the poet with whom we began, lengthening shadows were—or could seem to be—eloquent of security:

> et iam summa procul villarum culmina fumant
> maioresque cadunt altis de montibus umbrae
>
> *Eclogues*, i. 83–4

Now in the distance smoke is rising from the roofs of the farms, and the shadows from the high hills are growing[19]

---

[17] *Fatal Venture* (London: Hodder and Stoughton, 1939).

[18] *Young Hamlet: Essays on Shakespeare's Tragedies* (Oxford: Clarendon Press, 1989), 11.

[19] Laurence Lerner thinks that these lines are simultaneously reassuring and threatening. See his 'The Eclogues and Pastoral Tradition', in *Virgil and his Influence: Bimillenial Studies*, ed. Charles Martindale (Bristol: Bristol Classical Press, 1984), 193–213, p. 196.

In our own century, in the paintings of de Chirico we see, most disquietingly of all, the shadows of people who themselves, unlike Crofts's murderer, remain for ever out of sight. It is so with this book. We have come to the edge of an uncertainly illuminated area and can only guess at how much lies beyond.

Index